SOE's
Secret
Weapons
Centre

STATION 12

SOE's Secret Weapons Centre

STATION 12

DES TURNER
Foreword by M.R.D. Foot

The History Press

First published in 2006
This edition published in 2011

The History Press
The Mill, Brimscombe Port
Stroud, Gloucestershire, GL5 2QG
www.thehistorypress.co.uk

British Library Cataloguing in Publication Data.
A catalogue record for this book is available from the British Library.

ISBN 978 0 7524 5944 8

Typesetting and origination by The History Press
Printed in the EU for History Press.

Contents

Foreword

The Special Operations Executive (SOE), otherwise known as the Ministry of Ungentlemanly Warfare, had outstations all over Great Britain. In one of them, in Aston village near Stevenage, still more knavish tricks were invented during the last world war, to frustrate the knavish tricks of our enemies.

Des Turner lived through the war as a child in western Essex. When he moved to Aston forty years ago, the village had become a suburb of Stevenage new town. He heard vague tales of wartime secret goings-on at Aston House, lately demolished, and piece by piece put together its story. It was Station 12 of SOE; its tasks were to invent and to manufacture devices for undercover warfare. Here, time pencil detonators were made by the million to set off explosive charges planted by brave men and women on innumerable pieces of enemy equipment; here, the charges were prepared that destroyed the dry dock at St-Nazaire; here the Welbike, later renamed the Corgi minibicycle, was developed; here were dreamed up into reality no end of odd devices for improving the secret war.

The author has combined, with great ingenuity, recollections from long after the events by those who took part in them and what he has devilled out for himself in the archives written down at the time, many of which have now gone public at Kew. In the depth of the Cold War, all this sort of information had to be kept secret; hardly any of it appears, either in agents' memoirs, or in the official histories written in the fifties, sixties or seventies of the last century. The modern age is more relaxed. A lot of what appears below used to be unpublishable; that makes it all the more interesting to read.

M.R.D. Foot
November 2005

Acknowledgements

I would like to thank the many individuals and organisations who have helped in the writing of this book.

In particular Colonel Leslie J. Cardew Wood who gave me such a wonderful start when he could so easily have refused because the Official Secrets Act still applied at that time. Although he did not of course reveal any secrets, he gave me some important leads and a wonderful insight into the way he ran Aston House and the fun he had doing it. His contribution forms the foundation of this book.

Johnny Riches for workshop memories and personal photographs. Cicely (Scottie) Hales for information on workshop materials, her personal photographs and for allowing me to photograph her souvenirs of Aston House. And it was she who introduced me to Jimmy Welch, the son of her ATS friend the late Mary Wardrope. Jimmy gave me his parents' anecdotes of the design office and allowed me to copy photographs. Lucy Holdaway was also an ATS friend of Scottie's who, with her two sisters, chauffeured the officers around in their staff cars. She also loaned photographs. Joe Wardle read my appeal in the British Legion magazine and volunteered his memories of the workshops and supplied me with photographs. Richard Bignell was located and introduced by Keith Bone, who spotted my appeal in a local Hertfordshire magazine *Village Affairs*, Richard provided memories of the stores and magazine areas and loaned photographs. I located Ishbel Orme and June Wilmers via the same magazine and they helped me with their experiences of FANY and loaned me photographs. Maurice Christie located me via the web and provided his father's memories of the Aston House engineering laboratories and also photographs of Arthur Christie.

Dr John H.C. Vernon provided the text of his interview with Scientific Officer Colin Meek plus additional technical information and Margaret Meek added memories and photographs of Colin.

I would also like to thank Professor M.R.D. Foot for providing the foreword. Other agencies and individuals who helped were: the Public Record Office (National Archives); the Imperial War Museum in London and at Duxford; Stevenage Museum, especially its manager, Jo Ward, who inspired me to complete and publish a local history on Aston House, the forerunner of this book, for an SOE Exhibition held at that museum during January 2004; Stevenage Library; the Carpetbagger Aviation Museum; the Bletchley Park Trust; Past Times and Stakis Hotels for their very informative 'Secret War' weekend hosted by Colin Burbridge and Clive Bassett who also provided me with technical information on SOE weapons; John Amess; Lord Balniel; Lynette Beardwood (FANY); Wally Bennett; John Billington; Fredric Boyce; John and Anne Clarke; Jim and Vera Edwards; Durwood W.J. Cruikshank; Professor David Dilks; Judy Hull; Agnes Kinnersley; Dr David Malan; Nita Pulley; Edward Marriott; Peter Martineau; Robin Mills; Christopher Murphy; Phil Nussle; Jack Pallett; Betty Randles; Margaret Richards; Jennie Spicer; Peter Robins; Mark Seaman; Donald Sommerville; Michael Summers; Jack Whitney.

In addition, two anonymous collectors of SOE equipment kindly allowed me to photograph rare and valuable weapons without imposing copyright restrictions.

Patricia Crampton proofread both my local history edition and the drafts for this book and gave much advice and encouragement.

Finally I thank my wife Mavis for her tremendous support and encouragement and my three sons Ian, Jamie and Simon for help and support with this book and many local history projects.

Introduction

When I moved to Aston, near Stevenage in Hertfordshire, with my family in 1966, I was curious to know its history. There was very little written about it, so I decided to set about finding out what this small parish might reveal of its past.

During my early taped interviews with villagers it became clear that Aston House had played an important role during the Second World War. I was told stories of its being very 'hush-hush'. – 'Explosives are still buried there, you know.' – 'Winston Churchill came here.' – 'A German spy was caught.' – 'There was a big fire there one night and we thought the whole place would blow up, you see it was full of explosives.' I was intrigued, to say the least.

The Second World War had a great effect on my life. As an impressionable young schoolboy in the Essex village of Ugley, I found the war frightening at times, but always very exciting. Our cottage was almost hit by a stick of jettisoned German bombs one night. We heard the air rushing through the fins as they passed low over our roof and my family and I dived to the floor. The air raid siren at nearby Stansted had not sounded a warning. The bombs landed around our village hall some 300 yards away and by sheer good fortune one bomb that landed very close to some sheltering village lads failed to explode.

I observed dogfights in the sky and fires caused by bombs. I cycled with friends to collect a piece of the latest crashed aircraft and it became a schoolboy hobby to collect bomb shrapnel and 'chaff' (strips of silver paper tape used to disrupt radio location, or radar as we know it today).

Then there was the build-up of tanks and military vehicles en route to the south coast for the D-Day landings; some would stop and park under the trees with camouflage netting over them. I watched the overhead air armada of bombers towing gliders to Arnhem, masses of them, some of which broke away and landed or crashed nearby. Then V-1 Doodlebugs (pilotless flying bombs) came over and when the engine cut they fell silently to earth, exploding on impact. One night a V-1 suddenly flew very low over our cottage. It was being pursued by a fighter aircraft that was machine-gunning it – now that *was* a shock! There was no time to dive to the floor and it exploded in the next village of Manuden. American servicemen were everywhere, so I became one of the 'Got any gum chum?' kids. One Yank gave me an orange. I hadn't seen one for years, so you can imagine how delicious it tasted!

I watched a Spitfire shooting down a rogue barrage balloon that had broken from its mooring, but the most exciting and unbelievable event of all was to see a Horsa glider snatched up from a field by a Lancaster bomber that flew just above it and hooked it into the air.

With these vivid childhood memories in my mind, I wanted to know what had happened in Aston – the locals must have witnessed similar events to those I observed at Ugley? I learned that two USAAF Flying Fortress bombers collided and came down in the neighbouring village of Weston, with tragic consequences.[1]

But what actually happened at Aston House, I wondered. I didn't realise just how difficult finding out was going to be.

'Don't tell dad – keep mum!' was a slogan from a wartime prop-aganda poster and in the 1970s when I began my research it still applied. The 'goings on' at Aston House remained TOP SECRET. At first I was surprised and disappointed by the abrupt refusal of personnel involved to tell me anything about it, due to their having signed the Official Secrets Act. One exception was a former Aston House soldier who agreed to tell me some of his memories, but he insisted I must not write them down or reveal them to anyone and would only talk to me as we walked in a field, lest we be overheard!

Peter Martineau, then resident at Holders, a large house at Aston End, offered to help me by contacting the former adjutant at Aston House, Stanley Elton-Barratt, whom he knew as a business associate at the Bassett sweet company. The officer's reply stated:

I was there first (Aston House) in 1940 as adjutant and then camp commandant until the end of the war so naturally knew much about its activities during that time and saw it grow from about a dozen officers and men to about thirty of the former and over a thousand other ranks, including 200 ATS. We had our own Military Police, (Bluecaps) who had their HQ at the guard hut by the main gates, also an army Fire Brigade but I am afraid before giving you any more information I must get in touch with the security authorities.

The subsequent letter stated:

I regret that I am not permitted to give you more information concerning Aston House.

This was very disappointing. I could not believe that it was still in the national interest to keep these secrets so long after the war had ended, so I wrote to my local MP for information about what I had identified as ISRB (Inter-Services Research Bureau) at Aston. The reply I received was as follows:

From The Minister of State
The Rt. Hon. Lord Balniel
Foreign and Commonwealth Office
London SW1
6 February 1973

Dear Mr Turner,
    ISRB was the cover name for the Special Operations Executive (SOE) which came into being in July 1940 as the organisation responsible for the carrying out of and co-ordinating underground resistance activities in enemy occupied territories. SOE took over Aston House from another War Office branch known as MIR (Military Intelligence Research). A small Research Unit had been in existence there for studying weapons suitable for use in subversive warfare. This secret establishment E.S.6. (WD), which at the outset had a complement of a few specialist officers and men, was greatly expanded by SOE in the course of the war. By 1942 the number of personnel employed on communications (W/T) research and manufacture was 280 and on special weapons and explosives 600. The research activities were subsequently transferred elsewhere. The experimental and manufacturing workshops employing well over 1,000 men were engaged in the production of special devices for sabotage operations, and a wide range of miscellaneous items. All these

were despatched, in some cases by parachute, to occupied territories in Europe and the Far East for use by the Resistance organisations formed and supplied by SOE.

I am afraid I cannot provide a list of types of weapons and associated equipment. But I hope that the above will be of some use.

Yours sincerely,

Balniel

This letter confirmed for the first time that Aston House was part of SOE and had played a vital role in the secret war. Many of those working there would have been completely unaware of SOE. They wouldn't have known what it stood for anyway.

Now that I knew the reason for the top-secret security rating I became even more curious to discover what were the weapons and special explosives that were made there, and on what special operations they were used. Also if Aston House was part of SOE, a countrywide organisation that requisitioned many large country houses and estates, how did it link up?

The background was that in March 1938 a new department was created within MI6. Section D (D for Destruction) was given the task of developing plans for subversive operations in Europe. At the same time the GS(R) Department – later MI(R) Military Intelligence Directorate – of the War Office was examining the potential use of guerrilla warfare. The two groups worked together in the months leading up to the war. Section D began to establish 'stay behind' sabotage parties in those countries threatened by German invasion. Meanwhile MI(R) investigated the feasibility of 'secret armies' of guerrilla fighters to resist German occupation.

After the triumph of Germany's armies on the continent and the Nazi occupation of most of Western Europe, Winston Churchill set up SOE to 'set Europe ablaze' by helping resistance movements and carrying out subversive operations in enemy-held territory.[2]

The Prime Minister has further decided after consultation with the Ministers concerned that a new organisation shall be established forthwith to co-ordinate all action, by way of subversion and sabotage, against the enemy.

War Cabinet Memorandum by the Lord President of the Council, Neville Chamberlain, 19 July 1940.[3]

Jack Pallett, a villager in Aston, gave me the next lead, producing a letter signed by the commanding officer of E.S.6. (WD), Major Wood.

War Department,
Aston House,
Stevenage.
20 January 1942

Dear Mr Pallett,

I wish to convey to you my thanks for the splendid way in which you helped to extinguish the recent fire which necessitated long hours of night work.

Your promptness in arriving on the scene, and the determination and cheerfulness with which you set about your task, was greatly appreciated.

> Yours truly,
>
> *Major Wood, R.N.*
> Commanding E.S.6. (WD)

So the story *was* true; there *had* been a serious fire at Aston House during the war, and Jack had helped put it out. He was employed there and told me in his rich Hertfordshire accent:

There was a terrible fire there one night, good job Jerry won't over, there was all these 'ere incendiary things, sheds and sheds of 'em. What caused it was the 'eat of the 'ot water pipes, an' all this packed up ag'inst it. I think tha's what started it. It even scorched the banks right down to the corner. The pond was emptied at the Dene and in the park during the fire. There was eight of us up there in the carpenters' shop, makin' ammunition boxes and detonator blocks an' the likes of that. We knew what was up there.

I decided to try to trace Major R.N. Wood and searched Army records but found no trace of him. Some years later I had a wonderful piece of luck. Agnes Kinnersley, who had worked with SOE at Aston House and The Frythe during the war, visited Betty

Randle's Patchwork Studio, then at The Stables, Dene Lane, Aston. Obviously she talked about her wartime experiences at Aston and Betty, knowing of my interest in this subject, discovered that Agnes knew of the whereabouts of Major, now Colonel, L.J.C. Wood. Upon much closer examination of Jack Pallett's letter (a poor copy) with a magnifying glass I realised that the initials R.N. were not Wood's but were R.E., indicating Royal Engineers!

I wrote to Colonel Wood immediately and he kindly invited me to visit him at Oatlands Park Hotel in Weybridge, Surrey, where he was then residing. But our plans to meet were interrupted several times by his appointments for treatment of a severe disability, coupled with the fact, he told me later, that he kept putting me off to see how persistent I would be. Here are some extracts from letters I received from him before our first meeting.

29 August 1984

Dear Des,

I must make it clear that I am 86 and suffer from peripheral neuritis as a result of a truly representative collection of tropical diseases collected in India where I served as Colonel Q to Force 136 and built and became Director of the Special Forces Development Centre. This is a dying of the nerve endings – a kind of creeping paralysis which is incurable and progressive. I can walk short distances, say 25 yards with the aid of a walking frame – after that a wheel chair, so that to visit you in Aston would be very difficult. Nevertheless apart from my lack of mobility I am fit and normally work (writing and finance) up to midnight every night.

I don't know what you really want from me?

However, when you visit I will tell about those sweet people, the Ashers, caretakers at Aston House when we took over, and who aided me when I decided to keep my own pigs. The Hun having a go at me with a stick of bombs in the early days and subsequent huge fun with two local ladies. (I had been over in France with their Deuxième Bureau just before the Germans invaded and some of them went over to Vichy – I was known to the Free French as Captain Blood!) Catching a red-hot spy on our own premises. Training Commandos in use of explosive devices we invented and made just before a raid – entertaining the heads of all the Commandos for a night (they said it was worse than Dunkirk!). I invented the totally illegitimate title of E.S.6. (WD) as a cover for us and got away with it. Dealing with greedy local senior people by illegitimate but very effective means. Maintaining secrecy by all manner of tricks. Staving off nosey-parker Generals from the War Office who tried to tell me how to run my establishment – plenty of rhymes of which I have copies and plenty of photos, (heaven knows how I will find them) – Oh! And the very happy Aston Ghost. That's just a start. The only thing for you to do is come here . . .

12 October 1984

I very much regret that I cannot manage Saturday 16 October. I have been under the weather . . . With my sincere apologies for the behaviour of my body and legs . . .'

20 January 1985

I've failed you on photos at the moment. All I can find is one of the Ashers, myself testing our silent mortar (the one that removed the newspaper from the hands of the vicar while he sat in his garden!), one of my dog 'Spats', my 'repaniel' (half retriever, half spaniel), loved by the whole station and responsible for many good yarns, even the poor chap's death was dramatic and as he would have wished it. I have another good one of Spats with Sergeant-Major Stallard and my formal farewell parade when I left for India. Some of my memories fall outside the scope of your 'local history', save for Aston's direct and sometimes tragic connection (the son of one of my senior civilian staff came to Aston to be instructed before a raid on which he died), with some of the daring exploits of the War.

17 February 1985

I greatly enjoyed meeting you in person at last . . . I really enjoyed speaking into a recorder for the first time. In retrospect it was unbelievable that I should roar with laughter at some of my own stories when you played back some tapes this morning!

Thank you for the gift of the new book 'SOE' by M.R.D. Foot . . . I have had quite a bit of correspondence with him . . . He made no real mention of Force 136 operations in Burma which were pretty spectacular.

As ever,

Leslie

The sound recordings we made were produced over two wonderfully entertaining weekends at Oatlands Park Hotel. He was living in a cottage within the grounds of the hotel, occupying the whole of the ground floor, which was ideal for his wheelchair. He was totally self-sufficient but evening meals were cooked by the chef and brought over from the adjacent hotel by a waiter, his regular tip for this service being a large glass of vintage wine.

Soon after I arrived laden with recorders, mikes and cameras, we had lunch and he told me the itinerary for the day. He said 'I usually have a sleep in the afternoon, you do what you like. We will have a glass or two of wine, the waiter will bring us dinner about seven, after that we will begin our chat about Aston.' This we did, and talked until about three in the morning.

Aston House and The Frythe, Old Welwyn (Station IX), worked closely together, but a good deal of research, development and testing of explosives and special equipment was carried out at Aston. He said:

We invented, made, supplied and trained personnel in the use of 'toys' not only for the resistance but for all the special forces: Commandos, Small Boat Section, Airborne Division and Long Range Desert Patrol. We had about forty specialised army officers and civilians, guards and several hundred soldiers, FANYs and ATS [First Aid Nursing Yeomanry and Auxiliary Territorial Service – the women's services; by WWII FANY had no nursing connections] and a few civilian technicians. We had magazines for explosives, and sheds in which to handle them and large storehouses for incendiaries and all the rest of our 'toys', and workshops wherein to experiment and manufacture. We designed and made up special explosive charges tailored for the job in hand and simple to place and fire by any commando or resistance worker. Many tons of explosives as well as the devices we supplied were dropped by parachute to the resistance to blow bridges on D-Day. The whole essence of helping the special forces was speed in both invention and supply.

Some of this may sound a little grim but I can truthfully say that we regarded the whole thing completely impersonally as tremendously funny and the more hideous the devices we invented and made to confound the enemy, the funnier we thought it. The same gaiety of spirit imbued the Commandos. I met nearly all the leaders and many of their officers and men when they came to Aston for last-minute briefing and training in demolitions, just before a raid. Most of what we did was bloody hard work but I will tell you about the fun we had.

He certainly did, I was in stitches most of the time. What a sense of humour and what a sense of fun!

Here was a very exceptional man who had packed so much into his life. To keep his brain exercised he learned and recited poetry; he loved the English language, the sheer beauty of the words; he was a man of great sensitivity. It is difficult to relate this to his wartime responsibility of innovating, designing and manufacturing devices with just one aim: to kill or injure enemy personnel. He also loved fly-fishing, was President of the Piscatorial Society when he retired from industry, and was an expert on the subject, writing articles in *The Field* magazine under the pseudonym 'Black Pennel'. Leslie Cardew Wood was deeply religious and attended church every week. He told me that he fell out of his wheelchair one day onto the floor of the flat. He could not get back into the chair, could not get up. He tried pulling himself up on various pieces of furniture but they fell over. As he was becoming exhausted, he decided to pray. He said, 'I prayed to God for help, I said, "God, I haven't asked you for much lately but I really would like some help now please", and do you know, I got straight up!'

When I was back home, Leslie would ring up and chat. He made light of his disability. I would ask him how he was. 'I'm in awful pain at the moment but never mind that', and he would always end with a joke, a funny story or odd ode. One I clearly remember went like this:

> There was a young barmaid from Yale,
> Whose breasts bore the prices of ale.
> And on her behind, for the sake of the blind,
> Was the same information in Braille.

It was like talking to Q – Ian Fleming's fictional gadgeteer for special agent James Bond – but much more revealing, for here is the real Q. At least that was his code in India.

When the government began releasing SOE documents to the Public Record Office on 26 October 1999, I renewed my search for veterans of Aston House. The fifty-year rule of silence has ensured that most of the older staff have sadly died. Fortunately I did discover a few with valuable memories that I have included with those of Colonel Wood.

Notes

1. Amess, John, *Mission 179*.
2. Imperial War Museum, Secret War Exhibition.
3. *Ibid*.

The First CO's Story

Lieutenant-Commander A.J.G. Langley was the first commanding officer at Aston House, having arrived with the initial party from Bletchley Park in November 1939. He invented the time pencil fuse and was also the first person to purloin and experiment with plastic explosive as a sabotage weapon.

John Langley was born on 9 September 1899 at Frogmore Farmhouse in the village of Sixpenny Handley, Dorset. While he was still young his parents emigrated to Canada, but later John was put on a ship back to England to get an education. At the age of thirteen he became a cadet at the Royal Naval Colleges at Osborne and Dartmouth and in 1915 he was assigned to HMS *Lord Nelson* as a midshipman. The ship joined the fleet that attacked the Dardanelles. John helped to operate a 9.2-inch gun inside its enclosed turret and suffered a permanently injured eardrum caused by the continuous explosions. When he was fifteen he experienced his first burial at sea, an event that soon became commonplace. Many of his fellow midshipmen were killed in the first attack on enemy positions at Gallipoli.

Promoted to sub-lieutenant, he was appointed first officer of HMS *P 59*, a small torpedo boat engaged in the anti-submarine campaign in the English Channel and in July 1918 he was appointed to HMS *Tenacious*, a large destroyer escorting convoys in the North Sea. Promotion to lieutenant in 1920 enabled him to serve on the battleship HMS *Benbow*. But alas, four years after the First World War, the Navy was forced to make financial cutbacks and Langley was very disappointed to find himself axed from the service that had become his whole life. He returned to Canada in 1923 and studied for a science degree at McGill University, Montreal. During his holiday break he worked with a survey party at Climax, on the southerly branch of the Canadian Pacific Railway in western Saskatchewan, surveying virgin prairie from Climax in the west to the White Mud River in the east, a distance of some fifty miles. After graduation John worked his passage back to England as a stoker on SS *Metagama*. Back in London he was awarded a fellowship at the Institute of Physics and learned to fly in his spare time, gaining a pilot's licence in 1931, but he still longed for the sea and adventure and accepted an invitation from the Oxford Exploration Club to join them as mate on the schooner *The Young Harp* for a three-month voyage to the Canadian Arctic. It was a difficult and dangerous expedition that resulted in recognition, albeit many years later, by the Canadian government, which honoured Langley and his colleagues for the valuable work that they had done in the area by naming geographical features after each of them.

In 1936, Langley was back in London working at the Admiralty. He married 'Toni' Antionette M.P. Viguie, his French sweetheart of many years, and together they built a house in Kent and raised two children. This idyll was not to last long for Langley would soon be called upon to serve his country in naval uniform again, but this time his ships would be landlocked country houses. After the Second World War he established the Scientific Intelligence Section at the Defence Research Board in Ottawa, and later became a director of Computing Devices of Canada. He died in 1979, and his wife in 1983, they are survived by three daughters and nine grandchildren. This is Langley's description of the changing times:

It was early in 1938 and I was frustrated. Not long previously I had spent a short holiday in Italy and Germany. In Italy Black Shirts were everywhere. In Germany Brown Shirts. Both countries were obviously being converted into efficient war machines. The dictators of both of them were clearly not doing that for fun. In 1936 the Italians had conquered Abyssinia; Hitler was already, in 1938, making threatening gestures towards Czechoslovakia, and Mussolini towards Albania.

Any innocent tourist – as I was – could see with half an eye that trouble was brewing. I hadn't an idea of what our high-priced ambassadors and military attachés were reporting to London; if they had any grains of common sense, their reports must have been completely ignored.

When I got back to my London office I found the government continuing to lull the population into a spirit of comfortable complacency. The ship of state seemed to be calmed in the doldrums where it drifted about listlessly. There was little enthusiasm for anything to be found anywhere.

Much of the research being sponsored by the Admiralty was long-term; its results, if any, would not bear fruit for years. I am sure my chief was worried, but there was not much he could do about it. I tended to lose interest in it; my work seemed to me to be irrelevant to the tense situation on the continent. I grew restless. Surely somewhere, somehow, such capabilities as I had could be put to better use? I was accordingly in a receptive mood for suggestions when I received a rather strange telephone call.

'Langley?'

'Speaking.'

'This is Slocum calling; you may remember me; we were together at the Naval Gunnery School after the war.'

'Why, yes. What the hell are you up to now?'

'I was axed as you were; I'm in the War Office now.'

'An ex-naval officer in the War Office?'

'Well, it's a civilian department concerned with future planning. Lord Hankey thinks the future is not too bright.'

'I couldn't agree more.'

'Anyway, I've a friend who wants a scientifically minded chap to do a bit of future planning. I've heard about you; how would you like to do a little research on what might happen if war breaks out? It could be a bit risky in the present climate of pacifism.'

'Count me in; I was in Italy and Germany not too long ago; I'm certain that trouble is brewing.'

'All right. I thought you'd be interested. I want you to see this friend of mine who would like to meet you. Can you be in the lobby of the St Ermin's Hotel next Thursday at 10.30 a.m.?'

'Sure'.

'He's a tall, thin, good-looking chap who will be wearing a carnation in his buttonhole. Keep all this under your hat.'

The proposition put to me by the tall man sporting a carnation in his buttonhole [Major Laurence D. Grand] was staggering, at any rate for me. I said I'd call him tomorrow morning to let him know my decision. I had to think of my family, my future, my pension, but I knew from the moment he shook my hand that I had met a man I would be proud to serve.

Thus it came about that I slipped quietly into the British Secret Service. I had been doing some temporary work for the Air Ministry that I could easily relinquish without causing the smallest flutter. My chief in the Admiralty accepted my resignation with a smile. 'You are a lucky chap', he said, 'I'm sure we'll meet again when war breaks out.' I hadn't said a word about where I was going, but he, I'm sure, sensed that I wasn't taking up a post in some ivory tower. To my friends I was still a minor civil servant who, as the saying went, emulated the fountains in Trafalgar Square by 'playing from ten to four'. I continued to catch the same train to London and the same train back home I had always taken. But now it was no longer play for me. It was all rather exciting in a James Bond-ish sort of way. (The James Bond stories were not written then but when they were I realised that their author had been one of my colleagues. No doubt his association with the SIS [the Secret Intelligence Service, MI6] had some influence upon his tales.)

The conditions of employment with SIS were simple. One was not officially employed by anybody. One was paid in cash; there was no security, no pension or health plan. One did not render any income tax return. Officially one had ceased to exist. An assignment would be given to fulfil as best one could, usually outside the law; if one was caught either by the police of one's own country or the counter-intelligence organisation of another, one would be officially disowned. The conditions were not too comforting when one had a family to think of, but I was convinced that a European war was not far off and, when it broke out, everyone would be in much the same boat. I did take one precaution, though. I went along one day to a wholesaler in the City of London and bought a dozen fifty-pound cases of corned beef and half a dozen sacks of green coffee beans. With that and the large vegetable garden we had at home, I felt the family could tide over any drastic food shortages which might occur in the event of war. Of course the local villagers got to know about my purchases when the stuff was delivered; they thought we were crazy but a year later they abruptly changed their minds, and every now and again some friend would call diffidently on my wife to enquire whether she could spare a pound of coffee.

In London I was given a tiny office in an elderly, unassuming building on an elderly, unassuming street, ostensibly concerned with government statistics. It was one of the camouflaged SIS hideouts; there were others, I suspected, but where they were and what went on in them I never enquired. The less one knew, the safer one was. Secrecy is always difficult to maintain. Most people are so proud of having a deep secret that they almost invariably give away by one hint or another the fact that they are 'in the know'. After that it does not take a counter-intelligence man long to nail them down. Stalin is alleged to have said that the only man who could keep a secret was a dead one; if he discovered someone on his staff who was in the least indiscreet, he had him bumped off or sent to Siberia. In more democratic countries the treatment for breaches of secrecy cannot be so drastic, the best one can do to guard against them is to confine secret plans to the fewest possible people, preferably chopping the plan up into small components and allowing each person concerned to know only one facet. In that way, if the person is caught, only a small piece of the whole is blown and the damage can probably be repaired without either the complete plan being abandoned or the other participants in it being discovered.

In those days I thought the Secret Service was rather old fashioned. Hardly any of the personnel I met had any technical or scientific knowledge; the sort of intelligence it gathered seemed to me to be very similar to that collected in World War I, if the account of its operations given by Somerset Maugham in his fascinating book *Ashenden* was any guide. I only saw the chief of the service [Admiral 'Quex' Sinclair] extremely rarely but I could not help but be reminded of the chief described by Somerset Maugham. However things were starting to change. My own chief [Major Laurence Grand], a brilliant engineer, had been recruited. The service had also taken on another outstanding executive engineer who, at that time, was busy having our embassies abroad fitted with radio communication facilities much to the disgust of some of the older ambassadors who were still living in the horse and buggy age and preferred to send their dispatches by courier rather than make use of these new-fangled gadgets. Nevertheless, change was in the air. When I joined in 1938 I could sometimes sense a feeling of veiled resentment at this 'nuts and bolts' character who had been thrust upon the service; by mid-1939 that attitude was rapidly changing. I am sure that the service was receiving more and more requests from the defence ministries for technical information about the latest Nazi weaponry; many such technical queries were unintelligible to the traditional intelligence officers who had to sink their pride and come along for advice from the despised 'nuts and bolts' section.

To begin with I had to adapt myself to a totally different world inhabited largely by rather strange people. Some were experts in this or that area; others had odd international connections, unspecified of course. They would occasionally disappear from their offices and reappear again as mysteriously as they had gone; sometimes they never reappeared. No one ever made any comments; no one asked any questions. Eventually a new face would appear in the vacant office and we would guess that he had the job of rebuilding the 'X' intelligence network, the previous one presumably having been 'blown' and the agents concerned having been quietly liquidated, perhaps after having been tortured to obtain confessions from them.

My own assignment was not too risky provided its objects could be kept secret and I didn't do anything stupid if I had to go abroad. The objectives were probably inspired by Lord Hankey, a far-sighted statesman who felt sure Hitler would try to destroy us and would employ every subversive trick to do so. The tricks I was to study first were the sabotage attacks made, mostly against our shipping during the First World War, by German agents in foreign ports who concealed incendiary bombs with time-delay fuses in ships leaving for Britain, mixed high explosives in cargoes destined for Britain, usually arranged to go off when the cargo was discharged so that the wrecked ship would block the port, and so on. The examples were very varied. Having found out what they did twenty years ago, I had to imagine how they would update their sabotage weapons and what the latest models would be like. Finally one was asked to devise effective counter-measures.

I remembered a wise remark I had heard years previously: if you wish to defend yourself successfully, you must know how you are going to be attacked. Clearly, the heart of nearly all sabotage attacks is a time fuse that can be set to go off after an interval from half an hour to half a month.

It must preferably be very small, easy to operate, easy to make, silent (no ticking from a clock), immune to vibration or bumping about, unaffected by changes of ambient temperature (to function equally well in the Arctic or tropics), have a good shelf life, be safe to handle and, finally, be constructed of common easily available materials in wide supply with no identification marks on them, so that if found by an enemy he would not be able to prove where it was manufactured.

That presented an interesting problem. I first of all researched everything I could find about what the Germans had used in World War I then what guerrillas had used in South America and the Middle East. I had to be most circumspect. The very word 'sabotage' was anathema to most respectable citizens in those days, even outwardly bloodthirsty military people would, at the slightest hint of anything of that sort, edge away muttering 'Gad, sir, the fellow has no idea of Marquess of Queensberry rules.'

My own small office had no place in it to carry out experiments except an old fireplace. After much trial and error I evolved a little time fuse about the size of a pencil. It could set off incendiary bombs or high explosives. For its time delay it depended on a corrosive solution eating through a fine steel wire. I was desperately in need of some chemist who could experiment with solutions of the different strengths required for eating through the wire in different times. The date was now early 1939. The world still thought that Hitler could be peaceably restrained. Morally I was in the position of an anarchist wishing to blow up the Houses of Parliament and having to seek the help of some innocent academic who would more than likely report me to the police as soon as he realised what I was up to ... then suddenly I remembered a professor of chemistry in the University of London whom I had met when I was doing some minor research work there. He'd been in World War I; he was a realist; he had a wry sense of humour and of adventure. Surely I could try him out very tentatively. My chief agreed.

And so it happened that, in an obscure corner of a university laboratory, thin steel wires were stretched in corrosive solutions of differing strengths to find out how long it would take for them to break. And then the solutions were doctored so that the time did not vary much when the solutions were at different temperatures. I never knew what the professor's students thought he was doing; no doubt just another eccentricity of the old so-and-so.

By mid-1939 we had accumulated a good general grounding in sabotage methods and possible modern sabotage weapons. If I, with my meagre resources, working in a generally hostile environment, had been able to dream up better weapons than the Germans had twenty years ago, there was every reason to suppose that the Nazis would have done equally well if not better when working with enthusiastic official backing. We found out later that they hadn't. That was probably because they had not worried about what to them would have appeared an utterly insignificant phase of warfare. You do not waste time on feather dusters when you are busy making sledgehammers capable of crushing entire nations at one blow. [Poland was crushed in eighteen days. A year later France was crushed in a month.]

Anyway, with the help of my immediate chief, we had now amassed enough information about sabotage to enable us to describe suitable counter-measures. A handbook containing these counter-measures was drafted; it would be issued to 'naval boarding officers' if war came. One of the duties of these officers would be to board all merchant ships just before they entered British ports, search out any sabotage devices and neutralise them. Prototypes of our 'pencil time fuse' were made secretly so that boarding officers could recognise the sort of device they might be looking for. Making them wasn't difficult. All you needed, except for a little ampoule of corrosive liquid, could be bought at the local ironmongers or hardware store. Any chemist capable of doing a little glass blowing could produce an ampoule.

By this time, August 1939, I had made a number of useful contacts. My chief, who was wonderfully versatile and a most charming person, introduced me to the Director of Research, Woolwich Arsenal, another fine character who agreed with us that we were on the fringe of war and entered fully into the spirit of our operations although, officially, it was absolutely against all regulations for him to have anything to do with us. Other patriotic people my chief helped me to have on our 'mobilisation list' in the event of war were the director of a large international company [L.J.C. Wood], a first class mechanical engineer [Ramsay Green] who had lost a leg in World War I, and a Fellow of the Royal Society [Francis Freeth] who had been a consultant to a great corporation. And we could always depend upon our university professor [C.R. Bailey] to help us in any way he could. The 'nuts and bolts' section of the Secret Service, unknown to anyone but ourselves, was ready to go into action as soon as an emergency called for it. Although most of us felt that war was imminent despite the government's complacent attitude, we did not realise how imminent it was, nor how soon our roles would be brutally reversed. From the purely defensive stance we had so far assumed, we were to be plunged suddenly into the thick of the attack.

My chief suspected, as did almost everybody else, that London might be heavily bombed as soon as war was declared against Germany. He had accordingly arranged for a fair-sized country house in a five-acre park thirty miles to the north of London [Aston House] to be requisitioned for us. At the outset of war the 'nuts and bolts' section of the SIS immediately occupied it and set about preparing it for our work. Our chief said that we should camouflage it under some sort of official cover. We should wear appropriate uniforms. Within a week a large official-style notice was erected at the gates of the estate:

WAR DEPARTMENT
INTER-SERVICE EXPERIMENTAL DEPARTMENT

A high wire fence was put up around the park. Our company director and our university professor appeared as Army majors, I was granted wartime rank as lieutenant-commander RN; only our FRS remained a civilian, but as his appearance was so distinguished he added great cachet to the 'management'.

The local villagers were naturally more than curious about what was going on in the old aristocratic home. To satisfy this we would arrange for one of our men to drift occasionally into the local pub where, after everyone had had a few pints of mild and bitter, he would let out – very confidentially, of course – that we were experimenting with special aircraft flares, special rockets for the Navy and special star-shell fillings for the Army. 'But don't whisper a word about it to anyone . . . We don't want any German bombs dropped round here, nor do you . . .'

I cannot say for certain, but I believe that by subterfuge we really did keep secret the real purpose of our establishment. To support that story we bought a good supply of local fireworks that we would let off from time to time at night. When I was in Germany towards the end of the war, we came across, in a Sicherheitsdienst [Security Service] headquarters a list of British spies and saboteurs who should be shot on sight if taken prisoner on the continent, or in England when it was invaded. I was glad to find no mention of anyone in our section, although there were a number of people listed who worked in other intelligence sections.

One of the questions that intrigued us was what type of explosive enemy saboteurs would be likely to use. Dynamite is not normally too difficult to acquire, if necessary by stealing it from stocks kept at quarries or mines for blasting purposes. But that brand of dynamite is usually rather weak: it is far from having the punch of an undiluted high explosive. Also it is not too handy to carry around or make up into convenient charges for special purposes. Gun cotton, used for blowing up bridges and so on by the armed forces, was quite unsuitable for saboteurs even if they could have got hold of it. I had, however, heard of a new high explosive called 'cyclonite' which was said to look and feel like putty. I went to see my friend at Woolwich Arsenal to find out about it. 'Sure,' he said, 'we have recently made some experimental batches.'

'Have the Germans got it?'

'Oh yes, they are usually well ahead of us in this field.'

'Could I take out some samples?' He looked at me with a grin.

'You have a car here?' I said 'Yes.'

'Well' he said, 'mine's at the garage, maybe you could give me a drive home; they won't search your car with me sitting in the front seat.'

So, after dropping him at his home, I uneventfully delivered a hundredweight of cyclonite (more commonly called plastic explosive) to our labs at Aston House. It indeed turned out to be the ideal explosive for saboteurs. From experiments we carried out in our remote deserted quarry, we soon knew exactly how much was needed to derail a train, to blow a sizeable hole in the side of a ship, to detonate an ammunition dump, to destroy an electrical sub-station, to shatter the tracks of a tank, in brief to do a great deal of damage behind enemy lines with not much more than what looked like half a pound of butter and a tiny pencil time fuse.

We worked feverishly through the Phoney War still thinking always of our defence. Then suddenly in May 1940 the Germans struck in the West. The French reeled in retreat. My chief asked me to rush over to Paris to try to make some arrangements with French military friends of his, for us to come to their assistance. But it was too late. The heart had been knocked out of the French. By the time I arrived in Paris the French government had fled south. It was hopeless. They were completely demoralised and disorganised. The Germans were not far away. I hurried to Le Bourget, hoping to get a plane from there to England. Le Bourget was deserted. A few disconsolate Allied military men and diplomatic couriers were wandering around the empty tarmac. Then I spotted a small passenger plane in the shadow of a distant hangar. Hurrying over I found the pilot and mechanic. They had for some reason been sent to Le Bourget a few days previously from Scotland. They were completely out of touch with the course of the war and had not been able to find anyone to give them orders. 'Well, now you have,' I said, and then explained the situation. 'We take off for England immediately.' 'But we've no flight plan, no met forecast,' objected the pilot. 'Never mind,' I said, 'I'll take full responsibility.' I was in naval commander's uniform. He gave in. We collected the other stranded people and took off.

We flew below the cloud which steadily got lower. At the French coast we skimmed over the chalk cliffs, then northwards close to the surface of the sea. The visibility worsened. In those days there was no radar. The pilot had told me that he had been ordered always to fly below the clouds when he left England because he might be shot down by British or German fighters if flying above them. 'Never mind,' I said. 'In this fog at this height (we were about fifty feet above the sea) the risk of running into a ship or the cliffs of Dover is greater than being shot down. Up you go above the clouds.' He hesitated. I was sitting in the co-pilot's seat alongside him and reached for the joystick. I still had my pilot's licence. Under my armpit in my shoulder holster was my little 0.38-inch, revolver. This was no time for dilly-dallying around. Maybe he saw my rather grim expression. Up we went. We weren't shot down, of course, but we did have a little excitement when we finally saw land below us through a hole in the fog. We hadn't a clue where we were. Those old-fashioned biplanes cruising at about a hundred miles an hour could get drifted far off course if you didn't know the wind force and direction. To decide whether to turn left or right, we flipped a coin. We turned right and by great good luck spotted the windsock of some small airfield ten minutes later through a gap in the fog. It was not far from Dover. Had we missed it we might well have run out of fuel somewhere over the North Sea, to be seen no more.

On reporting the failure of my mission to my chief in London the following morning, he said he had expected it, but it was worth trying. 'Go home for the weekend and report to me on Monday; I may have some news for you.'

'The situation is like this,' said my chief when I reported to him on Monday. 'With Dunkirk behind us, there is not a single effective Allied soldier left in Europe to fight the Germans. Until we can land another Expeditionary Force, we have to rely upon the underground or clandestine resistance forces mounted by our defeated allies. As our position gets stronger, and I think the USA will eventually have to intervene, more and more French, Belgian, Danish and Norwegian brave men will become anti-Nazi guerrillas. They have two essential requirements: weapons to fight with and communications with Britain. The SIS Director of Communications will see to the second need. You will see to the first. Have you designed your time fuses and incendiary bombs so that they can be mass-produced? Can we get enough plastic explosive to keep our resistance friends busy?' I replied in the affirmative to both questions.

'OK, I want ten thousand time fuses, a thousand incendiaries and half a ton of plastic available within a couple of months.'

'Ten thousand!' I gasped. 'So what?' he commented with his absolutely charming smile. 'I know it's a bit faster than Ministry of Munitions turns things out, but I'll give you a man who has every sort of pull in Birmingham.'

I knew next to nothing about the techniques of mass production. I did know of course that our gimmicks could be made out of plentifully available common components that would not interfere with strategic materials in short supply. Most fortunately the young company director in our group was intimately familiar with the world of engineering business. (He wasn't actually so young – maybe around thirty-five years old – but it required exceptional competence to be elected to the board of a large company at that age.) The man mentioned by my chief called the next day and turned out to be a real business tycoon; our company director left for Birmingham with him immediately. I felt sure that if anyone could come near fulfilling our chief's order, those two could.

I have absolutely no idea of how the financing was done nor how it was arranged, in that frantic period, to have men taken off other work to make our time fuses, but it was. In two months' time we had the complete order ready for export. There is no doubt that the achievement was greatly helped by the amazing change in public feeling. Since Dunkirk everyone knew we had our backs to the wall. Churchill was in command. Everybody was willing to do almost anything at almost any sacrifice to help the war effort. Traditional customs were thrown away, peacetime rules abandoned. People who had never said a word to one another in peacetime became the best of friends in the emergency. All that was vividly demonstrated to me when I went on one of my rare visits to home. I managed to catch the 4.50 train from Cannon Street Station, in the heart of the City of London, to Sevenoaks, a small Kentish town near home. That train, which I had caught hundreds of times before when I was working at the Admiralty, was referred to as the VIP express. I was far from being a VIP but the price of a first-class season ticket was well worth the advantages of being able to travel by it. There was nothing but first-class carriages on it; it only stopped once between London and Sevenoaks, which was a dormitory for extremely wealthy City people. The Lord Mayor of London was one of them. Others were the sort of people I had never heard of: great bankers, members of the Stock Exchange, international financiers, company directors. I would slink aboard, insinuate myself unobtrusively into a seat and meditate while my co-travellers, never even glancing at me, would bury themselves behind the *Financial Times*. Even when something untoward happened – say, an hour's delay owing to fog – no words passed. Everyone clung grimly to the tradition that no one ever spoke to a stranger.

But now all that had dramatically changed. We were all in the same boat. My uniform had somehow transformed the character whom they had previously taken for some minor civil service clerk into someone who could save their bacon. They introduced themselves, squeezed up to make room for me in the carriage, asked me how the war was going. Could they do anything to help? They had obviously thrown away their bowler hats and rolled umbrellas, and were ready to roll up their sleeves to assist the war effort in any way they could. The same outlook would have prevailed in Birmingham when our two crusaders went to have 10,000 time fuses produced. In the meantime, secret radio communications had been fixed up between SIS radio centre and a few loyal groups on the continent. Supplies were flown over by light planes on moonless nights and parachuted to secret rendezvous. The underground war had started. No longer were our naval boarding officers searching desperately for enemy sabotage weapons in ships coming to Britain; the roles had been completely reversed: it was now the German military police who were searching desperately in occupied territory for our sabotage munitions.

To begin with, this secret war did very little more than inflict minor pinpricks on the German war effort, although it had valuable side effects for us. Good resistance fighters were few and far between, but there were good informers. From them came reports of German troop movements, of the sailing of German warships and submarines, of the airfields the Germans were constructing along the French coast, of what the Vichy French were planning, of how we could rescue our aircrews who had been shot down over occupied territory and managed to reach the Channel coast, generally with the self-sacrificing help of the resistance people who knew only too well that they would probably be shot if found out. A week later I was to get mixed up briefly in the rescue business.

Our chief was visiting Aston House. We were all as busy as bees perfecting the designs of our munitions, bringing out little pamphlets in French giving instructions on how to handle them, arranging for the steady delivery of them to some secret airfield [probably RAF Tangmere] on the south coast, whence they were flown by night to a secret resistance movement rendezvous in France.

'You seem to be pretty well organised here,' said my chief. 'Could your second in charge look after the place for a couple of weeks?'

'Of course,' I replied. 'For the next month or so we shall be busy supervising production and testing products, after that we imagine that we may have some training to do. I'd like to be here for that.'

'OK. I have another small job for you. Come to my office tomorrow morning. Wear uniform, but bring a suitcase of nondescript civvies and night things with you.'

My chief explained the position. The French resistance people were really doing their stuff in helping shot-down RAF pilots and escaped prisoners of war evade the Germans and reach the French coast. The SIS Director of Communications was in touch with them and the first batch, consisting of three pilots and a sailor, who had escaped at Dunkirk, were hidden in a farmhouse near an isolated cove on the north coast of Brittany. This was one of the first sea rescue operations of this type to be attempted and I was to be the Operations Officer at the headquarters of the Senior Naval Officer (SNO) Dartmouth, who, of course, knew nothing at all about the plan. The Admiralty would send him a signal requesting his co-operation. At Dartmouth, under the SNO's command, there was a small flotilla of high-speed motor boats manned by Royal Naval Volunteer Reserve (RNVR) personnel – mostly amateur yachtsmen – splendid men, even if a trifle looked down upon by the regular navy. One of those yachtsmen had been far-sighted enough to have special silencers fitted in his boat so that it could cruise almost noiselessly. My chief gave me his name. There were other details about recognition signals at the Brittany coast, communications with the resistance group concerned and so on. I pointed out that the operation looked a bit risky for the personnel involved (not me); it is a 240-mile trip across the Channel from Dartmouth to Brittany and back, with often rough weather and always fierce tides. The coast of Brittany was edged with dangerous reefs and shoals; it was closely patrolled by German P.T. [Patrol Torpedo] boats. He smiled at me. 'I'm glad you appreciate the tactical position,' he said. 'That's why I thought you might have a good chance of pulling it off. We considered an air rescue, of course, but there are absolutely no safe landing fields in the area. Good luck.'

The SNO Dartmouth was a grizzled old retired admiral. I didn't meet anyone on his staff who wasn't elderly and retired. These so-called 'dug-outs' were doing a fine housekeeping job for the Navy. They looked after the guarding of the coasts, managed the inshore patrols by motor boats and the like, were responsible for the security of minor ports such as Dartmouth, saw to the refurbishing of small shipyards and superintended the building of a multitude of small craft required by the Navy.

'What's this all about?' he asked me, glancing at the signal he had received from the Admiralty. I explained in vague terms, requesting that *Patrol Boat 317* might be allocated for this job if the crew would volunteer for it. A few minor changes would be necessary. The topsides should be painted a darker grey, all the identification marks obliterated. Before they sailed, all their codes and confidential books would be landed. The prize was three pilots and a sailor.

'My son is in the RAF,' he said. 'Go right ahead. I'll give the necessary orders for all concerned to give you every facility. If the crew of *317* don't like the idea, try some of the other crews. These amateur yachtsmen are a daredevil lot.'

It was not long before *317* was all ready to sail. The crew were enthusiastic; one of them even knew the Brittany coast like the back of his hand, having yachted all along it two summers previously. Still, yachting in daylight in the summer is not quite the same as creeping into a rocky cove in the middle of the night when all the lighthouses and light buoys are extinguished, and enemy boats are on the lookout for you.

We now had to wait for suitable weather conditions. There must be no moon and we'd prefer dark, rainy overcast with not too much wind. I kept the Director of Communications in London in touch with progress via a prearranged secure telephone channel. Three days later conditions looked about as promising, from our point of view, as could be expected. The skipper of the *317* was anxious to sail and I agreed. The D of C, London, was informed. The party in Brittany would shine a shaded lamp to seaward from the cove at intervals beginning at 10.00 p.m. If *317* got into trouble, she was to send a prearranged signal by her little radio to SNO Dartmouth. Now all I had to do was to spend the night in the Operations Room of the SNO. I must admit that I am no tough warrior. The business of sending those fine youngsters off on a trip from which they had perhaps a fifty-fifty chance of returning alive was not easy. Time passed. The wind freshened. A nasty sea was running up the Channel. God knows what it would be like off that treacherous Brittany coast. Midnight passed, then 4.00 a.m., then 6.00 a.m. The sun was rising, still no sign of them, still no signal. I had a lookout man sweeping the horizon with a powerful telescope. Another patrol boat was standing by to go to their assistance if they signalled a breakdown in mid-Channel. At last, around eight o'clock they hove into sight, limping rather slowly through the rough sea but outwardly, at least, intact. I hurriedly changed into my civilian clothes before going down to the dock to meet them.

At nine the SNO came to the Ops Room. I had changed back into uniform and had another couple of cups of coffee – making a total of about a dozen since the previous evening. I saluted. 'Operation completed, sir,' I reported. 'I took the liberty of granting, in your name, the skipper's request, that he and his crew take the day off; they are all a bit tired. They will report to you tomorrow, sir, if you so desire.' 'Perhaps you had better take a day off, too,' he answered. 'You don't look as if you've slept much. What's happened to the rescued men?' 'Well, sir, the skipper and crew of the *317* asked that they might look after them today. As you know all of the crew belong to the yacht club, where they can arrange for the others to get baths, meals and a bed. They will also fix up some decent clothing for them; on arrival they were hardly in suitable attire for a naval mess. I have arranged for the next of kin to be advised that they are now in England.' The old admiral looked rather quizzically at me. 'You don't seem to be quite like an *ordinary* naval officer,' he remarked. 'I regret it sir,' I said. He smiled at me. 'Perhaps I'm not quite like an ordinary retired admiral; what are the rescued lads like?' 'The pilots are just what you'd expect, sir, terrific. They were seasick coming across but regarded the whole operation as great fun, as indeed *317*'s crew seems to have, too. I understood from you, sir, that you are not unfamiliar with RAF pilots.' 'And the sailor, what happened to him?' 'He is a young yachtsman who took his boat over to Dunkirk to help. The boat was shot to pieces, he managed to swim ashore, was collared by the Germans, succeeded in disposing of his guard the same night and escaping.' 'Disposing of his guard?' 'Yes, sir, I understand the guard accidentally tripped over a hand grenade.' 'Oh . . . and the others?' 'Nothing special to report, sir. They did bump into a German sentry on a bridge across some river one night, but he unfortunately slipped off the bridge and was drowned.' 'I see. Maybe these young men would feel a little out of place in our mess with rather conservative staff. I wonder?' he enquired diffidently. 'Do you think they might all, including *317*'s crew, care to dine at my home tomorrow evening? I do have a couple of tolerably presentable daughters who might brighten the occasion. It would be absolutely informal, of course.'

I grinned at him. The old dear. 'I will see that your request is carried out, sir.' 'And could you come too?' I'm afraid, sir, that I had better get back to London. There may be more of these operations brewing. I probably won't be personally involved, but if I have your permission, sir, I would like to report to my chief what tremendous co-operation we have had from the SNO Dartmouth.' He looked at me severely. 'Commanders,' he said, 'do not usually thank admirals, but as these circumstances are a little unusual, maybe I could overlook it.' We shook hands. I never saw him again.

In June 1940 I was in the chief's office. 'Things don't look too good,' he said. 'Have a look at these.' He gave me a number of RAF reconnaissance photographs; they were of the ports along the coast of Belgium and France as far west as Cherbourg. Every port was chock-full of little oblong objects. 'What are those?' I asked. 'Invasion barges,' he replied. 'And these,' handing me another bunch of photographs, 'are of the new airfields they are constructing along the north French coast.'

Britain, I knew, was almost defenceless. The Army had lost most of its equipment at Dunkirk; the Air Force was insignificant compared with the Luftwaffe; only the Navy could be of help in preventing an invasion, but with the German air and submarine superiority, control of the Channel was not certain. If the Germans established a bridgehead on our south coast, it would be a miracle if we could repel them.

'Where's your family?' enquired my chief. 'Near Sevenoaks, between Hastings and London.' 'Are they doing any essential war work?' 'Hardly,' I replied. 'There's my wife and her elderly parents, with our two children aged six months and three.' 'Well, I suggest they might all take a holiday. Have you any other relatives in other parts of England?' 'Not really, sir; as you know I am actually a Canadian. My nearest relatives are in Victoria, BC, rather a long way from here.' 'Well, do as you please. But I suggest that you move your family out of the invasion route. I don't want any of my officers distracted by family worries if the Nazis land in Britain; there will be plenty of other things to worry about then.' 'OK, sir. I'll tip the other members of my section off and give them a weekend's leave if they wish to move their families.'

A week later an odd little convoy could be seen leaving the village of Halstead in Kent. In the first car, which I'd borrowed and was unlicensed, was a Navy commander complete with brass hat, an elderly Frenchman (his father-in-law), piles of luggage and two small Scottie dogs. In the second car there was his wife, two small children and his French mother-in-law. It is doubtful if ever a more suspicious outfit ever tried to cross southern England at a time when every foreigner in that area was assumed to be a Nazi spy. We got to the outskirts of Winchester without interruption, but there we ran into military operations. Armoured personnel carriers and tanks blocked the road. Traffic was being regulated by military police. My heart sank. There was I, a somewhat spurious Navy commander with an unlicensed car accompanied by a gang of French characters who, for all any conscientious military policeman knew, were French spies. The MP approached. 'Sorry about the hold-up, sir, let me guide you past our convoy.' It was perhaps my eldest daughter who was really responsible for our escape. She was frightfully carsick. Not even the toughest MP could but be sympathetic. Twenty tanks were held up and we surged ahead. Nobody had apparently noticed that my car was unlicensed. We had arranged for the family to spend a holiday in an old farmhouse on the outskirts of a small village in Dorset, Sixpenny Handley, where I had been born forty years previously. I hadn't revisited it for thirty years. It had changed hardly at all. Even the squire, Colonel Cartwright, and his wife were still there. My mother, who had a bungalow between Southampton and Portsmouth – a risky area in the event of an invasion – joined the family at the farm. I paid my respects to the squire, said hello to some of the old villagers who remembered my parents, and hurried back to my job at Aston House. A month later I was again in my chief's office discussing some problem or other. 'By the way,' he said, 'from what we can find out it looks as if the enemy invasion of Britain has been postponed. A number of the concentrations of their invasion barges have been dispersed and the barges towed back up the Rhine and elsewhere. Perhaps they have decided to crush our Air Force and neutralise our southern naval bases before their sea trip. So watch out. But I think you can bring your family home again.'

His assessment of the enemy threat was not far off, but it was not quite correct. The towing away of some barges was done to deceive us. We discovered what was actually happening from documents captured towards the end of the war.

The gist of the tale they told us is as follows: Hitler was furious that the British continued the fight and would not accept a compromise peace after the British Expeditionary Force had been ignominiously chased off the continent at Dunkirk. Hitler had plans for crushing the Russians, but did not fancy having to fight a war on two fronts. He called his chiefs of staff together at the beginning of June 1940 and directed Operation Sealion – the invasion of England. He had the enthusiastic support of Göring, who said that 'the Luftwaffe would soon smash the RAF to pulp and make every port on the English south coast untenable for any ships of the British Navy'. The Chief of the General Staff also supported the operation although he asked for a couple of months' grace in which to make preparations. He proposed that twenty-five divisions be landed in England. Admiral Raeder, the Chief of the Naval Staff, also supported it (he had little option when Hitler had made up his mind) but cautioned that the Navy would need the help of the Luftwaffe in protecting Army convoys from British naval attack when crossing the Channel. In fact Raeder was seriously worried about the whole scheme. He had a healthy respect for the Royal Navy. He had been more than impressed by the way the RN had rescued practically the whole of the British Army from Dunkirk in the face of heavy attack by his ships and the Luftwaffe. He knew that the British would sacrifice every ship and every man to counter an invasion. Göring had promised to launch his attack against the RAF on 15 September as D-Day for the invasion. He anticipated that by the end of September the German Army would be holding a line stretching from the Thames estuary along the hills south of London and Portsmouth . . .

I winced when reading those captured documents, four years later. My family home was situated right on those hills running south of London, my mother's bungalow was next door to Portsmouth. I had never realised the narrow escape they had had. But, at the time, I took my chief's advice and the family returned home. It was the end of July. An ominous quiet reigned over Kent. In the middle of August the Germans launched their great attack against RAF Fighter Command. We didn't know it at the time, of course, but this was the start of one of the decisive battles of the war – the Battle of Britain. Ironically enough I had brought my family back for a front seat at the battle. A large Fighter Command airfield lay a few miles to the west of our home; half a dozen others were within fifty miles of it. By the end of October the battle ended; the Luftwaffe had lost seven fighters or fighter-bombers for every fighter lost by us; it was too much even for Göring to stomach. He decided to bring England to its knees by his heavy bombers at night; bombers in the dark would be difficult for our fighters to locate.

That attack was the family's next trial – and of course a terrible ordeal for everyone living in London and living south of it. It persisted for months and months. The family had not been injured during the Battle of Britain although a number of German aircraft had crashed uncomfortably close to our house. During the ensuing months they miraculously escaped unharmed although there were bomb craters in almost every field round about. By the end of the war the Sevenoaks Rural District alone received over 3,000 high explosive bombs, over 45,000 incendiary bombs and over 130 flying bombs. As the war progressed, more and more anti-aircraft batteries were sited south of London. Every anti-aircraft shell fired into the air has to come down again, usually as a multitude of jagged steel fragments. The countryside was absolutely littered with them. On the few occasions I was able to go home, I found it impossible to mow the lawn as it was liberally sprinkled with steel fragments which ruined the mower blades at the first cut.

Through all the turmoil Toni maintained her usual cheerfulness and calm, something which I found difficult to achieve myself, although Aston House, north of London, was a haven of safety compared with my home. To my mind the unsung heroes and heroines of the war in Britain were the civilians who unflinchingly stood up to Hitler's might with never a thought of surrender or compromise. For night after night, month after month and year after year from the beginning of the terrible winter of 1940 they listened to the banshee wail of the air-raid sirens announcing another bombing attack. And among them I naturally had a special feeling for the thousands of mothers of young families, whose husbands were away with the armed forces or in other parts of the country on essential war work, and who had to face alone those dreadful nights.

Every evening Toni would get the children to sleep under the Morrison shelter which was a massive steel table about the size of a double bed, strong enough it was hoped to withstand a house collapsing on top of it and so save the children from being crushed to death if a bomb exploded nearby. We had removed our ordinary dining table and managed to squeeze the shelter into our dining-room. Everyone who could, slept on the ground floor because it was safer. Toni herself slept under the stairs, being careful to have handy a first aid kit and within easy reach a steel shovel by a couple of pails of sand for dealing with incendiary bombs. Outside the night would be dark and silent. Not a light could be seen; the blackout was complete. As enemy planes approached the coast, the soft music from her wireless would fade away; the wireless stations in Britain going one by one off the air so as not to act as guides for the bombers. Then, growing louder and louder, would be heard the ominous throb of the enemy planes. Suddenly the blackness of the night would be pierced by the light beams of a dozen searchlights, almost immediately to be followed by the flashes and bangs of the anti-aircraft batteries. The nightly battle had begun! The sky would be star-dusted by bursting shells. (Don't forget to wear your steel helmet if you have to go outside . . . jagged fragments (shrapnel) of the shells come down like hail across the land.) And next, if bombs landed in the neighbourhood, the deafening explosions were often followed by the lurid flames from burning buildings. As regularly as sirens would sound their warning after sunset, they would sound the welcome, long, steady note of the 'All clear' before sunrise. Life in the besieged island would then return to normal for a nation fighting for survival, that is to say the lives of those who survived. As a result of the bombing attacks on Britain during the war the number of civilians killed amounted to over 60,000 and the seriously injured to over 86,000, most of them in the southern half of England. You may now appreciate why I gave Toni a specially engraved memento for her bravery 'beyond the call of duty', as the official citations go, during that harrowing time.

Britain lost no time in telling the occupied countries about the stunning defeat of the Luftwaffe. 'Doubting Thomas' became a little less doubtful about Britain's survival. All the same it was one thing for the British to stave off a Nazi invasion; it was quite another for them to invade the continent and liberate the conquered peoples. Nevertheless, more and more men and women were encouraged to escape from occupied territory to Britain in order to join up with the free forces there or offer their services to the various resistance movements, which were still pathetically small.

As I suspected, our section at Aston House was now called upon to train more and more resistance people in the handling of our weapons.

My chief agreed that we should never permit any of them to come to our establishment. It was too risky. There was always the possibility that the German counter-intelligence would plant double-crossers among them or that the less fanatically loyal would weaken when they got home and give the game away or that any of them might be caught by the enemy and forced under torture to tell all they knew. After all, the position of Britain at that time still looked quite hopeless to any outsider, and the Nazi position impregnable. What was the point of risking not only one's own neck but those of one's family as well, in a hopeless cause? In consequence visitors who were considered to have legitimate interest in sabotage weapons were taken only to the remote quarry where we carried out our field trials. On such occasions, those of us who had to be present went in old civilian clothes, always wore sunglasses and were introduced by fictitious names. Looking back, it all appears rather childish but at the time, in those dark days of 1940, one was prepared to go to any lengths, no matter how melodramatic, to preserve secrets upon which other men's lives might depend.

And so we did our utmost to maintain our secret cover. The people who received our weapons knew neither where they came from nor who had made them. None of the defence ministries knew of our existence; with the exception of my chief, the only high-ups in London who were aware of our activities were the Chief of the SIS and a couple of Cabinet ministers. Even so rumours must have started to circulate. A Cabinet minister might ask himself what business the Secret Service had in running some sort of secret war. The SIS was supposed to concentrate on getting useful information, not be mixed up with a lot of piratical ruffians who might well blow up something which would sully the Allied name. On the other hand the policy of backing up resistance movements was obviously a good thing to be in on; it offered scope for setting up a 'proper' headquarters in London directed by the 'proper' people. I knew nothing of that, but began to smell a rat when my chief called up one day to say that a Cabinet minister had expressed his desire to inspect our place and he would be bringing him along in two days' time. We should have a demonstration ready for him in our field testing area.

The great man [unnamed] duly arrived. He was very small, had a pinched look and a bad cold. He obviously had absolutely no technical knowledge. After touring the establishment, he was taken to the quarry where we did our field trials and trained resistance people. By that time our boys were pretty adept at putting on demonstrations. It had been explained to our distinguished visitor that the time fuses to be used were for training purposes; they were set to go off five minutes after actuation, to save time.

The quarry looked deserted when we arrived. Down one side of it there was a length of railway line. At another spot there were some 40-gallon oil drums; at another, a pile of lumber. Near the entrance was parked a condemned military truck we had scrounged. It was the late afternoon of a typically English autumn day. Light drizzle was falling from low grey clouds. In the humid half-light the old abandoned quarry took on a sinister appearance. The minister looked far from cheerful as he shook raindrops from the brim of his hat. 'Go ahead,' he growled. My chief blew a short blast on a whistle. A man leading a frisky dog came walking along the gravel road through the quarry. Every now and again the dog would drag the man aside and leave a calling card at some convenient spot, the oil drums for one. The man was followed by an untidy-looking woman carrying an umbrella and a shopping bag (one of our secretaries took that part). She stopped to light a cigarette near the woodpile, threw the empty cigarette packet away and trudged on. The last character, dressed as a farm labourer, arrived riding a rickety old bicycle with a basket of potatoes tied by string to the carrier. Near the further end of the quarry the basket slipped off, the potatoes rolling all over the place. The man stopped, gathered up the spuds, retied the basket to his bike and made away. 'Just stand back a little, sir,' said my chief to the minister. 'There's absolutely no danger, but there may be a bit of a bang.' Almost immediately there was a slight hissing sound and the pile of lumber burst into flames; next a slight report was accompanied by a spurt of flame and streams of burning oil began running from an oil drum. 'A minute to go,' said my chief, looking at his watch. Then a blinding flash followed by an ear-splitting crack as half a pound of plastic explosive blew a gap a foot long in one of the rails of the track running near the road. 'That charge is normally set off by the train itself,' explained the chief. 'We have a little pressure switch which is slipped under the sleeper. Military vehicles are also easy targets. Would you care to see us deal with this one, sir?' pointing to the truck. The minister shuddered. He had jumped back when the explosive detonated. I was sure he was frightened. 'I have seen quite enough, thank you.'

I am always amazed by the number of important people directing wars who have so little appreciation of what war is really like when it comes to the crunch.

Sure enough, my rat-smelling was justified. A month later my chief summoned me to his London office. He told me that the government was much impressed by our activities, felt that they should be greatly expanded and removed from the SIS, intended to set up a new organisation to be called the 'Special Operations Executive' [SOE] which should be placed under the Ministry of Economic Affairs. The nucleus of a headquarters staff had already been formed. A good many advertising executives from a prominent agency in the City of London were among them. 'An advertising agency?' I muttered. 'Yes,' answered my chief. 'They are very competent men who haven't much to do in wartime.' He looked me straight in the face. 'Security will be a bit of a problem at first, but they will learn quickly.'

Words failed me. It was all so sudden. Yet I had seen the writing on the wall. Our work was indeed becoming more and more like a regular military establishment. Production would have to be increased, our training facilities enlarged. The thrust, enthusiasm and spontaneity of the 'Robin Hood' phase of our activities at Aston House were drawing to an end. No longer would our FRS slip away in the early hours of the morning to supervise manufacture of the incendiary arrows we had devised and which were being used against the Italians in Abyssinia. All that sort of thing would be regularised. Proper Ministry of Supply forms would have to be filled out and approved by God-only-knew-what channels, and products passed by 'proper' official inspectors. By the time they reached enemy-occupied territory, German intelligence would probably know as much about them as we did. Oh well, that was the way wars went. I remembered remarking to my boss at the Admiralty before the war that if such and such wasn't done soon, there would be a hell of a muddle when war broke out. He looked at me sympathetically and said quietly, 'John, war is a muddle.'

My present chief was a real 'Robin Hood'. I knew he must feel deeply about these developments. 'What are you going to do, sir?' I asked. 'Keep this under your hat John, but I have requested another posting.

Meanwhile I will do everything in my power to help you and your staff. If any of you do not wish to be transferred to SOE, you may depend upon me to ensure that you are suitably relocated. As a matter of fact, the Director of Communications of the SIS has already asked me personally that you be transferred to his section if you wish to remain in the Secret Service. Go back to Aston House, discuss the position with your staff and let me know the result. Good luck to you all.'

It was nearly dark. I drove slowly northwards with dimmed headlamps through London in the blackout. The sirens had already sounded to warn of a German air raid. The wrecked buildings on either side of the road harmonised with my feelings. Sad as I felt, I was cheered by the thought of the Director of Communications. Like my chief, he was another 'Robin Hood' and he had asked for me. My mind was made up. I had a fair idea of my weaknesses and my not very outstanding capabilities. I knew I wouldn't fit usefully into a large organisation. Such contributions as I could make to the war effort would be much more effective with another 'Robin Hood'.

Calling the officers together the following morning, I explained the situation to them. They were flabbergasted. They implored me to reconsider my decision. It was terribly nice of them. 'Look,' I said, 'let's not be sentimental about this. The war changes and we have to change. This ship has been in commission for two years. In the best traditions of the Navy, it will be to everyone's good for it to be re-commissioned under new command. If you all agree, I propose to recommend to our chief that Leslie Wood (he was our company director) take over. He knows the City of London, he figures in the Directory of Directors, he can talk turkey to the MEW [Ministry of Economic Warfare] boys and is fully competent to protect your interests.'

In the end they all agreed. I reported the result of that agreement to my chief. Three weeks later I received my official (as far as anything can be official in the Secret Service) transfer to the Communications Section (Whaddon Hall). They gave me an absolutely smashing farewell dinner and presented me with a silver mug on which was engraved, 'To A.J.G.L. from his happy ship.' I was deeply moved. It was the only souvenir of those adventurous years I took away with me. None of us had kept a diary nor retained a single copy of any memorandum we had written; we were all too conscious of security to retain records. For the next three years that silver mug was the only souvenir I had of an episode in my life which I shall never forget.

But after the war I acquired another memento. In 1946 I was going to visit a friend who lived north of London and noticed that the road went close to my old 'happy ship'. I detoured to see it once again. It was a sad sight. The house had been de-requisitioned at the end of the war and never occupied since then. One of the great entrance gates was sagging off its hinges. I drove up the weed-covered driveway to the house. Deserted and empty, its windows looked with blind eyes onto unkempt lawns. I peered through to see paper peeling from the walls in the erstwhile handsome rooms. Outside the great oak front door there had been a large brass bell – similar to a ship's bell – hanging from a wrought frame. I looked for it. Its frame had toppled over, and the bell was half covered by weeds at the bottom of a ditch. I 'rescued' it. For the last twenty-five years it has hung in a proud position outside a cabin on an island I own in a beautiful lake in Canada. I think the island has been a 'happy ship' for the family, which spends most of the summer holidays there.

I had a moment of great pleasure when I was asked to call at the offices of the British High Commission in Ottawa ten years after the war ended. I had not the least idea what it might be about. When I got there a genial official handed me a cheque and told me that it came from the British Royal Commission on Awards to Inventors and was in recognition of my invention of the time pencil fuse. The cheque wasn't for very much, but that was beside the point. For me it represented the happy ending of a long and rather hazardous journey – the little time-fuse born secretly like an illegitimate child in an obscure back room before the war, had reached honourable manhood during the war and achieved official recognition.

Note

The above extracts are from Arthur John G. Langley's Memoir. Ottawa 1974. Imperial War Museum.

The Second CO's Story

A bank manager's son, Leslie John Cardew Wood was born on 4 August 1898, and educated at Dulwich and the City & Guilds Mechanical Engineering Department. In 1916 he volunteered for the Royal Flying Corps and, while learning to fly, was involved in an incident worthy of P.G. Wodehouse. Having made a forced landing on an estate in Staffordshire owned by the third Lord Hatherton, he was informed by his lordship that one of the farmhouses had been made available to a troupe of chorus girls. He eagerly accepted the invitation to 'come and join us'.

Next day, Lord Hatherton loaded the fledgling pilot's Vickers Gunbus with strawberries as a present for the mess. Inevitably this hospitality led to further landings there, though Wood was permanently grounded soon after the incident, when it was discovered that he had a heart condition. (Nothing to do with the chorus girls!) By pestering a general to the point of being threatened with arrest, he remained in the RFC and was posted to Heliopolis in Egypt as a navigation instructor. On demobilisation, by then a lieutenant, he completed his education with a degree in engineering at Imperial College, London, and published a paper on air navigation, which was acknowledged by his election in 1920 as an associate fellow of the Royal Aeronautical Society.

The next year he went to India, where he was responsible for installing refrigeration plants. On his return home in the mid-1920s he joined Bells Asbestos & Engineering which later became Bestobell and is, at the time of writing, Bestobell Aviation.

Wood married Vera Marion Kells in 1922. They had two daughters, Patricia and Jennifer. In civilian life between the wars, he gained a considerable reputation for inventiveness. He developed an asbestos fire-fighting suit, which, while heavy and ungainly by today's standards, was greatly admired at the time, and was adopted by the RAF and civil airlines. A sculpture of this suit is still to be seen outside the entrance of the factory in Slough. The press was particularly delighted by his willingness to don the suit and demonstrate its efficiency in test blazes. Less spectacular, but of more permanent significance, was his part in the development of silicone rubber for aviation purposes.

In 1938 Wood was recruited by Major Laurence Grand, who had been asked by the then C, the head of the Secret Intelligence Service (Admiral 'Quex' Sinclair), to start a secret service section, known as 'D', shortly to be part of the new SOE.

With the resignation of Lieutenant-Commander Langley on the inception of SOE, the former RFC lieutenant was now a lieutenant-colonel with responsibility for Aston House, Station 12, which he surreptitiously renamed Experimental Station 6 (War Department) in order to run it without interference from, as he said in his letter (*see* Introduction) 'nosey parker Generals from the War Office who tried to tell me how to run my establishment'.

Colonel Wood's contribution was particularly important to SOE because of the sabotage weapons and equipment that his E.S.6. (WD) produced. He relished playing with his 'toys', which included anything from firing a silent mortar to testing powerful explosives and lethal devices to evaluate their effectiveness before they were employed in the field. As the war progressed there was an increasing requirement for special 'toys' in the Far East, and Wood was posted to the Special Forces Development Centre, which he established at Poona and Meerut in 1944. There his staff concentrated on the research, development, training and camouflage of special explosive devices. Although the jungle offered less scope for ingenuity than Europe, some unusual toys were produced at that time, aimed at attracting Japanese Army souvenir hunters. One was a fake Chinese lantern made of wood and plaster rather than the customary heavy stone, with its five compartments filled with explosive. There were also Balinese carvings, moulded in high explosive and finished in wood, sandstone or porcelain as a disguise, as well as tins of soya sauce and kerosene with Japanese labels, which exploded when opened.

Wood's daughter Patricia, who incidentally was a translator at the Nuremberg Trials, revealed recently that his general knowledge of natural history was truly outstanding, while another area of genuine expertise centred on English silver, seventeenth to nineteenth century, and the now much-sought-after Calcutta silver. She had been surprised to learn that he was co-founder of the Silver Collectors' Society. He collected Chinese porcelain, including some pieces of enormous interest. He was generous to a fault and some of the finest of these and his earliest silver items were quietly donated to museums.

He adored parties and his enjoyment was infectious: his grandchildren used to say they preferred to watch *Tom and Jerry* with grandpa because he laughed so much it made them laugh even more.

Colonel Wood stated:

To start off I'll give you my background. I was in the Regular Army Reserve of Officers as a Sapper [Royal Engineer], and before the war I was trained for Intelligence, the background being rather intriguing. There was a chap called Laurence Grand, he was a Sapper officer up on the frontier in India before the war and he was full of ideas. Amongst others he got fed up with the Pathans raiding and stealing ammunition. He had the delightful idea of letting them steal ammunition of which about one in ten rounds would be loaded with high explosive instead of ordinary cordite, so that when they fired their bundook that would be that! It was a brilliant idea but to the dear old boys out there – 'By God, sir, the man's a cad! God! I've never heard anything like it!' and he was absolutely deplored, they couldn't stand the fellow – 'You know, the Pathan's a gentleman!' Well, gentleman be damned, I've had little to do with them, but they're certainly good fighters.

He was cursed for this, but they remembered it, and before the Second World War something eventually called a Special Operations Executive was dreamed up and they thought that Grand would be a very good chap to put in charge of all the sabotage and raids. He knew a friend of mine and I was recruited and called up before war had actually been declared, to go to what was then the Intelligence Headquarters in England at Bletchley Park, Station X.

Author M.R.D. Foot confirms Grand's role:

In late March 1938 the head of SIS, Admiral 'Quex' Sinclair, known as 'C', borrowed Royal Engineers officer Major L.D. Grand and told him to start a new section of the Secret Service. It was to be called Section 'D' (D for Destruction). Grand's task was to look into the theory of secret offensives: How could enemies be attacked otherwise than by the usual military means? While peace lasted he was to do nothing; but he was to think about sabotage, labour unrest, inflation, anything else that could be done to weaken an enemy, and if he could he was to make outline plans for them. He was to consider who could do the work on the spot – communists, perhaps, or Jews – and he was to consider means of propaganda, to shift enemy opinion. No wonder Grand noted, when he put in his final report years later, 'Examining such an enormous task, one felt as if one had been told to move the Pyramids with a pin.' He was a striking personality, tall, handsome, well tailored, with a heavy dark moustache; wore a red carnation; smoked cigarettes, almost without cease, through an elegant black holder; had an equally elegant wit. He was brimful of ideas and energy, and he had a rare gift: he gave full trust to those under him and backed them up without question against outsiders. Unhappily he had a gift of rubbing staid men up the wrong way.[1]

Kim Philby observed that Grand never had the resources to carry out his ideas, though they were given freely to his successors. Thus Grand's demands on the Treasury and on the armed forces were often blocked within the service. At best they were given lukewarm support.

Grand was 'D'. Subsection heads were coded DA, DB – Guy Burgess was DU and Kim Philby was DUD! Incidentally it was Guy Burgess who proposed the establishment of a school for training agents in the technique of underground work. He suggested it be called the 'Guy Fawkes College' to commemorate the unsuccessful conspirator who had been foiled by the vigilance of the Elizabethan SIS.[2]

Colonel Wood continued:

We were quartered at Bletchley Park for a short time. It was there that I met the cadre of the people with whom I was going to work.

There was a Commander John Langley, RN – he was loaned from Naval Intelligence – and Colin Meek, a brilliant young scientist, from one of the scientific establishments; he was a civil servant, and I think they'd already recruited a very good chap called Captain Bailey, who was in the First World War; he was a professor at University College [London]. Then there were a couple of first-class staff sergeants who had been employed at Woolwich Arsenal, named Doe and Stallard, the latter was a hell of a chap! Well, we were only there a short time – it was an idiotic place, it was supposed to be secret. I was not allowed to tell my wife where I was but she was told all right, because somebody met me accidentally in town and said to her later, 'I've just been talking to your husband in Bletchley.' You see the whole thing was a nonsense. The other thing I remember about Bletchley was that we behaved like schoolboys – we were given a password for getting back in the evening. Nobody ever remembered it, so the word went down the long line of people back from high jinks in London or elsewhere, 'What's the password?' Somebody remembered it and it was shouted all the way down the line at the top of their voices.

I also found that there was a leakage of intelligence there through wealthy people who asked officers to dinner. I had been trained to look for that kind of thing and I exposed them, which did a bit of good. The people with whom I was going to work were already engaged on one of our most famous gadgets, or toys as we called them, and that was the pencil fuse, of which more later. It was a very small device, exactly the same size as a pencil, that could be used to fire a detonator any time between half an hour and two or three days. It wasn't dead accurate but it was accurate enough for the purpose. So it wasn't an exact timing device, but they were working on that and flexible explosives and ways of carrying out demolition by virtual amateurs using only what they could carry. Very quickly a suitable site was found for us, because it was obvious we were going to develop like mad, and that was Aston House in Hertfordshire.

And so, in November 1939, I travelled to Aston House, and spent the first night there alone, surrounded by files and things, and that was when I first met, or heard, the ghost of Aston, a charming thing. There was a great ballroom with the grand piano still there and someone played the piano in the night. It was heard quite a few times while we were there; once or twice we watched but there was nobody there and it stopped directly we went into the room. It was just one of those very pleasant little episodes.

Well, we grew until we had a very big staff indeed. There were hundreds of ATS, FANYs, troops and so on, I don't know how many we finished up with, many hundreds, possibly a thousand altogether.

Among the people, they must forgive me if I don't remember all their names, but there were some very good people in addition to those I have already mentioned. Ramsay Green, a friend and good engineer, he was a Gunner in the First World War, where he lost a leg, Francis Freeth, a very famous Fellow of the Royal Society, a delightful bloke, the inventor, incidentally, of the triangular equation. And he was a great asset in the mess, because it was easy to pull his leg. I'd turn to somebody and say in a loud voice, 'I can't see much good really in this profound long-distance research. In my business and private life the kind of idea is you employ an inventor and there is only one way to get answers out of him and to stop him going miles away on esoteric ideas which won't bear fruit in the year two thousand, and that is wall him up and every time he puts out an answer with some good commercial sense, you put in some food and water!' Dear old Francis, he had a lovely sense of humour and would suitably explode. He got an OBE in the First World War and he wore an old-fashioned cut of uniform.

We sent him on a kind of weird little expedition to America; it wasn't a secret trip, it was to make contact with our opposite number in OSS [Office of Strategic Services, the forerunner of the CIA] there. When he came back I remember I met him on the steps of the War Office and knowing his views on the subject the first thing I said was 'Hello Francis. Welcome home! Tell me, I expect the American press were waiting for you?' (I knew he hated the usual journalists.)

And so I said, 'What did you think of them, Francis?' I've never forgotten his reply. He drew himself up. He said, 'My dear Colonel, when you consider that there are brasses to be cleaned in public urinals, pianos to be played in houses of ill-fame and many other comparatively gentlemanly pursuits to be had for the asking, it passes my comprehension how anybody can work for the daily press!'

There was my PA, I think she'd been in the Red Cross, Mavis Martin-Sperry, from the Martin-Sperry gyroscope family. She celebrated her twenty-first birthday in the mess, which is something she will remember, because we did play hard when there were no operations on. She was an extraordinary girl. When we had a new gadget and it needed very clear-cut instructions that could be understood by really anybody who was given the gadget to use, she would produce sketches and words with absolute clarity and did a really marvellous job.

Incidentally, I remember when Langley left to return to Naval Intelligence, he wrote me an extremely nice letter; he mentioned one or two people by name and he said, the one woman I would always want to stay behind, this was if we were invaded, to give us a hand, would be Mavis Martin-Sperry. I gave her a copy of that letter and she was delighted.

Well, we grew and we grew and my basic idea was to continue to run a happy ship and one had to kind of tone down military discipline and use a different kind of discipline because these were the early days. REME [Royal Electrical and Mechanical Engineers, established in 1942] hadn't properly started then and I had a mixture of civilians, and also soldiers who, when they joined REME, might be absolutely top-class craftsmen and very much worthy of promotion, but you could not promote them because they couldn't handle men. But that was not what they were there for. So it was all very tricky, and very amusing to sort out. The great thing was that I insisted that everything was fun. We did produce some pretty evil devices, very evil some of them and evil ideas, too. But we used to roar with laughter about them. It reminded me of Kipling when he said something like, 'Meet the she-bear at its lair, warm the frozen dynamite, but oh beware my English when my English grow polite'. Well, I think our motto was 'Oh beware my English when my English start to laugh', because the more hideous things we produced, the more we laughed. I paraphrased that to 'The Jap he Kamikazes, the Hun he likes to strafe. But oh beware my country when my country starts to laugh.'

The other thing I did was to nickname most people who joined us. There was 'Longfellow', he was about six foot six, and my wife was very annoyed with me, 'Do you realise I have been talking to someone I thought was Captain Longfellow all the evening, and calling him Captain Longfellow and his name isn't Longfellow at all!' And then I remember one ATS officer joined us and she was a plump little thing and I said she's like a partridge. She was known as Lieutenant Partridge thereafter. And there was 'Crafty' and 'Sweetypie' Bertie (poor chap, his real name was Barratt and he was a director of Bassett's Sweets Company). It was all good fun and we were a very happy ship indeed.

Under the instructions of the Chief of the Secret Service, the terms of reference for Station 12 (Aston House) were as follows:

> To study how sabotage might be carried out.
> To make experiments on carrying out sabotage.
> To produce special sabotage ammunition.
> To train saboteurs.
> To study methods of countering sabotage.[3]

Colonel Wood continued:

To give an example of the kind of demand we would get: the Commandos would come back from a raid and say the Germans had got a new barbed wire, high tensile steel, our standard wire cutters could make no impression on it. In under a week they were going on another raid, could we produce something that a man lying on his back could use to cut this wire silently, and our chaps managed to do it. This was the sort of thing we did early on in the war before we really started on the high explosive game.

We were obviously going to serve SOE but, in addition, the Commandos, Special Boat Section and a host of other semi-irregular forces; also I found I was being consulted by all manner of people, the War Council, Admiralty, etc. and I needed a complete alibi. I wasn't going to have us connected – be called Station 12 or SOE, so I had all our paper printed Experimental Station 6 (WD), and got away with it!

It was entirely my invention. I never asked for approval, the War Office just accepted it. They must have thought that high-ups had given me permission. We were a special and unique part of the SOE set-up.

The next thing I found was that the people at headquarters didn't really know anything about sabotage but they liked to think they did. I realised that we were going to work against time and there would be no time to get permission to buy this or permission to buy that. I had tons of friends in the engineering world and could get anything overnight. But it had to be paid for, eventually. And we had to get pencil fuses and the like manufactured by the thousands. I remember I wrote to a silly ass at headquarters and pointed out that I should need funds, and the only reply was, 'My dear Wood, You must realise that there are more important things, there is a war on.' He was supposed to be in charge of me! God help me and God help him, but it didn't worry me at all. So I went and saw a marvellous chap, Atkin, who was responsible for Vote 9 at the War Office. Vote 9 is an open-ended vote. You pour money in at one end and it comes out at the other and it doesn't accumulate. He introduced me to the head of the Treasury and they said, 'Right, we know all about you, there is your cheque book,' and I could sign my cheque for any amount. And I remember this same silly ass telephoned me one day and said, 'Wood, I hear you are signing cheques.' I said, 'Yes, sir.' 'How much for?' 'Any given amount.' 'What do you mean any given amount?' I said, 'Well, I've just signed one for about a hundred thousand.' 'What?!!! In future all these cheques will come to me.' I think the intelligence in the Treasury must have been enormous. A second after I put down the telephone, my green line went. 'Is that you Wood? I think a certain rather officious and obstreperous officer's probably been giving you instructions. Don't take any notice of him. His signature would not be honoured. Yours will be. Good morning, Wood.' That was all he did say!

The Station 12 history concurs with this:

The original organisation included a Research Laboratory and a Development Section which was also responsible for the placing of orders with outside manufacturers. Very little had been done to regularise financial arrangements, and the Station lived from hand to mouth on an account which was reimbursed by Headquarters, not always before it was overdrawn.[4]

Colonel Wood continued:

I thought, we have got to get explosives made and we have got to order this and that, so I went and made friends with the head of the Ministry of Supply, George Turner, who later became Sir George Turner [George Turner also came under MGOF – Master-General of Ordnance Finance Department].[5]

He was absolutely marvellous. We had a tacit understanding: I would never ask for anything that was not really necessary. Occasionally, when

I was up there seeing him, he would say, 'Have you got a few minutes to spare? Sit in the corner there.' And on one occasion – he was a wonderful chap – there was a deputation for him – I think it was from the Canadians, or somewhere or other, part of the Empire who were fighting for us, and they'd been to MPs and they wanted this and they wanted that. They came in and they said, 'Is there any decision, Mr Turner?' And he said, 'Yes, you can have what you want.' Their faces lit up. And just as they were leaving through the door, he said, 'Oh just a minute, by the way it's your responsibility but if you have that lot, the British Army won't have any small arms ammunition for a month.' Typical of the chap, right down to brass tacks.

We got on like wildfire, so I never had any trouble with supplies, anything I wanted I got it all. I got the first supplies of plastic explosive because I couldn't bear the thought – I mean, they were sending chaps on raids with 806 which wasn't too bad but they told me that it was quite safe. The first thing I did was to take some out on the range and fire a rifle at it. And of course it went off! These chaps were supposed to go ashore with this stuff in their packs.

The history of the R&D Section of SOE states:

By the end of 1940, production of certain devices was reaching a considerable scale: for example, quantities approaching one million each of Pencil Time Fuses, Incendiary Arrows and small Incendiary Bombs were required and quite elaborate arrangements had to be made for their mass production, testing and storing. Liaison with the principal Secretary of Priorities at the War Office secured the necessary release of materials, and the willing co-operation of the manufacturers enabled a manufacturing programme to be carried out successfully, which if undertaken through official channels in the normal manner would undoubtedly have required a much larger staff than was actually available.[6]

Colonel Wood was a maverick officer who could not stand red tape and did not suffer fools gladly. He knew how important the work at Aston House was and wanted to get on with the war and finish it as quickly as possible. Because of his stubborn and determined attitude he would not have been popular with some senior officers or civilian bosses in Whitehall. Under cover of his own secret organisation

E.S.6. (WD) he was able to provide special forces with urgent supplies tailored for their raids, seemingly without SOE or anyone else knowing too much about it. This is quite amazing: a secret organisation within a secret organisation! How *did* he get away with it?

As a consequence of this many of the unique devices that were made at Aston would not have been recorded in any *Secret Agent's Handbook of Special Devices*. Why bother anyway? These items were for a one-off raid. They were tailor-made for that job, and probably would never be needed again, be it for the resistance, the special forces, Commandos, Special Boat Section, Airborne Division or Long Range Desert Group. These various group leaders knew Colonel Wood would get it made, deliver it and it would work. He had probably tested it himself! The devices couldn't have been subjected to slow and painstaking quality testing; there was not enough time. Little of this would have been recorded, so the only people who knew what was actually being made at Aston would be the designers and the users.

The R&D Section history states:

Early in 1941 a considerable further expansion in staff took place at Aston House and it was soon clear that even greater expansion of the workplaces would be necessary as well as increased accommodation. At this time various schemes for reorganising the research and development organisation were under consideration. It was proposed to move the research side to Station IX, The Frythe, where a Radio Section was already established. Aston House Station 12 would then look after production, inspection, packing and dispatch of stores.[7]

Colonel Wood confirmed that magazines were built underground and additional stores were constructed. The production of the 'toys' was sub-contracted to British industry. Huge quantities of the standard everyday items such as time pencil fuses, limpet mines and others were made. Most factories were forced to turn over their expertise to the war effort. For instance locally in Stevenage, ESA (Educational Supply Association) converted from the production of school furniture to wooden parts for the de Havilland Mosquito aircraft. The pressed steel toy firm Triang manufactured the Sten gun.

There was friendly rivalry between the two neighbouring stations and a bit of resentment at Aston that The Frythe received all the credit after the war was over. Aston House had made a major contribution to items that were subsequently given the prefix 'Wel' for Welwyn.

Aston House was unfairly labelled as just a production unit, but it was much more than that. It did undertake small batch production in its own workshops, but not on a large scale until late in the war. The ATS sometimes worked day and night assembling explosives, but this was for specific urgent raids.

The Station 12 history states:

At the beginning of 1943, it was found that liaison between The Frythe (Research) and Aston House (Production) establishments was insufficient. Lieutenant-Colonel J.L. Bliss, RE, was therefore appointed co-ordinating officer, and a series of Co-ordination Meetings, at which both stations were represented, was instituted and continued throughout the remainder of the war. These meetings not only provided opportunity for detailed discussion at low level of various projects in hand but also enabled responsibility for action to be allocated to individuals at one station or the other. A further improvement in liaison took place when Aston House became represented on the Trials Committee – in the first place by Major Bedford, and later by a representative of the Production Department as well. This ensured that:

- Prototypes submitted for User Trial corresponded to tabled drawings.
- Amendments recommended after User Trial were incorporated and, if of major importance, further prototypes were manufactured and submitted to trial.
- Production models were submitted to Acceptance Trial.
- Station 12 (Aston House) views on production and inspection were fully presented to the Trials committee.

Major R. Gardiner, REME, took over the Production Department in the summer of 1943, on the departure of Major Moreland Fox to the USA.[8]

The design drawing office was at Aston House. Having worked in a design drawing office myself at British Aerospace, I know that having received a specification outline for a new idea from some boffin you don't just draw it up and that's it. You have to make the thing work and that involves a long process of group discussions with experts in different fields, further innovation, modification and amendment, testing of materials, motors, explosives and other components and then further discussion and modification in the workshops before you go into production. In the end the invention may well be very different from the initial conception because of design constraints, and in addition the initial specification is likely to change during the process.

There would have been an office at Aston House where all the orders for weapons were initiated and where the quality control, testing and delivery were managed – no small task when you consider that by the end of the war, over 12 million pencil time fuses had been made. If few people knew what was being made at least somebody was counting! It must have been the chartered accountants.

Colonel Wood took a poem by Rupert Brooke and rewrote it, line by line, in frustration one feels, with the obstacles he had to overcome to obtain funding. When reading it you need to know that the head of finance in SOE was coded D/Fin, hence the title 'A Finnier Heaven' and Messrs Price and Rivers were two of the finance staff. C.A.s refers to Chartered Accountants.

The Fishes 'Heaven' (Rupert Brooke)

One may not doubt that somehow, Good
Shall come of water and of Mud;
And, sure, the reverent eye must see
A purpose in Liquidity.
We darkly know, by Faith we cry,
The future is not wholly Dry.
Mud unto mud – Death eddies near –
Not here the appointed end, not here!
But somewhere, beyond Space and Time,
Is wetter water, slimier slime!
And there (they trust) there swimmeth One
Who swam ere rivers were begun,

Immense, of fishy form and mind,
Squamous, omnipotent, and kind;
And under that Almighty Fin,
The littlest fish may enter in.

A Finnier Heaven (Lieutenant-Colonel L.J.C. Wood)

One may not doubt that something nice
Shall follow when we've paid the PRICE
And, sure, the reverent eye shall see
A purpose in Parsimony.
We darkly know, by Faith believe,
It's *sometimes* blessed to *receive*.
Mud unto Mud! C.A.s draw near
Not here the appointed end, not here!
But somewhere beyond Space and Hours!
Is wetter water, slimier slime!
Is liquid money, broader powers!
T'wards which (we trust) there swimmeth One
Who swam ere RIVERS was begun,
Longish, of fishy form and mind,
Squamous, omnipotent, but kind;
And without that Almighty Fin,
The littlest sanction can't get in.

Colonel Wood continued:

In the early days when we started off we had no magazines [for explosives] at all, we just had Aston House with about half a ton of ordinary high explosive, not plastic, underneath the table in the billiard room and one or two rooms which we were able to use temporarily until we could build proper laboratories.

[Among] just a few amusing little incidents I remember, Sinclair Munro, a wonderful chap, a scientist with a good degree in chemistry and physics – I introduced him to high explosive, I gave him a 69 fuse on the top of what looked like a thermos flask. I told him, 'This is full of high explosive and is one of the ideas to throw at tanks. I don't think they are much good, but they were issued to the Home Guard and so on. But you'd better learn something about these things.' The 69 fuse had a cover to it and when you took the cover off you quickly put your thumb on a little piece of lead that was attached to a piece of tape. The moment that lead was let go it uncoiled the tape, which fell away and the thing was then armed. It had a little ball inside and any slight tilt would send it off.

I left Sinclair with this and presently someone came along and said, 'Oh, Captain Munro says that he is sorry to bother you, sir, but the tape has fallen off and he's got the object in front of him on the bench, what does he do now?'

I had to laugh! 'What you do now is you clear everybody out of this part of the building because there's enough high explosive in that thing to wreck the place.' Then I went in and said, 'Don't move for a moment', and I got somebody to open all the doors and somebody to put a sheet of metal out on the lawn at a reasonable distance from the house but absolutely dead level. Then I said, 'Now all you do is, you hold the flask in both hands and I am going to hold you from behind by your elbows. I'll warn you about your feet, don't look at your feet, don't look at anything else, only look at that device and make sure it doesn't tilt.' And so we slowly paraded out through the door and across the drive and on to the lawn, and he put it down, and I got someone with a 0.22 rifle to fire at it and of course there was a big explosion. Which was a very good introduction to explosives!

We just escaped another disaster in the laboratory inside the house. Somebody came in and said, 'Excuse me, sir, there is nobody in the laboratory but there's smoke coming out of it.' I dashed along. There was a drying cabinet made of copper on the wall which was heated to dry whatever you wanted to put in there. There were fumes coming out of this. By this time quite a lot of chaps had come chasing along and so I thought, well, here's an opportunity. I said, 'I've got here a bit of asbestos blanket – we are not going to ruin this place with water – I will now show you how to immerse this in a blanket, pull it off the wall and get it outside.' A voice said, 'I say, sir, ought all these people to be here? That cabinet is full of CE.' (Composition Exploding, which is so sensitive, because it's what you use to set off other explosives.) This bloody fool had put it in there to dry and forgotten it! It was approaching detonation temperature at any moment, so – 'Out everybody except the fool who put it there. You stay behind.' I said,

'Now, look, there's the fire extinguisher. When I say "Now" you start the fire extinguisher going, and when I say "Now" a second time I am going to open the doors of the cabinet. Don't worry about me. You have got to have that aimed at the door of the cabinet so that it goes straight in, because the moment air gets to this stuff it's going to put the temperature up.' He managed to do it and it didn't go off. It was a hair-raising moment – it would have blown the side of the house out. He aimed it accurately enough and as I opened the cabinet doors, so this jet of foam and water went into it and over me. I had a chat with him afterwards!

I found out that the average poor Sapper before the war was only allowed to fire one detonator and to watch the sergeant-major explode one block of gun cotton. Well, that wasn't much good.

Colin Meek was working on the 'Neumann' effect, which is the focused charge, and he perfected it. You can focus an explosion from high explosive exactly like you can focus the light from the sun with a magnifying glass. It is quite extraordinary.

You took one ounce of plastic explosive, put it up on a tripod of three pieces of wood and underneath it, pressed in so that it absolutely fits, a paper-thin concave copper plate the shape of a lens, and you stood that up so that the focus of the lens, if it had been a lens, would be exactly where the little tripod was standing. You put that on three-quarters of an inch of armour plate and set it off and stand quite close by because there is no fragmentation and it will drill a hole clean through, marvellous stuff, and that enabled us to jump forward a lot.

We had the job of cutting the penstocks where the Germans were making heavy water [deuterium oxide] at Norsk Hydro at Rjukan, near Vemork in Norway.

We at Aston were asked to supply everything. I did all manner of experiments. I knew a lot of people and found everybody who was willing to help. I got a copy of the penstock from one of the big water companies, about a 6-foot diameter high-pressure pipe. But of course ordinary high explosive didn't have any effect, especially when the pipe was full of water because the opposite and equal reaction to the water prevented it cutting. So Colin Meek produced the charges and we made webbing belts to go round our parachutists' waists with a weight of high explosives of only about one ounce per inch, something of that order, in hinged aluminium casings with focused charges. All the attackers had to do was join up two or three of these belts, put them round the penstock, and cut it like a knife; the plan was to cut it well above the power station. The whole of the hillside of course would come down through the power station, and cover it with debris and rocks and so on – there was about 700 foot of water, the weight of the pressure of course is fantastic.

I know that well because I once saw the result of some silly ass testing the valves in the valve house at the top of some penstocks. They forgot to leave the windows open so that when they tested it the whole valve house disappeared with the vast suction of this great column of water chasing away down. The whole of the building fragmented and went down too. The power of water is terrific.

We used to tailor-make explosives, every device was made specifically for the job in hand so there was no hit or miss. If it had a ring – our instructions said put it there and then pull this ring and then go away from there. We did that on the Lofoten Islands raid [Operation Claymore].

I was really annoyed that I wasn't allowed to go on that raid, it must have been enormous fun, except I lost a friend there. That was where the Germans had stored enormous quantities of fish oil, it was very, very useful to the Hun, great storage tanks full of it, very valuable. The thing was to destroy this. We knew very well that if you try and set things on fire with high explosives you are more likely to blow the flame out than to set it alight, so you have to mix your high explosives with powdered magnesium and things like that. We'd made all these discoveries in our own experimental work. Well, two or three days beforehand, they sent me a young Sapper officer and I looked at his orders and I did what I did on several occasions very naughtily and told him that I'd been phoned by headquarters and they'd left it to me to change them. It wasn't true but the people who'd sent him down didn't really know very much about the modern ideas. 'There are two Lancashire boilers, we know that; the first thing you do, my lad, is to tie down the safety valves and open the draught full, so as to get a terrific head of steam and put these two saddle-bags over each boiler. Just pull these little rings and you have got one minute. You go away from there.' (The flash charges for the fish storage were of course linked to the boiler charges.) He came back to see me when he was back quite safely and said, 'Oh, it was glorious, you know, you never saw anything like it in your life.'

I could believe it, I was really annoyed not to see two great Lancashire boilers under a full head of steam, both of them exploding at once, plus all the steam and all the chunks of metal; totally wrecked, beautiful, oh a lovely job!

A letter revealed that 'Captain' Wood also sent fighting knives for the raid:

Major Munn, R.A.
Arisaig
13 February 1941

Dear Munn,

At the request of Major Wilson, we are despatching today by passenger train 46 Fighting Knives which are for 'Claymore'. This is the most we can supply at the moment and we hope they arrive in good condition.

Yours sincerely,

L.J.C. WOOD,
Captain R.E.[9]

The Lofoten Islands are 850 miles north of the Orkneys near Narvik. The islands were important to the Germans because there were oil installations to serve shipping but more important were the factories that processed herring and cod extracts, from which fish oil was produced in large quantities for a variety of uses, including the manufacture of nitro-glycerine for high explosives. The orders were straightforward: to blow up the oil installations and any enemy shipping they could lay their hands on, capture prisoners and Norwegian quislings, and carry back any Norwegians who wished to volunteer for the British-based Norwegian forces. Nor was there any mercy to be shown to shipping which carried the local products under duress from the Germans. 'They were to be burned without compunction,' ordered Lord Lovat, who had just been posted to No. 4 Commando, which would combine with 3 Commando, each with 500 men, plus a force of fifty Norwegian troops for the raid.

Many of the soldiers were mightily sick. The convoy reached the Lofoten Islands in the early hours of 4 March 1941, and the force, armed to the teeth and faces blackened, was ferried ashore under freezing conditions in a dozen landing craft, each carrying 35 men. There was little opposition. Two of Goebbels' Propaganda Ministry officials were caught sleeping. The door was locked. One shot blew it open and, upon entering, a chamber pot was seen below the bed. No one could resist such a target and so another shot was put into the pot. The two half-conscious bodies performed a feat of levitation unmatched by any magician!

Lieutenant R.L. Wills sent off a telegram from the telegraph station at Stamsund. Addressed to A. Hitler, Berlin, it read, 'You said in your last speech German troops would meet the British wherever they landed. Where are your troops?' Sixty Quislings and 225 German prisoners were captured at the cost of one casualty, an officer who accidentally shot himself in the thigh when he slipped on the ice. One success that could not be announced at the time was the seizure of a set of spare rotors for the Enigma cypher machine which were of help to the cryptanalysts at Bletchley Park, Station X. Eleven ships were sunk (22,000 tons), eighteen factories blown up, and seven fish oil and petrol installations burned to the ground or blown up.

This was the first real Commando landing and it achieved complete surprise. There were no British losses.[10]

The Prime Minister's personal minute to the Director of Combined Operations was as follows:

The unequalled success of CLAYMORE says much for the care and skill with which it was planned and the determination with which it was executed. Pray accept for yourself and pass to all concerned my warm congratulations on a very satisfactory operation.

W.C. 16.3.1941[11]

Colonel Wood's friend was probably killed on the second Lofoten raid, Anklet, on 26 December 1941, or Archery which was directed against Vaagsö and Maaloy on 27 December 1941.

Seventeen Commandos were killed including Captain Martin Linge. (Martin Linge became a Norwegian national hero. A sculpture of him now stands at the spot where he fell leading the attack to capture German headquarters at the Hotel Ulvesund.)[12]

The demolition party sent back a report to Aston House about the effectiveness of the weapons with which it had been supplied. It clearly demonstrates how precise the performance of every piece of equipment needed to be, to enable the operative to transport it easily, quickly plant the devices, set the fuses and get out before being captured or worse. It was vital for the operators, knowing that they had risked their necks, to be confident that the explosive would work and do the job intended.

NOTES ON THE EXPERIENCES OF THE R.E. DEMOLITION PARTY IN THE LOFOTEN RAID FROM THE TECHNICAL POINT OF VIEW

Some of the boilers were found to be much larger than the information indicated but the 10 lb charges provided were quite adequate for the destruction, though naturally they were unnecessarily large for the smaller type of boiler.

The blast effect from the 10 lb charges was particularly severe and in every case buildings housing boilers were severely damaged. In one case a party was somewhat short of explosives as they found no less than twelve small factories where one had been indicated. The other parties had more explosives than they needed.

The supply of loose sticks of plastic explosive was found most useful for destroying smaller targets such as electric motors.

The packing of the charges was considered to be very good but some trouble was experienced in loading them on to the crowded auxiliary landing craft as the sappers were the last to board vessels and the crates were somewhat large. One party split up some of their charges but the cold water made this somewhat difficult.

None of the charges failed to explode, though in eight cases commercial detonators failed and had to be replaced before success was achieved.

It was found that the crimping tools provided tend to bevel the edge of the fuse and prevent it fitting. Jack knives were found to be much better for this purpose.

The heads of the copper igniter tubes were easily broken off when striking and many of them failed to ignite. This was attributed to bad storage conditions on board ship.

The fuses were found to be very effective and in no case failed to ignite.

The limpet mines all fired satisfactorily and were very effective, though in some cases detonator failures referred to above occurred when using limpets.

Considerable difficulty was found in placing limpets under water against the side of the ship, as the craft which were being used for this purpose were also made of steel and tended to attach the limpets to themselves rather than the target.

The tar-babies were very effective.

Bombs Incendiary 1.5 lb Mark 1 [described as resembling a red Brasso tin] were most unsatisfactory owing to faulty cap mechanisms. N.B. As far as can be discovered these incendiary bombs were not supplied by the organisation but obtained from another source.

The wire provided for lashing the charges to the targets was too springy, and as soon as it was taken out of the bag it at once became tangled.

THE FOLLOWING RECOMMENDATIONS WERE MADE FOR IMPROVEMENTS TO, OR ADDITIONS TO THE EQUIPMENT SUPPLIED

If possible the waterproof bags provided should have a wider neck to allow more scope for the varying shapes of the charges enclosed in them.

The white colour of the bags would have been very conspicuous had a last minute change of plan necessitated a landing at night.

Cordage should be provided in preference to wire for lashing charges on targets.

A greater length of cordtex should be provided on charges which are intended to be placed in large buildings, ships etc., and fired from outside.

Some form of hooked stick should be provided for controlling the movements of limpet mines when being applied under water. [This tool was made and supplied for future raids.]

A smaller edition of the bakelite detonator case should be provided holding say 10 detonators to enable each man of a party to be provided with detonators.

A similar bakelite case should be provided for the copper igniter tubes.

An eye should be provided at the bottom of the tar-baby bag to assist in slinging it when it is being carried.

Jack knives should be provided for personnel who are not issued with these as part of their normal equipment (i.e. other than Royal Engineers).

Safety fuses could, with advantage, be placed in the neck of the bag of made up charges as an additional standby method of firing.

The following method of destroying boilers was found successful: Throw one hand grenade into the boiler, when this bursts it cracks the boiler in many places. Throw in a second hand grenade, the explosion of which will completely destroy the boiler.

A 7 lb sledge hammer was found to be a most useful weapon and its utility would have been further increased had one end of it been pointed, the point could then have been used for smashing barrels, drums, light gauge tanks etc. N.B. This will probably involve making special sledge heads of cast steel instead of cast iron.

A larger scale of issue of fireman's axes is desirable as these are particularly suitable for attacking all forms of electrical gear owing to the insulation of the handle.

Short crowbars or tommy bars could with advantage be included.

Adjustable spanners could with advantage be included for turning taps, nuts, etc. when the appropriate keys are not found on site.

The limpet mines as at present packed are very heavy, and when they have to be carried some distance, it is suggested that a rubber cover similar to the beach mine cover might be substituted for the wooden case.

It is for consideration whether suction grips might not be substituted for magnets on limpets and other charges where saving of weight is important.

Scaling ladders could be usefully carried when attacking large mechanical plant, as it is often difficult to place charges in contact with overhead shafting, roof tanks, etc. [These were later developed at Aston House.]

Instructions in the best methods of opening safes should be included in the curriculum for training personnel for operations of this type.[13]

Colonel Wood continued:

I was out in Paris before the Germans got in, working with the French Deuxième Bureau, their Secret Service, teaching them sabotage, because it was obvious that the Germans were going to take Paris. And I have always thought that I ought to have had a VC because anybody who teaches – who tries to teach – a Frenchman to use high explosives deserves a VC, if he lives to get it. It was appalling and also it was sad because I then saw for myself the lack of preparation for war. These chaps had got First World War fuse and as often as not it went out and they were begging me, almost with tears in their eyes, could I get some English Bickford. This is absolu\tely accurate, one centimetre per second, you can rely on it with your life, as we had to, but theirs . . . ! I remember on one occasion, 'It's gone out!' they cried. I couldn't stop them. And they all ran forward. It went up, of course, fortunately nobody was killed but I could see what was going to happen. I had to dive into a muddy ditch and it was the middle of winter. It didn't please me at all. I hadn't another change of clothes with me, either.

But honestly, trying to teach them to use plastic high explosive was the devil. I remember I was showing one Sapper major how to cut a railway line with a very small charge. I said, 'Well, you've got to come back a quarter of a mile with me.' I almost had to frog-march him back. And I said, 'Now will you lie down.' 'Ah non, lie down for that little bit!' Anyway, I waited; I'd got my stopwatch ready and at the critical moment I tackled him low; down he came and a second later there was a clang! as a piece of rail went through the metal signpost just where his head had been – went right across the lake at the Champs des Manoeuvres and with a crash hit the top of the roofs of the corrugated buildings opposite. And after that I didn't have so much trouble.

I had a comic adventure at the Gare du Nord railway station in Paris. It was like a 'Whodunnit'. There am I in a first-class carriage, night, everything dark, it was well after the war had started. I was on my way back from this expedition to the Deuxième Bureau and I was sitting in a corner in an otherwise empty carriage when suddenly a man appeared carrying a small suitcase and he really did look like a stage villain. He'd got a cloak and a black hat pulled over his eyes and he slung a suitcase, it was a little suitcase, onto the rack exactly opposite

me and disappeared – and didn't come back. I thought, that's funny.
The train started off and we began to cross from the Gare du Nord,
I think it was, where you go across a lot of viaducts over the Seine –
something like that. Suddenly I heard tick, tick, tick from this suitcase.
So I thought, by God, I'm taking no risks and I let down the window
and I seized the suitcase, with one swoop, I'd nearly let go of it when
I realised it was exactly in front of a hot-air ventilator, which was going
tick, tick, tick! That chap nearly had his suitcase thrown into the Seine.
He never came back and what was in the suitcase I don't know. But
really, it was too damn funny. Because he looked so – you know, the
whole thing – this mysterious stranger, you see, in the dark.

When the Germans arrived, some of these officers in the Deuxième
Bureau, I don't know what the percentage was, went over to the
Germans, to Vichy, but a high percentage found their way back to
England. And they were most gallant chaps. They had their faces
changed by plastic surgeons so that they shouldn't be recognised and
tortured if they got back.

And they did go back, I remember two of them kept on saying that
they must have a job to do. There was a small radar direction station on
the coast that was being a nuisance, and we said it would be nice if you
could do that in, we've got a photograph of it. So I had them down to
Aston House and we showed them the photograph, we gave them time
pencils and beautiful little charges with magnets tailored for the job and
all they had to do was attach them and get out. They went over in a
submarine and swam ashore. They not only brought down the wireless
mast, they dropped it clean across the sending station and were back
dusting their hands and saying next please. Marvellous chaps.

I wondered if I'd been given away because while we'd still got this
half a ton of explosive underneath the table in the billiard room (later on
we had big underground magazines and everything you could think of)
the night sergeant/guard came round with his hurricane lantern – it was
about midnight and I'd been working late in my study – and suddenly
there was a boomp, and I said, 'Hello, a bomb out here?' (Aston was very
isolated.) 'This is strange.' There was another boomp much closer and I
said, 'It seems to be in a straight line for us.' There was another boomp
and all the lights went out and I said, 'Gosh, he's got our range! Well,
there is nothing we can do about it.' So I said, 'You lie down on that

side of the sofa and I'll lie down on the other. We'll await events.' And I thought to myself, well, in any case, quite a happy ending because with all that explosive we wouldn't know anything about it at all. Then we heard just thump, thump, the other side of Aston and the next morning I went out and discovered that the last two bombs which would have hit us bang-on had stuck in the bomb rack and fallen on to a low hillside the other side of the church, and failed to explode. Later on, I wondered whether they knew about me, because I was known to the Free French as Captain Blood.

There followed one of the lovely amusing sides that we had in war, thank God, although it is a horrible business. I went over with a staff sergeant to have a look for these bombs. And I thought, well, if they haven't gone off, we'd locate them and send for the proper bomb disposal people. It was a narrow country lane, and we rounded a corner and heard a hell of a hullabaloo going on. There was a baby Austin and a baby Morris nose to nose facing each other and they couldn't get past in this lane. One of them had got to go back to one of the passing places. I know one was a district nurse and the other was something to do with the locality, and they were saying, 'I'm senior to you, you go back.' 'No, you're not, I'm on more important work.' They didn't take any notice of me – it was like two cocks fighting. They were just bent on having a row with each other. So I said to my sergeant, 'Right, you back into a lay-by so that things can get past you and then you will see some fun.' I walked up to them and saluted and said, 'H'm' and they said, 'Oh!' I said, 'Excuse me, ladies, interrupting your conversation but do you see these two holes in the hillside?' And they said, 'Yes'. I said 'Well, those are unexploded bombs and they are due to go off at any moment so I don't think I would stay here if I were you.' And I have never seen such a priceless thing. They must have been extremely good drivers or driven by fear, because those two cars went backwards like corks out of a bottle, whoosh! And when I got back to my driver he was sobbing with laughter, his head was down on the steering wheel. You know, it was a marvellous sight!

I have never forgotten the first bitter cold winter at Aston, I think it was 1940. Anyway, meteorologists will tell you, because in hindsight they can tell you something, occasionally. We had bitter cold, deep snow, some of the local lanes were filled with drifting snow, literally level with the hedge. One of my sergeants said to me, 'You know, sir, I've just seen a sight that has turned me up. After all I was at Dunkirk and I've served a lot, a Regular, but I have never seen anything so horrible.' The British Tommy loves to find something to feed, some kind of pet. They were feeding the birds when some huge rats arrived. He said, these rats were jumping into the air and making a screaming noise to try and catch the birds that were snatching the food that they'd come to eat. It was extraordinary.

The ICI company was very helpful. They sent down a first-class explosives expert to spend a week with us and well, we always reckoned that any guest ought to be given an exciting life, booby traps and so on. So an orderly took this chap's suitcase upstairs and put it outside his door for him. When he went to pick it up I was with him and there was a bang and a small sheet of flame, quite a safe one you know. And this chap went absolutely as white as a sheet and kind of reeled back against the door. And I said, 'Good God man, I'm terribly sorry but I thought you'd be used to bangs.' He said, 'I am used to bangs but that suitcase is full of high explosives!'

Other guests at Aston House were all the heads of the Commandos, who came down for two days and a night to see what we were doing. We wanted to get ideas from some of them who had been on raids and we needed to know what they wanted extra in the way of stuff from us. They were magnificent looking blokes. And I remember I had a deputation from the senior woman officer at Aston House. She came in almost swooning; you see they had seen these terrific lads, so the girls asked, couldn't we have a dance tonight? I said, 'I'm terribly sorry, no.' Unfortunately, these chaps were here for hard work.

However, we decided to make it an interesting evening and I told everybody, 'Any ideas that you've got, do put them into practice.' I remember I had an attaché from the Canadian Sappers and one from the American Sappers. The Canadian Sapper was a hell of a character, I can't remember his name now but I know in private life he was a prospector and he used to go out in the blue. He came to me one day and he said, 'Sir, are there going to be any operations for a week?' And I said, 'No, not this weather, we're absolutely safe.' 'Then, sir, with your permission, I will get blind.' I asked what he meant. He said, 'Well sir, it's my way of life. You see when I go out on my expeditions looking for minerals, I can be away for as much as several months at a time and I never take an ounce of liquor. When I come back I have one almighty blind. And you may have noticed I have never had a drink since I've been here, but the time for a blind has come on, sir, if you don't mind, and I'll lock my door and I shan't be a nuisance to anybody.' He then added, 'I have an idea for the Commandos, it's an arse-lifter.' I said, 'That sounds lovely, what is it?' It consisted of a thick sheet of asbestos put under the mattress and under that was a coil of fuse instantaneous. Well, instantaneous fuse isn't a high explosive but it goes off nearly as fast and it's quite forceful stuff.

He got a coil of this underneath the mattress and underneath the asbestos cement and he worked out the statistics exactly so that when this chap lay down and it went off, he wouldn't quite hit the ceiling. One of the gadgets we had was a pressure switch, you see, and his weight would set this off. My contribution was a metronome that I put in an empty cupboard in a corner of the big dormitory where we housed them for the night. I climbed on the roof and lowered some fuse down the chimney and blew the chimney into the room and that shook things up a bit; everything they'd touched had gone off and we had a mike fixed up so that we could listen to everything that went on. I heard somebody call his mate and say, 'I can't sleep in this fug, all gunpowder and everything else, go and open the window George.' 'You open it, I'm not going to.' So at any rate they got the window open. We hadn't booby-trapped it. I waited until they were just dozing off and then I started this metronome going in the hollow cupboard. It went tick, tick, tick, by gosh, the scramble then to get under their beds before something went off! At any rate, we had a very good time.

I knew that they would invite me to Scotland under some pretext or other to get their own back. And sure enough, a chit came through from HQ – oh, by the way, I have talked about War Office all the time, well part of the time it was War Office and part of the time of course it was Baker Street. Anyway, a chit came through, I think it was from Brigadier Stockwell, saying he'd got a lot of explosive that needed an expert to look at it to see whether it was safe to keep it at this Commando school. Also he wanted me to give some lectures and there were quite a few things they'd like to talk over with me if I could be allowed to go up there for a few days. I thought, this is it.

My boys motored me up to London from Aston, to – it must have been St Pancras. I remember dear old Leslie Henson [a well-known stage and radio star]: 'St George for England, St Pancras for Scotland.'

Anyway they said, 'If you don't mind, sir, we'll push off while there's daylight, because there's an awful lot of bombing going on at the moment and we don't want to be caught in it.' And I said, 'No, God bless you,' and away they went.

I entered a hotel bar. All the windows were bricked up and suddenly there was a whoof! The bar lifted about a couple of inches and dropped back again. I'd never experienced London bombing before and I looked round at the faces and I could see that the men reacted a bit. The women took not the slightest notice, not at all. But the men kind of talked a little faster. Anyway, I went down below to dinner and then the bombing really started. It was an underground restaurant, but it was shaking like mad. Again I looked round and the women didn't take the slightest notice, not the slightest, I thought that's bloody marvellous.

After a meal I went to the hall porter and said, 'How do I get the train? I don't know this station or anything and I've got only a tiny torch.' 'Don't worry,' he said, 'You won't have any trouble, sir, that last big one cut the gas main just outside the station and it's like daylight out there!' Too true, but what I could not understand was why, hours after the train was due to leave, we were still in the station, broken glass raining down from the roof and a loudspeaker telling us to put on our steel helmets and sit on the floor. I recollect that I had a Wodehouse novel with me and found that for a time I was trying to read it upside down!

I eventually arrived at Glasgow early on a Sunday morning and the combination of war, place and day was depressing beyond belief. I was determined to get out of there rapidly and asked a policeman if he could help me on the Road to the Isles. Bless him, he told me of a bus that took me right into the hinterland where, of course, there was no worry about rationing. A most marvellous little inn right out in the blue where I had bacon and eggs and everything you could think of for breakfast. I phoned Jim Gavin, a great friend, at Lochailort and he came and fetched me in a kind of Land Rover affair, and our adventurous journey began. To save time, we hugged the coast (the west coast of Scotland) and tried to cross the inlets on ferries. I remember one ferry sank under us but we just got ashore in time. Then we approached Arisaig House, Lochailort. Arisaig was typical of the heathen lairds. It was built on the north side of a mountain, if you please, with no central heating whatsoever and this was the middle of winter.

Arisaig House is on the rugged coast, remote and inaccessible, the dozen or so buildings were protected from prying eyes by the lack of roads and designation as a wartime 'protected area'. Here would-be agents went through rigorous basic infantry training, handled demolitions and learned about sabotage, perfected their skills firing pistols and other small arms, picked up the rudiments of Morse code, and learned the arts of unarmed combat and silent killing.[14]

Colonel Wood continued:

As we entered the forest that surrounded it, I said, 'Jim, I have a feeling that the fun will start any moment now.' He said, 'Yes. Knowing that I am fetching you and I'm a friend they haven't told *me* anything. But I should imagine you're right.' At that moment there was a sheet of flame and a pine tree, a large one, fell bonk! behind us, so that we could only go on. We couldn't go back. There was another sheet of flame and another large tree was felled in front of us. So then we had to walk the rest of the way, tripping over awful devices that went bang in the night. However, when we got there it was all over, they'd had their fun, except that I badly needed to go to the loo. I was a bit fraught by then and like a bloody fool instead of thinking I sat down on the loo and ascended into heaven! They'd wound fuse instantaneous all round underneath the seat! They'd used a pressure switch, one of mine. Nearly singed the pants off me but I was all right.

Well, that night, I've never forgotten this, they said, 'It's going to be a bit of a wild night, but since you're a Cornishman you're accepted as a Celt. There's going to be a bagpipes competition.' It was Grant who was a piper, against, I forget the chap's name, but he was of the same clan as the pipers to the MacLeods of the Isles. He played wild music and Grant played classical. Well, these two chaps sat close to what was left of the fire, they'd burned most of the stuff in the place that was burnable, and the forms and the benches that were left to eat on, they'd piled up against the door. When I said, 'What's that for?' they said, 'Well, you see, its going to be a noisy evening and the Sassenachs won't like it.' They didn't! But these two chaps, having poured whisky into themselves and into their pipes, advanced on each other from opposite sides of the room, each playing a different tune. And of course, all hell broke loose, and they tried to break the door down, oh, it was a wonderful night, enormous, terrific fun. I wouldn't have missed it for all the world.

The next day they said, 'Well, now what about this explosive? Because it's really quite true, we have got a lot of explosive here and we are worried, we know it's been here a long time.' And I condemned it as it was starting to sweat, it was nitro-glycerine stuff. So I said, 'We'll have some fun with this. We'll take it down to the loch and see if we can get some fish.' I wasn't sure how fast it would sink and the Sassenachs had rowed after us hoping to grab the fish for themselves. I said, 'Well, we'll light the fuse (it was a Bickford fuse – burns under water) and let it go down to a decent depth.' I tried to guess, I hadn't got a clue how deep it would go. Then we watched the other boat, we were shrieking with laughter because it looked to us as if the other boat was right on top of the explosive. Then we saw that they too were shrieking with laughter and making motions about the tide; we'd forgotten this and the tide ensured that the boat kept exact pace with us so *we* were over it. It couldn't do any harm, it was right down under the water and there would be no fragmentation, we'd just have been tipped over, that's all. In fact it had gone down too deep and one little blenny came to the surface with huge bubbles round it and a seagull took it away. And that's all there was to it.

While I was there Jim Gavin was demonstrating one of the horrors, the 'toys', that commandos used to leave behind after a raid. This was a special cartridge that you pushed into the ground and when anyone trod on it, it fired a 0.303-inch bullet through your body. He was demonstrating this, forgot how sensitive it was, it was a live one, and it went off. The bullet went through the ceiling and there was a deathly hush, because Brigadier Stockwell, CO of the training station, was having a rest in his bedroom, exactly above.

We sat there, you know, perspiring, and then the door slowly opened, and Stockwell came quietly in, holding a completely mushroomed bullet – it had hit the triangle of his army truckle bed and flattened. So that's how close he was to it. And all he did was to walk quietly across, drop this flattened bullet on Jim Gavin's desk in front of him, and say, 'Jim, not while I'm asleep, old boy, in the afternoon, not while I'm asleep.' And just walked away again and never said another word about it. That was the kind of man people will follow anywhere and believe me, he was the spirit of the place.

When I was up at Lochailort we went along the coast somewhere, you could only easily approach this particular station by sea. I suppose it was something to do with the Special Boat Section. It was, of course, run entirely by the Navy. The only other approach was a kind of mountain track. We went there by sea and we were received by Commander Viner, I think it was, commanding the station, a nice bloke. We had lunch and then he said, 'We're expecting an Admiralty boat in.' I said, 'Yes, but all the station seems to be gathered around the quay.' He said, 'Yes, this may sound funny to you, Wood, but we have taken over one of these castles, a laird's castle, and we have indented for a Wren because it really needs a woman's touch to run it. And since we haven't got any women in the place, or for miles around, the interest is intense.' He and I went down to watch this Wren disembark and we burst with laughter, she'd almost got a moustache and – well really! The Admiralty must have had a sense of humour.

When I returned to Aston I was advised that the Commandos were sending down some haggis. I love haggis, it was a great change and a great privilege in wartime and it was on its way to us from Lochailort. I wrote:

> *Haggis*
>
> A Haggis from 'Auld Reekie' came
> A Haggis ripe and merry.
> (Oh boatman, I'll gie thee a siller pound
> To row me o'er the ferry!)
> The ferry-boat's beneath the tide;
> It couldna stand the strain.
> But the braw Haggis swam ashore.
> (The Tweed has a crimson stain!)
> The Haggis is on the Great North Road,
> Ah me, the awfu' slaughter!
> I winna tell ye wha it did

To the miller's winsome daughter!
The Haggis is nearing Aston House,
Turn out! Turn out the Guard!
Mak siccar, Duty Officer,
That a' the gates are barred!
The Haggis has leppit o'er the gates!
It hammers on the door!
Around the gates the gallant Guard
Lie sweltering in their gore!
The doom has come on Aston now!
What hand? What hand can save? . . .
'Tis then the Hand of Aston
Comes scrabbling from the grave!
Up from the moulderin' tomb it comes,
(The Haggis is afeared!)
Its nails they pierce the bloated skin
(The haggis drees its weird!)
Hail to the Hand of Aston!
Wha's saved our skins this day!
Pity the Lady Super,
Who'll clear the mess away!

When we began supplying arms for raids, we were looking after our own SOE agents being dropped behind the lines, the Commandos, the Special Boat Section, and the Royal Air Force, etc. We were kept very busy, and sometimes we worked literally forty-eight hours and on one occasion for three days and nights without stopping; the ATS were making up high explosive charges. I'll never forget a visit I had from the colonel in charge of personnel for the ATS. She came in for a chat and she said, 'Now, look, is it true that my girls are being used for dangerous work?' And I said, 'Yes, very.' (Incidentally, most of them were Geordies, and when they were doing this work they sang a repertoire of songs that made even me blush.) She said, 'What if they got killed?' And I said, 'What has that got to do with it? There's a war on.' And do you know, she sprang to her feet and did a most unsoldierly thing, she seized my hand with both hers and shook it and shook it. She said, 'That's what I wanted to hear! You'll get all my best girls in future.' And I got them – and by God, I take my hat off to them. They were marvellous. They never cared a hoot – never a hoot. They were a grand, grand, grand crowd.

I think the same goes for all the women of England, including the women who ran their homes – what they had to put up with was nobody's business. After all, we in the Army, we'd been risking our lives at times, but we were well fed, unless we were under very difficult circumstances, but they were risking their lives, a lot of them, getting bombed and so on and they had to pinch and scrape, and look after children. Vera, my own wife, I nicknamed Vicky – Victory V – because of what she did. I was in Intelligence well before the war and I knew perfectly well what was going to happen. I was building quite a large new house at that time in Beaconsfield, Bucks, and I built into it, so that they wouldn't have to go outside, a completely bomb-proof shelter that would withstand a blockbuster. I happen to be a civil and mechanical engineer and so I had it reinforced with steel and thick concrete, armour-plated doors, ventilation, electric light, reserve batteries, everything, and bunks for about eight. They never actually used it in the war, which the children hated because they knew there were lots of stores and nice goodies and biscuits and things and thought it would have been fun. But I was very glad they didn't have to use it.

My wife not only ran the house, looked after our two daughters and two friends who were living with us from India, but she also opened doors to any poor refugees from London. For them the bomb shelter was heaven because it was soundproof and they slept without a whisper or a bang or a bomb or any kind of disturbance like that and it did them a power of good. Well, my darling not only did all this, she also worked in a local munitions factory – she drove one of their heavy lorries and was a first-class mechanic. She was also an emergency driver, any time, day or night, for the local ambulance; she also did air raid warden's work, and found time to help with making escape equipment. When the war was over she was presented with a complete set and a letter of thanks which I still have. She told me about all this afterwards. I was in India; it was the only time we were ever separated. We had fifty-nine years of complete happiness and would have had our diamond wedding in several months' time. I've got over her death now and just look back on the happiness. But it was all so sordid during the war, beating sardine tins flat so that they could be collected for metal, and so on. Saving any kind of scraps and keeping half-fed chickens, and trying not to waste anything, and so on and so on. And never a word of complaint in letters or anything like that – and this went for all the women of England. I think they were bloody marvellous, I can't tell you how much I admired them.

I had the facility of selecting an officer from anywhere in the Army that I thought was right for my kind of work. But sometimes someone said, 'Will you try this chap?' Somebody that headquarters had sent down. I never allowed anybody else to do any of the testing of people or devices. When it was a question of high explosives I used to get up early in the morning and if it was something that was needed urgently and we'd got to know if it worked or not and it had to be taken to pieces, I used to do it. I never told anybody, naturally, because they would want to do it, but I didn't like that idea at all; they were young and I was in my forties and had the experience.

However, I used to take newcomers down into the magazine and tell them that they were surrounded by, shall we say five tons of explosives, and watch them. Now, sometimes perspiration used to run down their faces, and maybe this chap had got an MC at Dunkirk but he just wasn't suitable for the job. I mean, they used to say to me when they found out what I was doing afterwards, 'Oh, how brave.' But I would say it isn't brave at all, because I know that if anything happens, I shan't be here. It's not like the chaps in the jungle in Burma, who risked everything happening to them there, if they got wounded, and the Japs caught them, and all that kind of thing. High explosive's a good clean death. First you are and then you are not, you see.

I got the Triplex Glass people to make me a five-inch thick window for observation and blast protection for proper testing. But my method of teaching young officers about the accuracy and reliability of Bickford fuse was to take them down to our pond [now part of Stevenage Golf Centre]. There were no stones, so it was quite safe and there would be no fragmentation. I would take a bag of high explosive that needed to be got rid of, and I'd sit on this bag and invite him to sit by me. And I'd say, 'Watch me, I'm going to measure off "x" centimetres of Bickford and that will go off in exactly as many seconds.' And then I'd say, 'Well now, I've given you a stopwatch, I've got one, we're both synchronised.' I'd light the fuse with a cigarette. And then go on talking and this chap would say after a time, 'Excuse me, sir, but it's alight.' 'So it is,' and go on talking. And then, 'Excuse me, sir, but it *is* alight you know.' I'd say 'Yes, good Lord, yes, you're quite right.' Until there was about eight seconds to go and I'd say 'Well, you can make your own arrangements, I'm off!' And, of course, it introduced him to high explosive and a relaxed attitude at the same time. He had a hell of a shock but he took it in good part and knew that he could absolutely rely on that fuse.

In our assembly area where we were handling explosive material, the men worked in isolated compartments, so that if an explosion occurred the whole lot didn't go up. Mind you in no case was there any fragmentation. Because we were handling the high explosive charges to *cause* fragmentation. We never used anything that had solids with it, so it was a question of encompassing a blast, rather a different thing. All you needed was high mounds, that's all. We never had any difficulty at all. In all the years I had at Aston we only had one accident when a chap forgot about the fuse, and went forward prematurely. He survived all right, but he was in great pain, poor chap, at the time. And unfortunately I lost my loved, very much loved by all the troops there, my Spats – my 'repaniel' – half retriever and half spaniel. He loved high explosive bangs, and I came back from leave one day and was met by a sorrowing adjutant – Camp Commandant Sweetypie Bertie – who said, 'I'm terribly sorry, sir, Spats has died.'

He said, 'He sensed we were exploding,' nothing would stop him coming when there were bangs on, 'and ran forward on to the range and one of our chaps risked everything, tore after him, pulled him back, but he freed himself and shot forward again just as it went off. Killed instantly.'

But the fun Spats had given us. I remember poor old Sweetypie – we had a parade one day, we had to have an occasional parade, you know, keep things tidy, and to the joy of the men, he saluted and said, 'Parade ready for inspection, sir.' Took a smart pace backwards, not knowing that Spats was leaning against the back of his legs, just below knee level. Of course, all the ranks were trying to control their joy.

Perhaps there'd be an expedition setting forth on this 'Shetland Bus' business up in the north of Scotland, I had to send explosives up in a lorry, and the chaps would come to me – it was completely against King's Regulations, but they'd say, 'Can we take Spats for company?' Because he loved it and they loved him.

The Shetland Bus was a nickname for an SOE system of Norwegian fishing boats based near Lerwick in Scotland that provided a supply link with Norway. In 1940–3 these boats delivered nearly 150 tons of stores, as well as 84 agents, and brought 26 agents and 109 refugees out; but at a cost of eight boats and 50 men lost, mainly through stress of weather. Nevertheless it was so efficient and reliable that an exiled Norwegian naval officer used it to pop over to visit his wife, when he was on leave. He was never late back.[15]

Colonel Wood continued:

They sent me a Guards regimental sergeant-major because they thought that I'd got so many troops there then. Most of them were [medical] grade C3 of course, apart from the chaps who were actually working on things, but they thought I ought to have a disciplinary sergeant-major to keep things in order, but I was very worried.

Well, you can't very easily have a disciplinary sergeant-major looking after people who are largely working with their hands. You know, it's a different outlook entirely. Some of them really would be very senior chaps – probably only a private and not been promoted because he can't command men, but on the other hand he's a first class mechanic.

At any rate, this foolish private started off by spending a lot of time in the village and so that he could get back in the evening he made himself a hole under the wire, filled it up with branches, and used to roll under it. Well, he was not told that we'd suddenly been provided with guard dogs and he came back late from leave and used this short cut. He arrived at the sergeant's mess with a guard dog hanging on to his pants. Incidentally, the next day I saw the corporal with charge of the guard dog (a guard dog – like a police dog – has just *one* keeper, nobody else must feed it or have anything to do with it). And I said, 'Corporal So-and-So, it doesn't seem to me that King's Regulations with regard to the feeding of guard dogs is exactly being kept.' He said, 'Well, what can I do, sir? The whole bleeding camp wants to feed him!' They were all slipping him bits, you know, surreptitiously.

However, I took this regimental sergeant-major in hand. He marched the offender in smartly to my orderly room, a very young soldier back twenty-four hours late from leave. 'Cap off, etc. etc. etc.' 'Any excuse?' 'Well sir, well sir . . .'

So I looked at this chap and I said, 'I don't believe a word you've said. Will you accept my award or go to court martial?' Late from leave can be quite a serious offence in wartime. But he was green and young, you see. He said, 'I will accept your award.' I said, 'Right, seven days CB' (that's confined to barracks). I saw this sergeant-major's face, 'Right turn.' So I said, 'A word with you, after you've seen the prisoner back.' He returned, and I said, 'Sergeant-major, what are your intentions about that young man?' He said, 'Oh, I'll make him wish he'd never been born. I'll larn 'im.' I said, 'I thought so. You will not. Because if you do, I'll larn you as you've never been larned in your life. For God's sake, man, listen to me. This is not the Guards, this is a very important place doing a lot of very important work. Discipline we must have, yes, but I have just dealt with a very young, green soldier. And he's learned for the first time in his life that people senior to him can read his weak attempt at lying; it's a first offence, and he's found that it doesn't pay to tell lies. Now if you go and lean on that chap you'll ruin a potential good soldier, because he'll just get sullen. Don't do it, man. When a man's punished that should be the end of it.' 'Yes, sir, I see what you mean, sir.'

Very shortly after that, it was Christmas Day and as you know the officers serve the men on Christmas Day, and there was a large bunch of mistletoe at the end of the long dining-hall. I looked around and we had a delightful ATS officer, Wordsworth, she was of the poet Wordsworth's family, pretty girl, too. I stood under this mistletoe and said, 'Lieutenant Wordsworth, come here!' So she came here and I seized her in a terrific embrace and gave her a most enormous kiss that lasted quite a lot of seconds, then released her, and she kind of fell away and I turned round and said, 'Sergeant-Major X (I won't mention his name), your commanding officer has set you the example and you will now kiss every ATS sergeant in this room.' Which he did, most gallantly. And we never had any more trouble. It wasn't exactly standard army practice, but there was no loss of discipline, absolutely none, a very happy ship.

There were some comic attempts to tidy me up. There was a dear old general who came down to inspect the camp, purely from the camp quarters point of view, nothing to do with our business side of it. He said, 'It's all looking very tidy, Wood, but you've got no wire between the men's quarters and the women's.' I said, 'No, sir, advisedly, sir.' He said 'Well damn it, what do you mean advisedly?' I said, 'Well, sir, I'm only Regular Army Reserve, I'm not a regular officer, and I'm also, as a civilian, a rate-payer. And quite honestly, men will be men and women will be women and as far as I can see it's far better that the rate-payer should not have to pay for torn uniforms, because that's all that'll happen. Nothing's going to change human nature, as far as I know I can't.' He kind of went 'ugh' and went off. It was absolute nonsense, the whole thing. What is the good of putting up barbed wire and expecting men and women to change their ideas? They don't.

The following was an amusing criticism of a super security bag that Colonel Wood opened all too easily.

Super Security Bag from Baker Street

Dear L. I/C Security Despatches.
Please – no fuss is necessary re key.
Simply place bag on its edge,
Lean on it,
It bulges open;
Contents removed and pressure released
No signs of crime remain.
L.J.C.W.

The reply:

It may be very easy for a person such as thee,
To extract the secret papers from a bag without a key.
But due to my upbringing,
(My youth spent in choir singing)
Such tampering with baggage did not occur to me!
Beryl Ferguson.

Second Memo:

With baggage I don't tamper,
Have for choristers no key;
But I see that you 'tu-toi' me
And I am 'thou' to 'thee';
'Twould appear a little baggage
Is tampering with me!
L.J.C.W.

I was phoned up by the War Office one day and told that they wanted to put a new telephone scrambler line in to enable me to talk when an operation was on. And because we were a very secret station they gave me the identity of the man they were sending down to install it. He was bringing identity cards with him, and they phoned to say he was leaving now, and so on, so there was no question about who he was. He went up on the roof to put this thing in and I went up to have a look at him, to see what he was doing. I don't know whether it's to do with training or not, but at any rate I can feel evil. And the sight of this man literally hit me. I thought it was the foulest, most evil face I'd ever seen in my life. But I chatted him up very happily, took an interest in his job, said, 'Right, you carry on and I'll get on with my work.' I went downstairs and straight to the phone, got on to MI5, and I said I want to talk to Jim. Now Jim was the most unbelievable man. He carried in his head all the details of every villain that ever passed through their hands or anybody he'd ever known about. Jim came on, 'What is it, colonel?' 'I've got a chap sent by the War Office to put a new scrambler line in and he's bad, Jim, I feel it in my bones, he's really bad.' So he said, 'Oh, describe him.' I described him accurately. 'Ah, go up again and have another chat with him and see if he's got a scar right across the ball of his right thumb.' I came back and said, 'Yes, he has.' So he said, 'Right, we'll pick him up.' I said, 'Anything for me to do?' 'No, no, no, you don't want to go up again, we'll pick him up as he leaves.'

So I got on to him that evening and I said, 'Now look, Jim, as you know MI5 give me fun and games occasionally, little jobs to do and I think one of the things that they like is that I never ask questions. But on this occasion, on my own premises, I would like to know.' He said, 'That man has served time for the most filthy offences against young children. He's a member of the German Bund.' (A pro-German, pro-Nazi organisation in England before the war.) And he was fully passed by the War Office as being absolutely safe to put a secret line in at a very secret station. I afterwards found that there was – I can only repeat what I was told – that there was little co-operation between MI5, the War Office and CID before the war. They each got on with their own jobs, and you got these kind of messes. You see, if the War Office had consulted MI5 – 'Is this chap all right for this very, very particular job – putting in a scrambler line on a secret station?' they would have known at once, and prevented sending a member of the German Bund who'd served time.

Just at the beginning of the war when Commander Langley, RN, was still with us, one of the guards came in and said, 'Sir, a villager just reported finding a parachute in the hedge. We thought we'd better report it.' So I said, 'Lord, yes, that's right.' So Langley and I hurriedly put something on, took a small file of men and went down there – it was a rather cold night. Actually it turned out to be a parachute from a parachute flare which the Germans used. I'll never forget, because Langley said to me, 'It's bloody cold, isn't it Wood?' And I said, 'Well, since you've got nothing on other than a coat, I should think you are feeling a bit cold in some bits of you, aren't you?' He'd been in such a hurry he'd forgotten to put on even his pyjama trousers!

I had a lot of fun doing little jobs for MI5. One involved going out to dinner at a house owned by a senior officer where a number of curious incidents had occurred, including the 'accidental' death of the village policeman who was found with a broken neck at the foot of the stone outside steps, leading to the room of the German maid he was supposed to be courting. I understood she was whisked back to Germany the next day – this was early in the war. Lieutenant-Colonel Fairbairn and Major Sykes (more of them later) fitted me up with a sawn-off 0.45 strapped to a leather belt under my jacket with a short string to pull to fire it. I didn't have to use it but I did find out all MI5 wanted to know.

The biggest fun job I had – MI5 asked me to lay it on – was a county job, a lot of people involved. They'd caught a German spy, they'd been waiting for him for months, while one of our operators learned to imitate his Morse exactly. Skilled operators can recognise another man's Morse as you and I would recognise somebody's voice, so you couldn't replace this man with a bogus person and bogus information until somebody really talked the same language in Morse. And this was done. One of the last messages before they pulled him in was that the Germans said to him, 'You are giving us information but we want to see some action – what about these great food stores we've heard about?' So *our* chap Morsed back, 'There's one of these big fat stores (fats of course were important in war) on Salisbury Plain.' He gave them the location that we selected and I said, 'I'll see if I can blow it up and burn it at a fixed time';

night was selected. I took Sinclair Munro into my confidence, as I had to have somebody to help me. We found an old Dutch barn on the Plain and we filled it up with what I call 'dog's breakfasts' – tar and all that kind of thing, and an explosive charge to blow the roof off and expose the flames. MI5 provided me with a racing driver and he'd got some socking great racing car. He took the side of the car out and filled up the back with soft sorbo rubber and so on. The barn was at the bottom of a long dip on Salisbury Plain, the hill sloping up each way, and the road could not be closed for security reasons. The idea was to have a car at the top of each rise and when they both blinked their sidelights, quickly, it meant that nothing was coming. I lit the fuse – it had to be a short one because it was beside a public highway. I ran straight for the road and this chap timed it perfectly. He drove slowly past, I put my arms in front of my face and dived head first into his car and we were off. And then boom! I thought, by gosh, that's a bit bigger bang than I intended.

Actually, one of the chaps who was helping with this was young Rothschild, later Lord Rothschild, who came to spend the night with me beforehand. I've never forgotten it, because my younger daughter said to my wife, the next morning, 'Who's that nice man that played games with me after breakfast?' Vera said, 'Well, that was Lord Rothschild.' 'But who's Lord Roth?'

Anyway, Rothschild was in on this game and the lord lieutenant of the county and they had a hell of a party arranged at his house, on the heights, whence we could see this enormous blaze. And sure enough presently a German reconnaissance plane came over; they used to fly so high you couldn't hit them. All you could hear was a very, very high whine. It would be unarmed. So it was noted that this spy was doing his job. After that, of course, they could feed in slightly wrong bits of information. That's how intelligence worked in the war, you gave wrong information but you also gave some right information that didn't matter too much, to feed them. I went back the next morning to have a look. My heart nearly stood still because, true, I'd knocked the roof off this barn, but a bit harder than I thought. Luckily for me it had sailed clean across the road and missed all the telephone lines to the south of England. If I had hit those, my name would have been mud.

On another occasion the War Office phoned me and said 'We've got a rum job for you, Wood. We want a really marvellous fireworks display.'

It was for some chief somewhere in Africa. He was mad on fireworks and this was the kind of bribe that was needed. And would we select some really good stuff – well, of course, talk about fun! Young Brock [of Brock's Firework Company] had been at school with me, so I twisted his arm and we went down to the factory and made our selection. And, of course, we did no end of tests. I remember one thing which we very vulgarly called 'An African Chief getting up in the morning (too late).' It was – whoops, zing, crash! I couldn't resist it. I got hold of one nice powerful rocket and one of the wooden benches in the garden and laid it on this at a nice angle and fired it in the general direction of people. It hit the side of the house, went round the corner and burned itself out on my great friend Ramsay Green's car. He wasn't a bit pleased. It did make people move quite fast. Z-I-I-I-I-N-G: a huge great rocket. There were no holds barred at that place at all.

Then there was the incident of the rector's garden, close to one of our boundaries [Gregor House]. The Rector [Revd Pugh] came to me one day and said, 'Really, Major Wood (or Colonel Wood or whatever I was then), the most weird things can happen in this place. I was reading my newspaper, it was a nice sunny day, in the garden in a deckchair, and my newspaper was torn from my hands by an unseen force. What could it have been?' I said, 'Good Lord, what *could* it have been?' I bloody well knew what it was. My young villains had been testing a silent mortar they'd devised. The noise of the mortar stayed inside, you see. Of course they were using blanks, but it would have taken his head off if it had hit him. They got it at the wrong angle and didn't know how far it was going, I suppose, and it had gone over the wall, out of our grounds, into the Rectory garden and swept the newspaper from his hands. But, of course, being a heavy large object, it didn't make a hole, it just pushed it out of his hands. He was lucky. I said to the men, 'I don't care if it takes the whole night and if you get caught I shall say that you were trying to steal apples or something. And I shall disown you. You've got to find that damn thing before dawn tomorrow morning.' They did. Took about half the night in the undergrowth of the garden, trying to find it.

Which reminds me, there was a thing during the war called the Blacker Bombard. It was used to hit tanks and it was used by the Home Guard. Well, they took this thing somewhere or other, and all the brass hats assembled to watch it demonstrated. It worked quite satisfactorily and one of the old generals said to the youngster in charge of it, 'What's its range, my boy, what's its range?' He said, 'I've no idea, sir.' 'Well, cock it up boy, cock it up.' So he cocked it up and fired it, and it disappeared out of sight. This old boy said, 'Where do you think that has landed?' and the youngster said, 'I should think smack in the middle of the A4, sir.' Well, these brass hats, they were all out of sight in, I should say, thirty seconds flat. They were not going to be associated with that.

While I was in India, I was asked to comment on what we would call, in the scientific world, a very clever and elegant device. It was designed to help our chaps to cross rivers in Burma, and this device went into a small 2-inch mortar. It was like an old-fashioned small harpoon, with the flukes folded back and a base that fitted the mortar. To it were attached several hundred yards of parachute cord, very strong and very light. This had to be flaked out on a ground-sheet. We tested it by firing it into a hillside. Sure enough, you pulled hard on it, the flukes opened and gripped and you couldn't shift it. A man would go across on this parachute cord and then he'd haul a heavier rope across and get all the men over. It worked very well. So I said to this youngster who was demonstrating it, 'What's its range?' And he said, 'I've no idea, sir.' So I said, 'Cock it up, boy, cock it up,' because I had seen the braking effect of the cord was all right and knew it couldn't go very far. However, the cord caught on a branch or something and broke, and this thing disappeared over the brow of the hill. I said, 'What is the other side of that?' And he said, 'The Governor's bodyguard camp, sir.' And remembering past lessons – and I am sure they learned one too – I was in my staff car and out of sight in a split second, disassociating myself from the whole affair. I wrote about this, with other amusing things, under the heading 'Top Brass' for one of the Christmas numbers of *The Field* magazine.

Anyway, to get back to the more serious side. I talked about pencil fuses earlier on. We produced and later had made millions of 'time pencils' which would fire an explosive charge or incendiary device at varying times from a few minutes to days.

The delay time fuse was controlled by the corrosion of a piano wire by copper chloride solution. Piano wire is uniform and standard and the delay times were remarkably consistent. The device was cheap, reliable and safe to set, easy to operate in the dark and easy to manufacture.

These, attached to explosive charges were, *inter alia*, left behind as presents after a Commando raid so that the enemy might not feel that our chaps had just made a quick call and then forgotten all about them.

Well, one of the really wonderful uses of these was in the Western Desert, with the Stirling brothers of the Long-Range Desert Group [in fact the Special Air Service – SAS]. An incredible pair of chaps, those two were. Jellicoe, now Lord Jellicoe, was with them. They started off by acquiring Jeeps fitted with twin Vickers K 0.303-inch machine guns, also 0.5-inch Brownings, a condenser on the radiator grille, fuel in a collection of American and German petrol cans (Jerrycans, hence the name) and searchlights, then literally driving into an enemy camp with searchlights blazing and shooting up the whole place and then pushing off into the desert where nobody could find them.

Later they had to work surreptitiously in the dark and had immense success, planting time pencils and charges near the fuel tanks of aircraft, using our explosives mixed with magnesium or something like that to make sure they'd get a good flare going.

The Stirlings would park their Jeeps somewhere out in the desert, crawl into an airfield, and, without a sound, cut a few sentries' throats with their fighting knives. The sentries would be found next morning which didn't make the rest of them happy. So then the sentries didn't patrol but sat with their backs to the aircraft, hunched up and listening.

And of course during the night up would go a machine. People would rush out and when they got there another machine would go up, and so on. I've heard that they accounted for more German planes in this way than were shot down in combat in the whole of the Western Desert campaign.

Between December 1941 and March 1942 the Long Range Desert Group made about 20 raids behind enemy lines and destroyed 115 aircraft and numerous vehicles.

The SAS insignia was adopted about this time. A winged sword, it symbolised King Arthur's sword Excalibur. Its colours, dark and light blue, were chosen because the original unit had a number of men from both the Oxford and Cambridge University boat race crews.

Rommel paid tribute to Lieutenant-Colonel David Stirling and the SAS in his diary, 'These commandos, working from Kufra and the Qattara Depression, sometimes operated right up into Cyrenaica, where they caused considerable havoc and seriously disquieted the Italians.' He described Stirling as the 'very able and adaptable commander of the desert group which had caused us more damage than any other unit of equal strength'.

Stirling became known to the enemy as the 'Phantom Major'. In January 1943 he was captured by German soldiers who had been brought in to track down the SAS. As a persistent escaper he was sent to Colditz Castle.[16]

Colonel Wood continued:

One day at Aston House the guard came in and said, 'There's an officer to see you, sir, at least he's dressed like an officer, he says his name is Jellicoe [Captain the Earl Jellicoe – commander of the Special Boat Section], and he's just dropped in.' He was brought into my room and I said, 'What the hell are you doing here?' He said, 'Well, I'd got a pal flying home so I thought it would be a good idea to come in and indent for some more of your pencils.' I said, 'You could have indented in the ordinary way, you know.' He said, 'I thought it would be better this way. Now, sir, with your permission I'll push off to London.' So I looked at him and said, 'Jellicoe, you have not got my permission and I don't know you and I haven't seen you.' Because I knew what he'd be like in London, back from the Western Desert and returning again the next day. I said, 'I completely disassociate myself from you, go away!' I knew what would happen. I think he would be amused if he knew but I haven't seen him since the war. This is a perfectly true story. I was phoned by Bow Street police station at about midnight that night and they said, 'Sir, we've got a gent here who says he's Lord Jellicoe.' I am not sure that he was Lord Jellicoe then or not, but anyway . . . 'He says you can identify him.' I said, 'Describe him.' They did. I said 'That's him all right.' 'What shall we do with him?' I said, 'Look after him like a father, because he's a damn good fighting man. Find out from him where he's got to report tomorrow morning and the pilot and aircraft and for God's sake make sure he gets on it.' They said, 'We will.' And they did. Wonderful chaps. I knew perfectly well what was going to happen, I was certain of it. Who should blame him?

George Jellicoe's SBS, acquisitive, well equipped and flamboyant, with a force made up of former SBS and SAS sections, bolstered and renewed after losses, had won medals by the bucketful across the whole North African arena and the Italian coastline, prior to and around the time of the Italian armistice. Jellicoe himself led some spectacular missions, by land, sea or floating in by parachute, routing Italians and giving little peace to the Nazis with his island-hopping raids off the Greek and Turkish coasts, around the Mediterranean and on into mainland adventures off the Adriatic and the Aegean.[17]

One such attack was on Crete. George Jellicoe led a contingent of SAS canoeists to Heraklion. The party included four French officers and a Greek guide. They were landed from HMS/M *Triton* in captured German inflatables and laid up while a recce was made of the airfield. Sixty-six aircraft were counted and the raiders moved off on the second day to do their worst. Unfortunately German guards discovered their wire-cutting entrance to the perimeter defences. Fortunately before the guards could seek them out an RAF Blenheim bomber followed three Stukas which were landing at the field and promptly dropped its payload, causing confusion and panic on the ground. This gave Jellicoe and his team the time they needed to set their explosives and pencil fuses timed to go off in 90 minutes. When the first of their charges began exploding, Jellicoe's party was still inside the perimeter, but with incredible coolness he and his men tagged on behind a German patrol in the darkness and walked boldly out of the main gate where they split up. Jellicoe and the Greek guide managed to reach their rendezvous by walking 120 miles across two mountain ranges before linking up with a rescue contact on the south coast.[18]

Colonel Wood continued:

I wrote about everything that happened at Aston House to kind of start and perpetuate our traditions, I suppose; every mess builds up traditions as quickly as they can. My chaps found a Victorian wooden glove stretcher in the grounds of Aston House and that became our mascot. It was decorated and hung up in the mess and called the 'Dead Hand of Aston'. There were various things that I celebrated in verse and I found they'd all been typed by one of my girls during the war so I kept them.

The Dead Hand of Aston

There's a fitful gleam of ghostly light
Glowing in Aston Hall.
My God! The Dead Hand's missing
From its place upon the wall!
There's a pool of ghastly crimson red
Gleaming upon the floor!
And the Dead Hand of Aston
Is scrabbling in gore!
Beneath each nail a tuft of hair,
Blond! With the skin adhering!
And between two grisly fingers
There's a broken diamond earring!
Tuck your head beneath the clothes
Tremble! Scream with fright!
No human hand can aid you,
This is the DEAD HAND's night!
My God! The Dead Hand's struck at last
The parchment's steeped in blood!
Another corpse perchance may lie
Fast sunk beneath the mud.

Rhubarbyat of Omar Khayyam

As round the board the evening meal hold sway,
The Lady Super's voice is heard to say
Partake of this sweet rhubarb, piping hot,
Grown in the garden, and fresh-picked today.
At those dread words, reviving old desires,
Commander Langley to the Hall retires,
Where the Dead Hand of Aston on the wall
Shines forth – should once it strike, a life expires!
I'll keep a rigid fast, and leave the lot
Upon the board, if they *must* serve it hot.
Unanswered let the gong peal through the house
Or let Miss King cry 'Rhubarb' – heed her not!
The worldly hope men set their hearts upon
Turns ashes – or it prospers, and anon

Upon the sideboard rhubarb *cold* is found –
Lingers upon the plate, and then is gone.
The Hand of Aston strikes; and having killed
Moves on: not all the First Aid, bad nor skilled,
Shall once revive the Lady Super, who
Serves rhubarb hot – it really *should* be chilled.

Also found in the grounds were the 'Lidless Eyes of Aston', a pair of human-size eyes on a metal frame to hold them and a weight – they were obviously part of a dummy. They must have moved when the head moved. These were hung on the wall to keep us from harm. A ring from a Christmas cracker provided the earring, the hair may have been from an old rug. It all sounds very childish but I think most people do it. There were lots of childish things in the mess; you need them when you are living alone – you see, we didn't have many visitors except one or two other stations' personnel who were near enough to dine with us occasionally. We never saw anybody from outside, we couldn't, except when we had the Commandos down. Sinclair Munro was very good at light relief, it was he that started some idiotic thing about imitating a firework rocket. When anything happened suddenly in the mess everybody would simultaneously say 'Ooooooo!' and then everybody would go pat-pat-pat-pat on the table with their hands and then there was a loud cry from everybody exactly timed 'Mind the stick!' Totally idiotic. Lots of silly little things like that, but they keep people happy, you know. And I think tradition is a great thing. At any rate, I established traditions with the 'Dead Hand of Aston' and things like that.

The Lidless Eyes of Aston

High on the wall in Aston's hall,
The Lidless Eyes stare down,
And never they flinch nor tremble
At the bloodstains turning brown.
For there's fearful sights
At dead of nights
That occur as the Eyes look out,
When the Whip and the Hand
In a ghoulish saraband
Dance to the tune of Captain Blood,

Wading knee-deep in the crimson flood
Loosed by his terrible knout.
Beware the Eyes that know no sleep,
The rimless gaze, the glassy stare
Which, penetrating everywhere
Eternal vigils keep.
And hail the Eyes that have no tear,
Nor pluckèd brow nor rougèd cheek
Nor carmined lips nor scented balm,
Nor smile nor frown –
Yet guard us all from harm.
But laugh with the Eyes,
As they look upon the Chair,
Where Naval honours had perforce to sink
For humour surely lies within their stare –
They do not even wink!

One of the most exciting things our chaps did at Aston and the fastest job they ever had to tackle was when we got a *cri-de-coeur* back from Tobruk. Some of our gallant chaps out there reckoned they could crawl out at night and purloin some German ammunition where the shell and the cartridge case were all in one, of course. Could we produce a puller that would remove the shell from its cartridge case without marking it in any way? It would have to be very powerful. Our chaps produced this tool in about a week, I think. It was dropped to them and then they crawled out at night and captured some German ammunition, brought it back, pulled the shells out, took out the charge, replaced it with high explosive and put it back again. And of course, every now and again when a German gun was fired it blew the gun to pieces and all the crew with it, and naturally this put them off a bit from firing their guns.

I helped to get Lieutenant-Colonel William Ewart Fairbairn and Captain Eric Anthony (Bill) Sykes over to us from the Shanghai Riot Police. They were not only first-class exponents of their craft, Fairbairn of unarmed combat (i.e. no firearms but not excluding knives) and Sykes in the use of revolvers and automatics, but they were also excellent teachers. Fairbairn and Sykes were guests at Aston House for some time, using it as a centre for unarmed combat and pistol shooting instruction and helping with the design and production of some 'toys' for use by the resistance.

The tricks they taught were only occasionally, but then very successfully, used under active service conditions, but our behind-the-lines agents told me that they greatly increased confidence and morale.

Fairbairn was the silent killing specialist, otherwise known as 'the Shanghai Buster' because of his thirty years' service with the Municipal Police in China's most chaotic and violent city. There he had learned the arts of ju-jitsu and produced manuals on self-defence for British imperial police forces throughout the Far East. Fairbairn worked closely with Sykes, a crack rifle shot who'd teamed up with Fairbairn in Shanghai while working for the Remington rifle company. Together they invented the famous commando fighting knife now widely used by special forces around the globe. It is a double-edged knife with an eight-inch blade. It fits exactly into the palm of your hand, it's beautifully balanced and you feel comfortable with it.[19]

Sykes emphasised that silent killing was as much an attitude of mind as a technique. 'This is war, not sport,' students were told. 'Your aim is to kill your opponent as soon as possible . . . forget the term foul methods. Foul methods, so called, help you to kill quickly.'

Fairbairn and Sykes also taught new methods for firing weapons which had been honed by Fairbairn during his career in the Shanghai police between the wars. The loss of nine policemen shot by armed criminals led to Fairbairn recommending new methods for using a pistol or revolver.[20]

They, Fairbairn and Sykes, taught instinctive 'double tap' (two quick shots) handgun shooting from the navel; the modification of handguns for quick drawing and firing; the use of the knife, silent killing with sticks from four inches to six feet long; coshes, longbows, crossbows, catapults, garotting, shovels and tin hat strikes and neck breaking. They taught the vulnerable parts of the body – mouth slitting, ear-trapping to break eardrums, eye gouging, the gralloch (or disembowelling), rib-lifting, 'lifting the gates' – temporary dislocation of the jaw, ear-tearing, nose-chopping, shin-scraping with the edge of the boot, shoulder-jerking – a sharp pull downward to dislocate the shoulder, and releases to get away from any hold. They also taught the 'grape vine' by which a prisoner could be secured without ropes to a slender tree or pole by a forced position of his knees and ankles. Fairbairn said, 'The average man in this position would collapse in ten minutes, and it was not at all unlikely he would throw himself backwards. This would kill him . . .' Every directive was followed by the order 'and then kick him in the testicles!'[21]

Colonel Wood continued:

It was one of my responsibilities to make or have manufactured what one might call irregular stores for SOE and the Commandos and the like. I was responsible for getting the well-known 'fighting knife' made and I seem to remember that I slightly altered the balance to ensure that they could be tossed from hand to hand without visual assistance; I expect Fairbairn and Sykes helped with this. I have reason to be grateful to them for some of the less lethal tips.

His [Fairbairn's] recipe for young women wanting to deal with nasty-minded old knee-squeezers was simple. I taught it to a young Wren officer who was having trouble with an admiral in the official cinema; it worked, so she told me, like a charm, all in the dark, no fuss, no bother, no scandal and thereafter, no trouble.

I was also able to pass on to some of our senior women staff a simple method of defence against serious frontal attack. The skilful use of the umbrella or parasol requires little strength and can very severely maim.

In my sixties, I twice used Fairbairn's tricks on the London Underground. The entrance port of a train was crowded with young women; two young men pushed in and started to jostle the girls. I quietly asked them to behave. They used foul language and made to jostle me. A second later they were senseless on the floor. I assured the girls that they were only stunned. I had been taught by Fairbairn that the unexpected, done with high speed and without hesitation, usually worked: I had simply banged their heads together.

On the second occasion, again the entrance port on an underground train was crowded, but plenty of seats were available down the aisle, to which access was barred by a large aggressive individual who, despite the pleas of a nice young conductress, refused to move. I backed her up by asking politely; all I got was a growl. I went close to him and said,

'After you!' A few seconds later he was down at the other end of the aisle. All I had used was a toned-down version of Fairbairn's recipe for coping with a man bigger and stronger than you who was holding you in a bear-hug. Bend your back and one leg as far as possible, feel for his shin with your instep, then straighten back and leg with all possible violence and you will smash his metacarpals.

I remember that incident very well because the train eventually emptied, save for my victim and me. We alighted together and he walked down the lonely platform behind me with his chest touching my back. I was praying that he wouldn't start anything because Fairbairn's method of dealing with an attack from behind entailed a roll and throwing your assailant over your head, and I feared he would go onto the live rail. However, he decided against further hostilities.

Fairbairn and Sykes also invented the 'thumb or crotch knife' which, from memory, was about two inches long and one inch wide and, in a tiny holster, it could be concealed in the crotch. [The leather scabbards/sheaths for the crotch knife were made by the local Aston cobbler Arthur Acres.][22]

Dorothea Fairbairn, daughter of Lieutenant-Colonel W.E. Fairbairn, was on the staff at Aston House under Colonel Wood and went to Poona with him. It was she who mentioned that the local cobbler had been asked to make the leather sheaths for the 'thumb knife', a miniature dagger. They may have gone to Force 136 in India with Colonel Wood.[23]

Colonel Wood continued:

Sykes's method of training in the use of revolvers and automatics was first to get your confidence and then to impress on you that successful use of his method of 'shooting to kill' meant that your every action had to be entirely automatic. Most of us used the standard Smith and Wesson 0.32 revolver, carving the wooden butt to suit our own grip. I told Sykes that, while I was a good shot with a rifle, I would like to be proficient at target practice with a revolver. He told me to hold it upside down, aim in the usual way at arm's length and pull the trigger with my little finger. It worked like magic! It was a perfect solution and he thereby won my confidence. Perhaps it was because wrist and arm were in a straight line, thus eliminating kick. I used a 0.38 Smith and

Wesson with a spring dip-fronted belt holster from which you could lift your gun or jerk it forward horizontally. I also had a shoulder holster with harness, both provided by the US police via Fairbairn.

The following tips are from an article 'Quick or Dead' by 'Town Gun', written by Colonel Wood's friend Colin Willock. They give a good general picture of Sykes's method, based on what Wood told him.

You have already carved the butt of your weapon to fit your hand. Grip it throughout as if it weighed a ton.

1. Stand with knees slightly bent.
2. Hold the weapon *at all times* parallel with the ground.
3. Drop the weapon, dead central, to your lower groin, elbow in centre of body. You will find this probably means locking the wrist.
4. Keep your head dead central to your shoulders, your shoulders and trunk all square as far as the hips; thus you are a kind of gun turret.
5. When you spot a target your eyes must face it dead front, at right angles to your head and shoulders. When your eyes are on target you are all lined up, and then and not until then, raise arm to horizontal position and pull the trigger twice.

If you spot another target you *must* drop weapon back to position 4 before repeating the rest of the exercise; if you just swing you will miss every time.

If a target is out of the orbit of your 'gun turret', use your already slightly bent legs to spring into a new position.[24]

Colonel Wood continued:

All this sounds very slow but, in fact, it is very fast and, above all, deadly accurate. I used to practise in front of a mirror every moment of my spare time. When proficient I could hit a playing card at twelve paces or, while myself running, a man-sized target at thirty paces.

My time, starting with my back to two head and shoulder targets which swung out at random, right and left, and swung back again was, if I remember rightly, under four seconds. This underlines the importance of doing exactly as you are told until you become an absolute automaton.

There were still lessons to be learned. When I was posted to India, my reputation as a revolver shot had preceded me. I was invited to an SOE training school where they had constructed a stone test house with a long passage, well guarded by dummies, leading to a large chamber where an English prisoner was being interrogated by a Japanese colonel. The idea was to rescue the Englishman and, using one of Fairbairn's tricks, use the Jap colonel as a hostage.

I entered the tunnel, dummy guards leaped out at me – I had drilled three of them – two shots on target apiece. I was feeling rather pleased with myself when a microphone whispered in my ear, 'And now, sir, you're dead! You've forgotten to reload' – an unforgettable lesson.

Fairbairn and Sykes were showing us some unarmed combat and wanted someone to demonstrate with. So I said, 'You'd better use me. I'm the heaviest bloke here.' As a grand finale, he [Fairbairn] said, 'I want you to charge me, sir, as hard as you can, and I shall catch you. I doesn't matter how hard you charge me, I shall catch you, you will somersault in the air and I shall lower you gently onto this mat.' Well, I charged him all right and I somersaulted – and I saw the room go round – I somersaulted and I finished up in the corner of the room on the stone flags. He ran over to me and said, 'Are you all right?' I said, 'No, I can't move my shoulder.' He said, 'Oh, that's easy.' He put his foot into my armpit and pulled – put it back, you see. But it's given me trouble ever since. Grand chaps!

I think some of those daredevil chaps may have found private life a bit tricky after the war and people who came across them in private life may also have found life tricky. I often wondered about that and remember that I wrote to headquarters when the war was approaching its end and asked, what about all these silenced weapons and God knows what we've been distributing in India, Burma, and all round there. Of course I suppose they couldn't get them back. I am afraid they were used against us later on. People wanted their freedom, and so on.

Here's an interesting story. My headquarters never knew about it, but I was consulted from time to time for advice by the Advisory Committee to the War Cabinet. They used to send me a chit along and say, what about this one? Privately, you see. Well, I got a chit one day, 'For God's sake, Wood' – you see, Mr Churchill, bless him, the world's greatest leader, but he did believe in magic, you know. You could sell him the most weird propositions. An MP had sold him the idea – they sold him several – I got into one of them, oh dear, I couldn't get out of it, wasted a lot of money on this damn thing, it was never any good.

The idea was that we should produce camouflaged pieces of coal which, in fact, contained high explosives. Our gallant boys were to risk their lives planting some of these in the bunkers used by the locomotives, which sometimes took German troops or ammunition down to the coast. Well, of course, it was absolutely ridiculous – it made me so angry, the thought of risking our chaps' lives for such a futile thing. Luckily, in those days I was still quite a good mathematician, and I'd got with me my very good volume on the Law of Averages. I worked out properly, so that it could be checked, the chances of one piece of coal ever getting into the fire-box of a French locomotive that happened to be at the right place and happened to be taking troops. It worked out about one in ten million, or something like that. I wish I had kept that file – I didn't like to. It came back – and this is absolutely true, this is a proper official War Office file, red tape and everything else, and across it was written 'Bless you.' But that was crossed out and underneath was 'God bless you.' And that was crossed out and underneath was 'May the good Lord shine the light of His countenance upon you for ever and ever, Amen. Signed.' That finished the whole thing, because nobody could refute those figures.

However, in spite of Colonel Wood's reckoning, the camouflage section at Station XV, The Thatched Barn, at Borehamwood continued to make explosive coal between 1941 and 1945.

One order was for 16 pieces of Explosive Coal, 65 Explosive Rats, 4 Explosive Logs and 50 Explosive Fish Plates (Railway). To illustrate the versatility of this station's work [for which Aston House would have provided the fuses, detonators, explosives, etc.] the first orders produced were a lipstick holder to take a small message, a pair of sabots (clogs) carved in wood and fitted with a false sole filled with plastic explosive and a time delay (No. 27 Detonator and No. 6 CE Pellet – 36 pairs were made) to act as an explosive device. The glass floats of a fishing net were drilled and filled with a fluorescent substance to act as night markers for hidden underwater containers. Pit props were produced in plaster to hide 3 in. mortar barrels, and latex rubber sheets, representing various barks of trees, were produced for the quick concealment of parachute containers dropped in enemy territory. The Demonstration Room and Lecture Hall, identified as Station XVB, was housed in the Natural History Museum in Kensington. Station XVA was next door in the Victoria and Albert Museum.[25]

Colonel Wood continued:

We made explosive charges at Aston House which Station XV disguised as mule droppings. [Droppings were made in the form of horse, mule and dog.][26]

I was responsible for inventing the method of making those droppings safe and making them work with apparently no thickness and an explosive charge and pressure switch. I came across Colin Meek who had gone over to The Frythe, and I said, 'What are you at?' He said, 'We're absolutely flummoxed. These damn things – we've got to have a safety device and they're too flat, there's no room.' So I said, 'Well, it's simple, isn't it?' 'Simple?' 'Yes, you've forgotten shear strength. Put a pin across. Use a very small spring.' Because if you use the kinetic energy of the spring, you can get enough percussion to fire the detonator without using a great big strong spring with a release mechanism or anything like that. All you do is put a little spring in, put a metal rod across, fracturable metal that won't bend but will shear when a certain weight comes down on it, the spring gets compressed against the rod and then it breaks. Bob's your uncle! And it worked perfectly, particularly against any form of transport. They used to sow these along the roads in Italy, you know, and you never knew when you were going along whether the goat pat was explosive, or not! That was one of my contributions.

I invented 'Exploding Dogs' Breakfasts' and got my own works to make them. The staff didn't know what they were for but enjoyed making them. They were a kind of sausage, about 2 feet 6 inches long by about 9 inches in diameter, and were stuffed with combustible material which won't go out – tar, wood-shavings soaked in resin, and all that kind of thing. These were to ensure that things really caught fire and stayed on fire. They were known to the Commandos as 'dogs' breakfasts'. I was phoned up one day from the War Office and again, those silly asses, 'There's a most extraordinary nomenclature going on in your station – damn it, dogs' breakfasts, and pencils, and things like that. These must all be catalogued and given a proper title and mark number in future.' I said, 'Well, willingly, sir, but you know the Commandos will take no notice. They won't know what the catalogue numbers mean and they'll just throw them away and still indent for dogs' breakfasts and pencils because they know what they are.' And they did too. One of these silly things in wartime – people trying to be officious who had nothing useful to do.

The Station 12 history states:

During 1942 a beginning was made with the long series of *coup-de-main* operations carried out against objectives in enemy-held territories by SOE and CCO [Chief of Combined Operations] personnel. Considerable trouble was taken in planning these operations to obtain very detailed technical intelligence, and a section was employed at Headquarters entirely on this work. This meant that as far as possible, the stores provided for the operations had to be 'tailor-made', and an increasing amount of work of this nature began to flow into the Testing Laboratory. A large number of 'ad hoc' designs for special charges and initiators were produced and towards the end of 1942 a separate department called Operational Supplies was formed out of the Testing Laboratory, with the primary functions of the design and supply of stores for 'ad hoc' operations, thus leaving the Testing Laboratory free to undertake inspection work.

The 'Operational Supplies' section worked from January 1943, under the general direction of a Technical Operational Planning Committee under the chairmanship of Lieutenant J.L. Bliss, RE, and on which Stations IX (The Frythe) and XII (Aston House), the operating section of SOE or other force, the training section and the 'G' staff were represented. The special stores for all SOE and CCO operations were thus almost without exception produced by this Department, and in the early days parties of all ranks, including secretaries, from the whole station, frequently worked all night to complete a rush order. The officer-in-charge was Major C.S. Munro who was succeeded on his departure to India in November 1943 by Major D.W. Pond, RAOC.[27]

Colonel Wood continued:

I was given another fascinating job, the collecting and batching of all the weapons, explosives, etc. in caches for the secret army of Great

Britain (the Auxiliary Units). [In February 1941 Aston House received an order for 1,000 cases of mixed stores for Auxiliary Units.][28]

If we were invaded, a lot of us were staying behind – I was one of them, and we were going to ground with silenced rifles. I was presented with one after the war and they let me keep it. I chucked it in after a time, it was far too dangerous to have about. The chaps responsible for finding hidey-holes really did find the most extraordinary places. I saw one myself, they found the most marvellous old country houses whose owners revealed that they had secret chambers nobody knew about. But the main thing was that they dug in woods and places like that, quite big dug-outs under the ground, removed the turf very carefully and pine needles and so on. Put them all back and had a trap-door with all this fixed to it, where perhaps a dozen men could live with food and ammunition and hidden vents for air.

Whitehall, anxious about the possibility of a German invasion of Britain, had decided that a British guerrilla force must be ready to go on fighting the Germans after they had occupied the country. The men of Laurence Grand's section D [Aston House] were told to do something about it. Grand's men scattered dumps of explosives and other stores in the hope that they would be used by 'stay behind parties'.

Major-General Colin Gubbins created the secret underground army that would be specially trained to use these weapons from the hideouts, attacking German occupying forces and then vanishing away back into their dugout hiding places. The purposely vague designation for this secret military organisation was 'Auxiliary Units'. All information being gathered at the time suggested that the Germans would invade somewhere between Yarmouth in Norfolk and Southampton in Hampshire, a coastal stretch of some 300 miles. Gubbins decided that his forces would have to cover a much longer strip. His Resistance cells would be set up from Pembrokeshire in south-west Wales, round the coast to Land's End, Dover, John o' Groats – to Dumfriesshire.

These specially selected men were trained in the use of explosives, how to make the least amount do the most damage, how to blow up railway lines, set booby traps, where to place charges on petrol tanks on vehicles and parked aircraft, how to blow up bomb dumps and destroy petrol stores and also how to improvise and make explosives when stocks ran low. When Plastic Explosive was introduced the Auxiliary Units were the first to receive it. It was nicknamed 'marzipan' because of its consistency and its smell.

Other arms supplied to secret Auxiliary Units were Thompson sub-machine-guns, sticky bombs, Piat anti-tank weapons, tyre bursters disguised as horse manure, the stick pencil or 'castrator' or 'debollocker', a booby trap that was inserted into the earth and fired a bullet vertically when stepped on. A sniper's 0.22 rifle with a powerful telescopic sight and silencer which fired high velocity bullets was lethal up to one mile range. The Fairbairn knife was also part of a massive armoury supplied by Aston House. These weapons were stored in over 500 secret underground hideouts in areas where the landings were expected to take place.

Major William (Bill) Harston taught silent killing at Coleshill House, near Swindon, HQ of Auxiliary Units, using the Fairbairn knife. He was uncertain how his pupils would react if they were actually required to force a dagger between a sentry's ribs. 'What I really need,' he remarked casually when visiting Aston House, 'is a body for them to practise on.' 'I can let you have one, old boy. Genuine German. It's in our freezer. I'll have it put in your car.' Major Harston hastily declined the offer, saying that the straw-filled bags were perfectly adequate.

In July 1940, Colonel Gubbins sent Captain Eustace Maxwell to Aston House for a brief course of training in sabotage techniques and then he was to go on to Scotland. There he recruited middle-aged men who eagerly welcomed the opportunity to serve the country in Auxiliary Units. Melville House at Ladybank became the Scots north-of-the border Coleshill House, with its own pistol range complete with spring-up targets, demolition practice areas, and training in hand-to-hand combat.

The men and women who served in Auxiliary Units kept their secret. No one else knew that Britain had a resistance group until it was revealed in April 1945.[29]

Colonel Wood continued:

We knew that the Germans had their tracker dogs, Pinschers I expect, or Dobermans, that would find these Auxiliary Unit hide-outs. So the Station IX chemists were given the job of finding something which would put the German dogs off the scent, and one of the ideas they came up with was, I think, selenium sulphide – one part in a million gives the stink to crude oil – the wretched girl chemist who was working on it didn't realise how pervasive this was and the smell went straight into her hair. I managed to arrange via the War Office, for twice a week treatment by the top hair specialist in London to try and get it out. Poor girl, she couldn't go out in the evening or go to a dance for ages.

However, there was a local Polish station near us, where the Poles who were going to be dropped back into their country were training. They loved our boss Colin Gubbins, and Gubbins loved them, he'd done some wonderful work in Poland, when the war broke out. He had a favourite Alsatian dog that always lived with the Poles when Gubbins was pushing off anywhere. The Poles phoned me and said, 'Look, we don't want to take a chance, we know you, will you come and observe an experiment? We have produced something which will stop any tracker dog.' Of course I said 'Yes' and drove over the next day. They had got it all laid out nicely in a corridor. There was the handler of this Alsatian at one end of the corridor and at the other end I was holding the dog. Halfway down the corridor was a plate of some awful-looking ghastly mixture or other. They said, 'Now you see, sir, if you let go of the dog the handler will call him, but he won't pass that plate.' He called the dog and sure enough he didn't pass the plate – he got straight down to it and wolfed the lot down before anybody could stop him! It takes a lot to frighten a Pole, but they were scared of Gubbins and went as white as a sheet, the whole lot of them, they were shaking with fear, watching this dog eating this chemical. It thrived on it! Nothing happened but – you know – 'Is he going to die? My God . . .' They thought so anyway. Laugh – I laughed till I cried. It won't pass the plate – of course it didn't pass the plate! You know how a dog likes nasty things.

I said to our camp commandant one day, 'I can't get to town, is there any way I can get a haircut?' He said, 'Oh yes, all the officers go down to the village, it's very good.'

I ordered my staff car and went down to the local barber. There were quite a few young officers – an extraordinary number – waiting to have their hair cut. I thought, this is funny. They all stood up and said, 'After you, sir.' I said, 'Nonsense. This isn't a parade ground. I'll take my turn.'

'No, no, we insist.' In the mirror I could see these chaps' faces and there was a look of eager anticipation and I thought, what the hell's up? Well, I knew the barber had gone off to the war and the daughter had taken it on and she was very handsomely built indeed. The next thing that I knew was that she stood close up behind me, my head was hauled backwards and held firmly in position between two most glorious soft bosoms. And there are these chaps splitting themselves with laughter. By gosh, it was really cosy but it was the wrong time and the wrong place for the whole thing! It made me laugh at the time though, and they thought it was grand. She was a very nice girl indeed.

In the garden of Aston House, just in front of the house, there was a kind of depression and when we had a little spare time, which we occasionally did, and had a visitor, we would ask him if he played bowls. We'd have little bets on this and we always made sure that the jack went into th'ole – this was known as th'ole because we had some North Country officers. What this poor sod didn't know was that in order to get the bowl near the jack, you bowled it fully at right-angles to the direction you wanted it to go and the contours took it round the most curious and devious routes and finished up in th'ole.

And we had an ancient old billiard table and some bent cues. All we could play on that was known as 'Slosh'. The great thing was 'a packet at the pink', because you could go in off it or cannon or anything else and it counted, I think five. We had lots of fun and also lots of very hard work. There were times when we didn't sit down at all for several days on end while there was an urgent operation for which to get ready.

An impressionable lady at first believed my tales of how I used my old plaited leather-riding whip in India in the early 1920s. My nickname with the Free French was Captain Blood.

Captain Blood's Corrector

By Gad Sir! When I was in Poonah,
I laid it on with a will!
To hear how I used my sjambok
Made a Lady Super feel ill.
For disobedience of orders
I would thrash a man till he swooned;
Then to show that I had no ill feeling

Rub HCl in the wound.
Yes! The way I used my kiboko
Was nobody's business at all.
I could weep tears of blood as I see it
Hanging idle on Aston House wall!

I remember one sad little thing during the war. Two of my officers came back from somewhere or other, they'd been up north to see something we were having manufactured. And they said it was the saddest thing. They came out of this factory in the dark and they said, we don't know the way, and there was very little light. The factory workers said, 'That's all right, follow Luminous Lu – follow Luminous Lu.' These people were putting luminous paint on operational watches and dials. And this girl – or woman – had always sucked this little camel-hair brush to form a point until she was literally imbued with, presumably, radioactivity, she glowed. She'd have died, I'm afraid.

We did a lot for Dieppe. [The Dieppe landing on 19 August 1942 was planned to test German defences on the Atlantic Coast prior to the D-Day landings.] To start at the earlier stages was very interesting. I was helping with the planning and so on. I said, 'There's an awful lot of dictation to do, send me one of your top shorthand typists from the War Office.' This they did, an incredible girl, you could dictate as fast as you liked, she took it all down accurately. Amongst other things, in the dictation was the planning aspect including Sheemy Lovat's [Lord Lovat] Commandos' part. He went up a gully and spiked their under-cliff guns with the charges we provided him with to put in the breech, which when fired blew the gun to pieces. I dictated all this and much more. When I had finished, she said, 'But you've left a lot of gaps.' I said, 'Yes, of course I have, that's for confidential names, places and times.' She said, 'Why? I'm an officer's daughter, I've signed the Official Secrets Act.' It was the kind of information you couldn't possibly dictate to anybody, whatever they'd signed. However, the silly girl got really hoity-toity and I said, 'Now, young woman, I'm going to quote Shakespeare to you, "And what thou dost not know thou canst not tell and thus far would I trust thee, Mistress Kate." She was out of that room and I thought my door was going to come off its hinges. I've never heard a door slam so hard in my life!

I was asked to send an observer to Dieppe and I felt compelled to volunteer myself. I should have sent a junior officer, but for certain reasons I didn't like to. I actually started off twice I think, the weather was wrong and we couldn't go. The need was to study the usage of scaling ladders, etc. which we had supplied. Then the Canadians took over, poor devils. If only they'd had a British sergeant with each platoon. They by-passed the pill-boxes which were only manned by the *Landsturm*, who just kept their heads down and didn't do anything. If it had been a British sergeant he would have posted half-a-dozen Mills bombs into every pillbox as they passed. This wasn't done, so they were enfiladed by these pillboxes when they were retreating. It was a tragedy, they were inexperienced – brave, brave men, but so inexperienced. The Canadians didn't come to Aston House before that raid because they were the main force, but the British Commandos had to come because they needed special guidance with explosives for their special jobs, theirs was quite a separate thing. It was lucky that I didn't go because everybody was killed in the tank landing-craft I should have been in. So I was born to be hanged, obviously.

Operation Jubilee was a raid on Dieppe intended as a dress rehearsal for the eventual invasion of Europe. The troops were to be ashore for 15 hours and then make an exit. A force of 6,100 men was gathered, 5,000 were Canadians. The role of British Nos 3 and 4 Commando was to get in ahead of the main group and destroy the gun batteries. The landing by the commando units was a shambles. No. 3 bumped into a German convoy and flak boat. There was quite a firefight and the landing craft scattered. Only four of their twenty-four landing craft made it to the shore. Many were killed or wounded as they came under heavy fire. No. 4 Commando fared better. Heavy fire rained down but they silenced some of the German guns. A No. 4 Commando demolition team with made-up charges moved in. They shoved in the charges and closed the breech, the 100-pound shell exploded and put the guns completely out of action. They left behind about 400 Germans dead or wounded. A massacre, no less, was occurring on the beaches in front of Dieppe under a barrage of fire from German artillery and troops, while overhead a massive air battle raged between Allied planes and the Luftwaffe, the latter coming in wave after wave with bombers and fighters to attack the Canadian troops now coming ashore and their boats and ships. What followed was 'ten hours of unadulterated hell'. The beach was an absolute killing ground. The incoming troops never stood a chance. The Canadians lost 215 officers and 3,164 men. The Commandos lost 24 officers and 223 men. Some 2,000 Canadians were taken prisoner. The RAF lost 106 aircraft for the Luftwaffe's 48 destroyed and 24 damaged. It was a disaster. Tough lessons were learned.[30]

Colonel Wood continued:

It was a New Year's Eve party and we were celebrating and having a whale of a time over at The Frythe (Station IX). A message came across that the Aston House incendiary magazines were on fire, and my God they were, we could see the glare from several miles away.

We went over there post-haste. I remember holding a sheet of galvanised iron so that a hose man could stand behind it on each side of me and direct their hoses. I remember turning to one of them and saying, 'By gosh, these flames have burnt all the leaves off the trees.' He looked at me and said, 'It is mid-winter, sir.' There weren't any leaves there at all. The heat was so terrific, and the glare, and I was so involved that for a second I thought it was summer.

The Station 12 history states:

A serious fire took place in the early hours of 4 January 1942. Fortunately the more dangerous stores did not become involved and the damage, though serious, was localised. After the fire the surplus stores were removed to Fawley Court, and a few Elephant shelters were obtained to afford improved segregation at Aston House.[31]

Seven-year-old Michael Summers witnessed the blaze:

The most incredible recollection of my childhood, at Aston, occurred when my cousin John Wheeler and I were staying overnight with our grandparents the Ashers, a special treat for us both. Some time during that night a fire broke out in newly developed buildings of the secret establishment at Aston House. It was mayhem, the noise of explosions, the shriek of corrugated roofs collapsing and seeing boxes and 50-gallon drums flying overhead was terrifying. We were soon evacuated from the gardener's cottage and taken to a home further away. I regret not being able to remember the house or family that took care of us. Incredibly on that night of all nights the enemy were not there to see everything floodlit for them. Furthermore I learned much later that, taking into account the major damage that was suffered, it did not severely slow down any technical developments.[32]

Another witness was farmer Howard White. He recalled:

I was a member of the Aston NFS [National Fire Service]. I remember that the Stevenage fire engine was a Dennis with solid tyres. They arrived and drove into the meadow to get to the nearest pond, and said, 'We daren't go down there with solid tyres, we shall sink right in.' So I fetched the Aston Coventry Climax pump that had been bought for us by Mr Vernon Malcolmson of Aston Bury Manor. I took this little trailer pump to the pond but the fire brigade said you can't pump water for more than seven hose lengths with that little engine. Anyway Stevenage put down their hose lengths across the road and through the churchyard and linked up to us and we began to pump the pond water. Problem was they had got a more powerful pump and they were sucking on us. Every now and again the hose would keep closing because they were pulling faster than I could pump it. But anyway they were getting a reasonable supply and had two hoses connected. If it hadn't been for the water from our little pump it would have been hopeless, a strong wind was blowing and of course the heat was terrific. They said the curtains of Aston House just got a hold.[33]

Colonel Wood continued:

Even that fire had its funny side because of the most amusing bloke. We will call him Bombardier 'X', the son of a certain sergeant of whom I was fond, a very old regular soldier, who had asked me if would have his son drafted to my station – he was a very willing chap and quite a character but not much good as a soldier. It was no good trying to discipline him, he just didn't understand it at all. For instance I'd seen him coming back to camp wearing his forage cap straight across his head instead of fore and aft, and it never occurred to him he was doing anything funny. Anyway, this is a true story. He noticed that some of the embers roaring up into the sky had fallen into the barn that led back to the house. Without saying a word, he gallantly rushed off to get a saw, climbed up onto the main beam at the top of the barn, sat on it, sawed it through behind him and fell with it into the flames. We managed to drag him out before he got too badly singed, but it was a gallant effort.

The next morning I got such an angry telephone call from the commander of the nearest fighter station. He said, 'Well, that was a nice waste of time.' I said, 'What?' And he said, 'That fire.' I said, 'A waste of time? Good God, it was very serious.' 'Yes,' he said, 'We thought with a fire like that it would attract every German bomber in the area and I had my fighters up all night searching, waiting for them, and they never turned up.' He was quite angry about it.

However there was a very pleasant sequel to the fire because our quartermaster, who was a grand chap and had risen from the ranks and become a captain quartermaster, had fought the fire most gallantly, and had been over at The Frythe with us where they had to rouse him because he had been carousing good and hearty and was just 'out'. But he sobered up completely for this fire and when it was all over he came into my orderly room, saluted and said, 'Fire completely extinguished and all safe now, sir,' and dropped at my feet stone-cold out again. Shows you what discipline will do.

The next day this quartermaster captain came to see me, looking very pleased with himself. He had brought with him a list of everything from the establishment that he reckoned was lost in the fire. I grinned and said, 'That's brought you up to date, hasn't it?' 'Yessir.' What an opportunity!

The Station 12 history states:

By the beginning of 1942, it had become apparent that a substantial expansion of the Aston House facilities would have to take place. Under the instructions of Colonel F.T. Davies, plans were made for an extensive building programme comprising general stores, incendiary and explosive storage, accommodation for explosive filling and also a light engineering workshop. This programme was substantially completed early in 1943, from which time considerable and progressive increases in staff took place, until a maximum of about 600 was reached in 1944–45.[34]

Colonel Wood's record of an incident on the way back from a very good party at The Frythe, 0100 hr, 24 November 1942:

A Solution of Abnegation in Alcohol

An earth-man stood and 'twixt his Atlassed legs,
Observed the stars.
He said 'I am the dregs
Of all creation,
The smallest greenfly this o'ershadowed earth
Has brought to birth!'
He little knew that this exalted thought,
Was due to his unbalanced aural balances;
Until a plangent voice across the void proclaimed:
'Oh little one, how art thou to be blamed?
Too green to know – not fly enough to see,
All this was builded for a pantheist Thee!'

Hailing the acceptance of staff from Station X (Bletchley Park) to dine with us:

A year has passed and our grey hairs,
Though still some inches from the open grave,
Are greyer still.
Now comes the news that 'X-es', in two pairs,
Are daring wintry elements to brave
And really will
By doubtless devious routes arrive at 12.
Now we all gloomy doubts and fears do shelve,
The very news does serve us as a dye;
Our grey hairs darken,
Birds sing, the sun shines in a cloudless sky,
Our years fall from us as the autumn leaves,
Our P.M.C. sends chits for wine in sheaves,
And we, we hearken;
Straining our ears for sound of distant horn,
'X-es' to comfort 'Maidens all forlorn',
And Eves to solace lonely Officers!

Colonel Wood continued:

I took men from Aston House with me when I went to India. One was a captain and they'd got a new idea for going ashore dry-foot, walking the water, it was really very brilliant using surface tension. We used lightweight canvas, rolled up, with canes positioned at regular intervals to keep it stretched out, and this was rolled out across the water. As long as you kept moving and didn't stand still, you went dry-shod ashore. They were asked to demonstrate the idea at Gubbulpore where there was a very big club swimming-pool. The equipment was laid out and this particular captain, with full equipment, wearing bandoliers, carrying a rifle and pack, started to march across the canvas, and some young devil of a subaltern said, 'Squad, halt!' And of course with all his old training, you see, he halted and went straight to the bottom!

It was a marvellous example of what discipline will do, but whether he got hold of the subaltern afterwards I don't know. If I had been him, I would have done and I'd have held him under! It was very naughty indeed.

We received a request from the French: they wanted something the ordinary civilian could do just to irritate the Germans and make them feel they weren't wanted. Not in the way of explosives but just something ordinary civilians could use without causing a riot or executions.

Well, of course, being a mad enthusiast for fishing all my life and knowing all the fishing tackle suppliers, I wrote off and obtained the smallest triangles ever made, less than an eighth of an inch across, but sharp as needles. We sent little packets of these to the French and the dear old ladies would tie about a dozen together with black thread. When they got on a bus or tram or whatever they'd gently hook one on to the edge of the trouser pocket of a German, preferably an officer, and then depart. Of course, this poor sod, it didn't do him any permanent harm, but he'd put his hand in his pocket and couldn't take it out again. All these little triangles drove straight in and acted like barbs. This made them feel that they weren't popular and it gave the old ladies no end of joy and so was a great morale booster for them.

Dear old Francis Freeth, whom I mentioned earlier, invented among other things an ingenious device that the French resistance or even the French citizens could use against the enemy. It was the use of an ordinary mousetrap to fire a charge.

Dr F.A. Freeth was a physical chemist with wide industrial experience. He was an ardent admirer of the Dutch school of physical chemistry and in particular their use of the Phase Rule, a very important scientific principle.

He would claim that his work had been a major factor in the maintenance of supplies of explosives in the First World War and hence to Allied victory. He claimed to have some credit for the invention of polythene. An indication of his somewhat eccentric character was that he always wore a black skullcap. To those who assumed he was Jewish he pointed out that its sole purpose was to keep his head warm![35]

Colonel Wood and Dr Freeth are credited with the invention of the Tyesule, an incendiary device. It was a gelatine capsule containing 2 oz of a petrol/paraffin mixture. At one end the capsule was coated with a match composition which, when rubbed on a striker board, caused the device to ignite. Targets needed to be selected carefully, for it did not provide any time delay in which to escape.[36]

Another well-kept and surprising secret was the involvement of Aston House in the assassination of Heinrich Himmler's deputy, SS Obergruppenführer Reinhard Heydrich, in Prague.

Colonel Wood and Major C.V. Clarke designed the special blast grenade and gave very precise instructions to the two Czech soldiers Jan Kubiš and Josef Gabčik at Aston House, where they rehearsed the attack on a slow-moving car.[37]

The device was a modified British No. 73 Anti-Tank Grenade. The standard grenade had a tin plate body 9.5 in long and 3.25 in diameter containing 3.25 lb of Polar Ammon Gelatin Dynamite, a nitroglycerine-based explosive. The grenade was fitted with the No. 247 fuse made of black bakelite which is often referred to as the 'all ways fuse' designed to function on impact irrespective of how the grenade landed. Total weight was 4 lb. However, the grenades that Jan Kubiš was to carry were a conversion of the standard grenade made from the upper third portion only. The filling was prevented from falling out by covering the open end with adhesive tape and then binding the whole with tape for added security. The effect of the conversion was to cut the size and the weight to just over 1 lb which would make the device easier to throw and to conceal.[38]

Kubiš would have to unscrew the bakelite cap, set the fuse and toss the bomb, taking care to avoid the powerful blast which followed.

In mid-October a series of experiments took place at Aston House with the agents rehearsing the attack using these converted grenades against an old Austin that was rolled down a ramp and around a corner at various speeds.

But there was a limit to the amount of preparation that the agents could be given, and it was recognised during the planning of the attack that they would have to seize any opportunity that presented itself. Consequently they took a positive arsenal of weaponry with them including: 2 Colt 0.38 Supers (with shoulder holsters), 4 spare magazines, 100 rounds of ammunition, 6 percussion bombs with PE, 2 detonator magazines, 2 Mills bombs (4-second fuses), 1 tree spigot mortar, 1 coil trip wire, 2 igniters, 1 spigot bomb, 1 4-hour time delay fuse for use with 2-lb PE charge, 3 electric detonators and 30 inches of wire and battery, 1 Sten gun, 100 rounds of ammunition, 32 lb PE, 10 lb gelignite, 2 yards cordtex, 4 fog signals, 3 time pencils, 1 lethal hypodermic syringe.[39]

Peter Wilkinson and Alfgar Hesketh-Prichard took over the personal training of the two agents for the Heydrich assassination and, with characteristic energy, tackled the technical problems of the operation. They spent several Arcadian afternoons at Aston House in the autumn sunshine carrying out more 'field trials' on the ancient Austin saloon. This vehicle had been rigged up with armour-plated panels and was now towed behind a tractor. Alfgar, whose father had played cricket for the Gentlemen versus Players at Lords just before the Great War, had no difficulty in hitting the moving target at speeds of up to 25 mph. Peter could also do it, but the two Czechs, Gabčik and Kubiš, without the cricketing background, were pretty hopeless. Also they didn't trust the percussion grenade to do the job, they favoured the Sten gun.[40]

On May 27 1941, the morning of the attack, Gabčik and Kubiš both carried battered briefcases. Inside, concealed under layers of grass, were the Sten gun, broken down into three pieces, and two fused bombs. The grass was to camouflage the weapons. Many Czechs kept rabbits and it was not unusual for people to collect food for their animals. Gabčik carried a light-coloured raincoat. The assassins caught a tram to the suburb of Zizkov, where they collected their bicycles and strapped their briefcases to the handlebars. They cycled to the chosen ambush spot, a hairpin bend in the road. Gabčik knelt down, opened his briefcase and put the Sten gun together under cover of the raincoat. Assembling guns blindfold had been part of his training. With the coat over his arm still concealing the weapon he crossed the street and stood beneath a small grassy knoll near a tram stop, to await fellow agent Valčik's mirror signal. Kubiš remained on the other side of the road in the shade of overhanging trees. The ambush ready, they waited for Heydrich to appear.

Heydrich was late. Eventually he got into the front seat of the Mercedes beside Klein his chauffeur and they moved off past the saluting sentries and turned into the road for Prague. He was on his way to visit Hitler in Berlin. There was no armed escort. Despite the orders to insert armour plate in the bodywork and seatbacks, nothing had been done.

The assassins watched the minutes tick by. There was no sign of the Mercedes. Where was he?

The tension was almost unbearable. Both men knew that this might be their last chance of killing Heydrich. If he had changed his plan or his route then Operation Anthropoid would end in failure. Another half hour passed and then Valčik's mirror flashed. Gabčik released the safety catch on his Sten and ran to the opposite pavement. Kubiš removed one of the bombs from his briefcase. Heydrich's car slowed down and came round the sharp corner. Gabčik dropped the raincoat, raised his Sten gun and at point blank range pulled the trigger.

Nothing happened! The gun had jammed at the crucial moment. The Sten failed to fire either because it had been badly assembled or more likely because there was grass jammed in the mechanism. Gabčik was helpless as the Mercedes passed. Heydrich then made a fatal mistake. He had seen his attacker fail to fire and instead of accelerating away he shouted at Klein to stop, stood up in the car and drew his pistol and fired at Gabčik. As the car braked Kubiš stepped out of the shadows and tossed his bomb at the car but in spite of all that practice on the old Austin at Aston House he misjudged his throw and instead of landing inside the car it fell short, exploding on impact against the rear wheel, throwing shrapnel back into Kubiš' unprotected face and shattering the windows of a passing tram. There were screams as passengers were hit by flying glass shards and metal.

The car lurched and smoke poured from it. Heydrich and Klein survived the blast that wrecked the car and appeared through the dust and smoke with pistols drawn.

Klein ran towards Kubiš, who had staggered against the railings half-blinded by blood, managed to grab his bicycle and force his way through the crowd of shocked passengers spilling from the tram, scattering them as he fired his Colt pistol into the air. Klein tried to bring him down with his automatic, but dazed and stressed by events he pressed the magazine release catch and his gun jammed. Kubiš pedalled furiously, outpacing his pursuer. He reached a safe house in Zizkov believing the assassination to have failed. He had seen Heydrich jump from the car and pursue his friend.

Gabčik dropped his Sten gun and tried to reach his bicycle, but was forced to take cover behind a telegraph pole. He drew his pistol and exchanged shots with Heydrich, who used the tram for cover. Suddenly Heydrich doubled over and staggered. Obviously wounded and in pain he collapsed against the railings. Gabčik took this opportunity and ran up the hill. He was bitterly disappointed about the failure of his Sten gun.

Heydrich was taken to Bulovka hospital, with a broken rib, a ruptured diaphragm, and splinters from either the bomb or the car in his spleen. His condition deteriorated as he developed peritonitis, rapidly followed by septicaemia. His temperature soared and he was in great pain. He began to slip into a coma and died. The bomb splinters had carried poison into his wounds, probably from the horsehair or leather of the car seat.[41]

This story ended tragically and is too long to be told here in detail. It was impossible for Gabčik and Kubiš to leave the city and they hid along with other parachutists in the catacombs of the Karel Baromejsky church, a Greek Orthodox foundation near the centre of Prague. Nazi reprisals began and the people and villages of Lidice and Ležáky were destroyed. The parachutists were betrayed and the Germans established a double cordon around the entire area of the church using 700 Waffen SS troops from the Prague garrison. The eleven parachutists resisted the SS for over six hours and the last to survive the siege committed suicide with their final bullets rather than surrender.

Colonel Wood continued:

We had some interesting official visitors. A lieutenant-general stayed for a night – he enjoyed himself no end. He hadn't been in a young men's mess for years because of his high rank, so we gave him a whale of a night. He joined in the singing of bawdy songs and all that kind of thing, we gave him the works and showed him everything. He wrote me a most delightful letter, 'My dear Wood, I haven't enjoyed myself so much for years. And quite frankly when I had my bath this morning and turned on the tap, I half expected to see a severed finger come out!' A really dear old boy, and to see his face light up – you know! He was a very old gentleman, lieutenant-generals often are, but he did enjoy himself.

A great occasion was an official visitation from Brigadier Robert Laycock, a Marine officer and the head of all the Commandos, and Bill Donovan, the head of the American OSS – Wild Bill, grand bloke. I gave him a fighting knife; he was very pleased to have it. About six others came with him, all senior staff, and I showed them the works and nearly overdid it in one case.

PROGRAMME OF VISIT TO E.S.6. (W.D.) 15.6.42

17.30 hrs Arrive. Party goes into the library. Short description of work of Station.

17.35 hrs Demonstration of Scaling Equipment. (Used at Dieppe)

17.40 hrs Conference Room. Devices on view, including special charges and mechanisms used at Lofoten, Bruneval, Vaagsö and St-Nazaire. Note the technique of the ready made-up charge based on the principle of utmost speed in fixing and thereafter 'Pressing Button A'.

17.50 hrs Proceed through Testing Laboratory to Workshops and Stores.

18.00 hrs Party proceeds to field for Spigot Mortar Demonstration. (Booby traps encountered en route).

18.10 hrs Party proceeds to Bombing Range.

The following demonstration will be witnessed.

A booby trap camouflaged time incendiary of the type which can be left behind in a raid, will be shown and 'set'.

Effect of small 'magnet' charge of explosive on petrol tank of car.

Demonstration of the laying and firing of three 'Lofoten' bags.

Demonstration of the 'cavity' and 'focussing' method of using small charges for penetration of steel plate. 1 in of mild steel plate will be completely penetrated by 1 oz of plastic explosive fitted with copper cavity focussing plate and backed by ½ oz C.E. primer.

Type 6 Grenades will be thrown against mock armoured and saloon cars. *18.40 hrs* Party will embus and return to library.[42]

Colonel Wood described 'nearly overdoing it' during the VIP visit:

I said, 'Now this is our method of dealing with cars that we wish to abolish, with people in them for that matter, for the resistance.' I used to buy up cars that were quite useless from the local garages, and use them for our trials. I was wearing a steel helmet, of course and I said, 'I'll now toss one of these into this car.' Well, I did it too accurately; it went in through the window and the car dismembered itself. I was trying to wriggle my way into the ground, steel helmet well down and my arms over the back of my neck, wishing that I was a blade of grass and could get further down than that. Things were raining down all round me, but I was very lucky and nothing touched me. They were laughing themselves sick.

Anyway, to finish up I said, 'Well, gentlemen, just to show you the accuracy of a time fuse, I've got some old explosive to dispose of and it will be really rather a lovely sight. We'll put it at the bottom of the pond and mark the time and the fuse, and you'll see how accurate it is. We'll lift the pond up into the air and it'll go back again.' Well, I positioned the viewers where I thought they were absolutely safe, lit the fuse and the pond went up in the air and the wind changed and the whole bloody lot shifted across and fell on top of them! All this ruddy water. Luckily it was a summer's day but they were *not* prepared for it. I will never forget Donovan, with a straight face, saying out of the corner of his mouth as he passed me, 'Wood, you know, old boy, I personally wouldn't treat senior officers like that.' They took it awfully well and just laughed it off, but I did feel such a fool. I didn't anticipate a terrific gust of wind that came from nowhere. Blew the whole mass of water about 150 cubic yards. Sock! It fell down en masse, it didn't just spray them. Oh dear, dear, dear.

They wanted me to have Mr Churchill down to Aston House. They said, 'Oh, if you do, you will get a gong and all manner of things; he will just love this place.' I said, 'I know he will, but I want to get on with the war, I don't want a bloody gong, what is the good of a gong to me, I want to get the war over and then get back to my family. If Mr Churchill comes here it will mess things up.' I loved the man, he was marvellous. I met him after the war, personally, and talked to him a lot. But he did like magic, we would have intrigued him and he would have given us comic tasks to do – his own staff knew this. I mean as the great overall planner and leader of men he was magnificent, but when he started to dabble in minutiae it was awful. Clement Attlee came once, but he seemed a nonentity, yes, a nonentity. I tried to keep them away, I didn't want them to delay us getting on with the job.

The above 'Programme of Visit' confirmed that Aston House provided special charges and devices for the raids at St-Nazaire and Bruneval. Both were extremely daring and bold attacks.

St-Nazaire had the only dry dock on the Atlantic coastline capable of taking the huge German battleship *Tirpitz*. Merchant ships in the Atlantic were already suffering heavy losses from U-boat raids. If the *Tirpitz* got into the Atlantic, she could devastate ships bringing supplies to Britain.

Destroying the dock would be a massive task. Quite apart from reaching the well-defended target there was the sheer size and weight of the structure. Each end of the dry dock had thirty-five-foot-thick sliding steel caissons, with internal compartments that could be filled with water. (A caisson is a lock gate that slides in and out rather than swings.) These caissons needed powerful winding gear, and each one had its own winding hut. To destroy these gates would demand enormous quantities of explosive and so the idea of an 'explosive' ship was born.

The plan (Operation Chariot) was that a ship, crammed with explosive on a delayed action fuse, would ram the front caisson. Commandos and demolitions experts would scatter to lay explosives on the back caisson and winding huts. They chose HMS *Campbeltown*, a lend-lease American destroyer, for the exploding ship. It was to be disguised as a German ship and loaded with over four tons of explosive encased in concrete. SOE provided and fused the explosive charge.

In the early hours of Saturday morning 28 March 1942, the Germans spotted the force advancing up the Loire Estuary. They pinned them with searchlights. At first they were fooled by the signalman with his captured German codes but as the ship and MLs (Motor Launches) continued to advance their suspicions were aroused. With only a mile to go to the target the *Campbeltown* ran down its German flag and raised the White Ensign and started firing. The German gun batteries opened up from all sides. There were something like seventy or eighty coastal guns dotted along both banks and in addition there was heavier stuff behind. All this was directed at the *Campbeltown*. Pinned by enemy searchlights and battered by gunfire, crammed with her cargo of explosives and men, she burst through a torpedo net and rammed into the massive steel gate. With a grinding sound and showers of sparks and flame, her bows crumpled like a tin can as she rose some twenty feet in the air and stuck there. The assault and demolition men made their way off the ship as best they could, stepping over the bodies of the dead and wounded. The sea-cocks were opened to scuttle the *Campbeltown*, leaving her firmly wedged at a forty-five-degree angle against the dock gate. Within half an hour, almost everything the commandos had planned to demolish had been reduced to a pile of smoking rubble. However, not all had gone to plan – all that remained of the motor launches that had been supposed to take them home was a sea of burning oil and driftwood. Of the sixteen that had set out from Falmouth only two made it back home. There were many casualties in the chaotic continuous firefight.

As daylight came, and survivors on land were being flushed out of their various hiding places by German troops, the one question in everyone's mind was: why hadn't the *Campbeltown* blown up, and was she going to? By mid-morning the ship was crowded with German sightseers and souvenir hunters, completely unaware that they were aboard a floating bomb. Germans from a destroyer that had anchored nearby were lined up unloading British survivors and looking up at the damage that had been done in St-Nazaire. One of them shouted down, 'There's a boat you won't use again in this war!' There was such a BANG – you've never heard anything like it.

It blew the *Campbeltown* to pieces and blew the lock gates to bits. There was dust and debris coming down, the ship's sides and wood, bits of arms and legs and bodies . . . there were about a hundred killed, if not more than that. The mission had been a success but at a terrible price.

Of the 611 men who took part in the operation, fewer than half made it home. A total of 169 were killed and 215 taken prisoner.[43]

The shower of decorations (including five VCs) after the raid did not include its most heroic figures, a pair of commando subalterns who were being interrogated in *Campbeltown*'s ward room, who kept to themselves the knowledge that she was about to explode, and died with her.[44]

Colonel Wood continued:

I remember a great disappointment. We knew that some German agents were going to be dropped in Ireland and they were going to be picked up. I said they are saboteurs and they have probably got some information that will be useful to me and I'd like to have the job of interrogating them. This was agreed and Mavis Martin-Sperry, by then my PA, and I worked out a scheme between us. We were going to – quite deliberately and obviously – these chaps were going to see it – clear everybody else out of the buildings, so that we had them at our mercy and would question them one at a time. She was a good little actress, she was going to pretend this and pretend that, so that the man who was being interrogated was kind of imagining what ghastly things were happening in the next room, not that we would touch them! We wouldn't allow anybody to torture anybody. Sweating with fear, he was going to wonder what was happening to the other man who was being prepared and what he was going to go through himself. We'd all this laid on.

Do you know what happened? These so-called saboteurs came ashore and, having thrown away everything, with glad cries gave themselves up! They were Spaniards who had been paid to have a go. Oh dear. I was so angry. I was looking forward to it so much, too.

We produced thousands of booby traps and railway pressure switches to blow explosive charges on the lines. The chap who did this one was a Sapper sergeant, a grand chap; he came to tell me about it. He was put on board a submarine that went into the Med. and started making itself a nuisance. I don't know whether the commander got a decoration – he should have got a hell of a decoration, because the enemy knew something was going on, and they were after him good and hearty. The submarine was lying doggo on the bottom while they searched for them with depth charges and God knows what.

The sergeant described how later he went ashore in Italy and the railway came close to the coast there. He put a really big charge of explosive on the line a few hundred yards into a tunnel, and one of our pressure switches, so that when the train passed over it would fire the charge. He said, 'Really, sir, it was a lovely sight. I couldn't resist it, I had to stop and watch and it was well worth the risk incurred, it was just like discharging a shotgun. It blew the whole bleeding train out of the tunnel.' He was so pleased.

I made some marvellous friends in the war. I borrowed a train once to see what would happen. I did it in, the whole train! I always believed in testing things properly.

I am not allowed to talk about all of the devices, silenced weapons, etc. that we produced. Some were easy such as buying up stainless big game fishing wire which the resistance stretched across roads at the right level for enemy dispatch riders who found that they quite lost their heads in the excitement.

We had one sad incident. I invited Alec Pooley, my old boss in India in the 1920s, to come back and work for me during the war. He was a first-class civilian engineer. Unfortunately his son was one of the Commandos that came to Aston House for instruction and was killed on a raid. He was a grand young chap.

I suddenly found I had to read the lesson in Aston church. The beauty of words had an awful effect on me and I wasn't warned, you see, and I came upon one of those beautiful passages, you know, 'Man goeth to his long home', 'Or ever the silver cord be loosed and the golden bowl be broken', etc. If I had been aware of it, I would have prepared myself, but there I stood in front of all my troops with the tears running down my face. I don't suppose it did any harm really, but I did feel a fool. I should have been told, I didn't realise I was going to have to read the lesson. Since then I have read the lessons in practically every church to which I've belonged.

Incidentally, when Colonel Wood heard his own voice for the first time on the playback of our taped interviews he later felt encouraged to recite poetry on cassette tape for the blind. The tapes reveal that he was again deeply moved by the beauty of the words and at times had difficulty in continuing.

The Germans began some rather accurate bombing by flying in on a beam. Well, typical lack of imagination, the code-name was Wotan, the one-eyed Norse god, so it didn't take our chaps long to think, 'Oh, one-eyed god, this is one beam' instead of a two-beam cross intersection. Enemy prisoners-of-war were in cells that were bugged, especially airmen, and by listening to their conversation we found out where this beam was coming from. We badly wanted the beam, so a Commando or Special Forces raid was planned to capture the secret beam equipment without destroying it.

We didn't know whether it was in a safe, or how it was kept, so I got hold of my friends in the CID and said, 'Look, I want to borrow a patriotic burglar.' The civilian jailbird was a grand chap and just loved it, adored it! He gave lessons in safe-blowing to the boys going on this raid and would have loved to have gone with them and done the job if it had been allowed.

We supplied them with everything we thought they might need. We didn't know what the building doors were made of so, in case they were made of metal, we gave them little charges with magnets to put over the locks and if they were wood we also provided little charges with ordinary screws, little corkscrew things. I still have a spare slim featherweight jemmy which seems quite unbendable and unbreakable. We tried to think of everything. They did a very successful raid but I don't know what they used, I never heard afterwards, but I know this burglar thoroughly enjoyed himself, he adored being in on things.

This was the Bruneval raid, which took place on the night of 27/28 February 1942.

In fact Colonel Wood's recollection was mistaken. Bruneval was a radar site for use in intercepting Allied aircraft and not connected with the Wotan bomber-direction equipment.

[The radar station] was situated on top of high chalk cliffs near Le Havre. An accurate model of the isolated house and its radar station was made to plan a precise operation. 'An experiment in radio-dislocation', as it was jokingly described afterwards. A company of paratroops commanded by Major J.D. Frost (later wounded commanding the attack at Arnhem Bridge), a party of engineers with the Aston House gadgets and an RAF radar expert were to land by parachute near the radar set.

Their mission was to capture the set and return it to Britain for our scientists to learn the secrets of its system. The landing was successful and they burst into the house, killing its only occupant. Moving to the radar set they killed five of the six Germans in the bunkers. The sixth had fallen over the cliff and landed on a ledge. Major Frost formed a defensive perimeter round the radar set as the local German garrison closed in. Flight-Sergeant Charles Cox, RAF, one of the best radar technicians in Britain, and Lieutenant Vernon with his Royal Engineers experience dismantled the equipment as quickly as they could by torchlight, ignoring the danger. Two bullets struck the equipment and damaged it while Cox was holding it.[45]

Despite the meticulous planning of the raid, and Colonel Wood trying to think of everything they might need, they didn't have a screwdriver long enough to remove a particular part.

When they used a crowbar to break it off, it came away complete with its frame. This later turned out to be a stroke of luck, as the frame contained the aerial switching unit, which was a vital part of the design.[46]

They completed the theft and all started the descent to the beach. They came under fire and there was a sustained heavy firefight to secure the beach because the men who were detailed for the job were dropped too far away due to German flak. Then there was an agonising twenty-minute wait for the Navy who had to evade German destroyers and E-boats. The raiders embarked with the spoils in the crossfire from the naval craft and enemy positions. The operation cost the British one life, seven wounded and seven missing. The Germans suffered six killed, an unknown number of wounded and the loss of secret radar technology. Three Germans were captured and brought back, one was the radar operator.[47]

Colonel Wood continued:

Somewhere on the French coast there was a German submarine base – I forget where it was but I know that the river was tidal there and we were asked to produce mines which would float down with the tide, and under certain conditions would explode and blow the gates and leave these things stranded.

We needed to test these mines, so I phoned the local authority and they gave me a lake to play with. I took some men down there and made sure there were no anglers and nobody about at all. I thought I'd have a last look-see myself, so I walked round and I saw a mackintosh sheet that was undulating in the most obvious and suggestive manner. I shouted out, 'Oi!' But no notice was taken at all. Well, I had to do something quick. So, not too strongly, I whacked down on the uppermost hump of this undulation and said, 'I'm terribly sorry to bother you; I'm going to turn my back at once, but you've got to clear out, there's going to be an almighty explosion in under a minute.' And presumably they departed. There was an almighty explosion. My crafty sergeant – I hadn't thought of this – it killed all the fish within hundreds of yards of course, but he'd got all his men there with sacks ready to take all these fish back to the mess. It was a welcome change. What the poor anglers thought, I don't know.

There was a delightful bloke – I've forgotten his name now but we were playing poker one night, it was terribly hot, and at about two o'clock in the morning this chap, who had been losing, disappeared. A quarter of an hour later he came back with nothing on at all, carrying one of these special live mines which were about a foot in diameter and two foot high, which he then put down and used as a stool. He sat down and said, 'If I don't win, I am going to pull the pin out.'

I devised a method of teaching young officers poker, remembering what happened to me in the First World War (a lot of youngsters, the junior officers, wanted to learn poker). So I said, 'Right, we will play with you, we older men, for an hour when we're free.' (Sounds as if it was nothing but fun but most of it was very, very hard work.) I evolved the idea of playing with them for counters and at the end of the evening we counted up how many counters the *biggest* loser had lost, and we said he'd lost a pound. The rest was worked out pro rata. So that was all anybody could lose, and the others won some of it, you see, so it was fair and they learnt to play poker without losing large amounts of money.

I found a bogus leg-pull copy of correspondence in my name, waiting on my orderly room table when I returned from leave. We kept pigs (Asher looked after them) to our great profit. Here is my reply:

Above: Aston House, the west end. These rooms enjoyed a view of the park. *(Author's collection)*

Left: Lieutenant-Commander John G. Langley, RN, the first CO at Aston House until SOE was created, shown here with his wife Toni at a party after the war. Langley invented the pencil time-delay fuse. *(Imperial War Museum [IWM] 76/151/1)*

Below: Pencil time-delay fuses. The fuses measure 5⅛ inches long by ⅜ inch in diameter. *(Private collection. Photo: Author)*

Colonel Leslie J.C. Wood pictured in 1943. *(Patricia Crampton)*

Scale model of Aston House made by G. Cowan and G. Elwood in the model shop of English Electric, Stevenage, which proposed to make the site the company's training college or social club. The plan did not materialise. The main REME workshops are at bottom right. *(Author's collection)*

Colonel Wood inspects the troops during his farewell parade before departing for India, October 1943. Aston Bury Farm is in the background. *(Colonel Wood)*

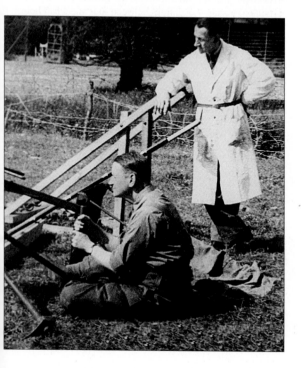

Colonel Wood tests the silent mortar. The weapon is out of the picture as it was top secret at the time. (*Author's collection. Photo donated by Colonel Wood*)

Above: Scientific Officer Colin Meek and his team at Aston House. *Back row, left to right*: Charles Erwood, Fred Stalton, ?, Wally Linsell, George Doe, ?, ?, Jack P. Owens; *middle row, centre:* Colin Meek; *front row:* Cliff Young. *(Margaret Meek)*

Below left: The Acetone Cellulose (AC) time-delay fuse. The body contained an ampoule filled with a liquid which dissolved celluloid, and a spring-loaded striker mechanism, the striker being retained by a celluloid washer. Six timings between four and a half hours and five and a half days were identified by the colour of the liquid in the ampoule. They were used mainly with the Limpet Mine Type 6. *(Private collection. Photo: Author)*

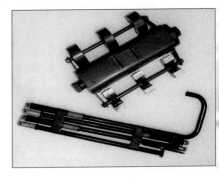

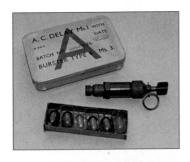

Above right: Limpet Mine Type 6. The mine was lowered below the target's waterline, using the folded placing rod, and secured by six magnets. *(Private collection. Photo: Author)*

Left: A tyreburster. This type of explosive could be disguised as animal droppings, stones, rocks, etc. and placed on roads. *(Private collection. Photo: Author)*

Arthur Christie, the Laboratory Assistant. *(Maurice Christie)*

Release Switch No. 6, a booby trap device placed under anything likely to be moved by the enemy. *(Private collection. Photo: Author)*

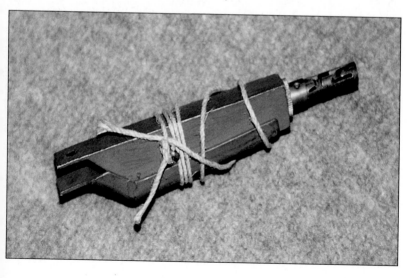

Aston House, the front entrance. *(Author's collection)*

ATS girls. *Back row, second left:* **Joyce Price**; *far right:* 'Scottie' Hales; *middle row, left:* **Nellie Burgess**; *front row:* ? Anderson. *(Cicely Hales)*

'Scottie' Hales, secretary at Aston House, wearing the staff badge, a coat of arms that was later withdrawn for security reasons. *(Cicely Hales)*

A secret message container, which could be hidden in the vagina or rectum. It measured 2⅝ inches long by ⅝-inch in diameter. This is Scottie's souvenir and was converted into a lighter. *(Cicely Hales)*

June Mecredy, 1944, wearing the FANY 'bonnet'. *(June Wilmers)*

Ishbel Hope Mackenzie, FANY 1944. *(Ishbel Orme)*

Some of the ATS girls, c. 1945, photographed on Aston House lawn. 'Scottie' Hales is in the back row, second from left. *(Cicely Hales)*

Above left: Private Lucy Redrup's driver's pass. *(Lucy Holdaway)*

Left: Lucy Redrup's pass to the magazine area. *(Lucy Holdaway)*

A furlough pass from 1943 belonging to Private Lucy Redrup and signed by Major Barratt ('Sweetypie Bertie'). *(Lucy Holdaway)*

Twins Lucy and Gertrude Redrup. *(Lucy Holdaway)*

The Spigot Gun was screwed into a tree using both hands. It could be elevated and aimed as required. Almost silent on discharge, with no flash or smoke, its position was difficult to discover. *(John and Anne Clarke)*

Light and portable, this weapon fired three pounds of plastic explosive over a distance of 250 yards. It was intended for use as a booby trap beside roads, set off by a vehicle passing over a trip wire. It could also be aimed at a stationary target such as oil storage tanks and could be fired by lanyard or a delay action device. *(John and Anne Clarke)*

This Plate Mortar fired the same mortar bomb as the tree spigot and could be aimed by the operator. It was capable of penetrating 2 inches of armour plate and would completely destroy a passing car or lorry. *(John and Anne Clarke)*

Hut 29, Aston House, 1944. *First left:* John Laidler, *third:* John Pigin, *sixth:* Ted Iles, *eighth:* John Lambourne, *tenth:* Bert Perkins, *far right:* Eric Wilson. *(Richard Bignell)*

Richard Bignell, storeman at Aston House. *(Richard Bignell)*

Johnny Riches, workshop engineer at Aston House. *(Johnny Riches)*

Above right: This booby-trap device was pressed into the soil vertically. When trodden upon the 0.303-inch bullet was discharged upward. *(Private collection. Photo: Author)*

Above left: A Liberator pistol. This American weapon, shown with its piece of dowel to remove a spent cartridge, was stored at Aston House. *(Private collection. Photo: Author)*

Left: Richard Bignell and Les Carter cycling near Aston. *(Richard Bignell)*

Veterans' reunion at the Coach House in 2003. *From left to right:* Richard Bignell, Johnny Riches, Cicely Hales, Joe Wardle. *(Author's collection)*

Joe Wardle, craftsman, married Doris on 4 April 1947. *(Joe Wardle)*

The REME dance band at Aston House. Joe Wardle, vocalist, is on the extreme left, with Harry Walters behind on double bass. George Hoyle, the leader, is standing, centre. Jack Hughes is on piano accordion. Harry Dent is standing to the right and Staff Sergeant Fletcher is on piano. *(Joe Wardle)*

The senior staff of Aston House, *c.* 1945. Unfortunately, most of the personnel cannot be positively identified. *Back row, second from left:* **Cecil Lake;** *sixth from left:* **Mr Cowdell;** *seventh from left:* **Mr Evans-Watt;** *middle row, far right:* **Mrs Taylor;** *front row: second from left:* **Major Barratt.** *(IWM: HU 74672)*

Research and Information Section, Secretarial Staff. *Back row, left to right:* **Gerry Stamper, Joyce Bidgood, Joan Whittle, Kathleen Skuse, Christine Watson;** *lower group in doorway, left to right:* **Pat Spillman, Mary Romset, Mrs Wanman, Dorothy Packman, Pam Ashley, Olive Taylor;** *group on right, left to right:* **Pat Dicks, Evelyn Amner, Jean ?.** *(IWM: HU 67317)*

Ernie Welch, wearing spectacles, and Mary Wardrope, the only woman, are here taking a break with friends at Aston House. *(Jimmy Welch)*

Captain Josef Gabčik (*right*) and Captain Jan Kubiš, both of whom were trained at Aston House for their mission to assassinate SS Obergruppenführer Reinhard Heydrich in Prague. *(IWM: HU 48669)*

SS Obergruppenführer Reinhard Heydrich, acting Reichsprotektor of Bohemia and Morovia, the 'Beast of Prague', was assassinated in May 1942 using an Aston House grenade. *(IWM: HU 47373)*

The German heavy water installation at Rjukan in Norway was successfully attacked by special forces in February 1943. *(IWM: MH 33999)*

The V-I Flying Bomb or Doodlebug. Aston House made various devices to be used in attempts to blow these up on take-off. *(Photo: Author; by permission of IWM Duxford)*

LW/594 3 May 1941
The Ministry of Food,
Meat & Livestock Branch,
Rydal Mount,
Colwyn Bay,
North Wales.
For the attention of Mr W.J. Hewlett

Dear Sirs,

1. Reverting to our application dated 17. 3. 41 for permit to slaughter one pig per quarter for consumption at the a/m Military Establishment

2. Your reply dated 27. 3. 41, reference C1/307, is considered unsatisfactory.

3. You are requested to reconsider our application, in the light of Para. 4 below.

4. Our establishment has been doubled since our last application was made.

5. Your reply, in duplicate, is requested forthwith.

6. If a slaughter permit is not granted, we shall be compelled to refer the matter to higher authority.

p.p. L.J.C. WOOD
Major, R.E.

P.S. On 1. 5. 41 one of our pigs strained a stifle chasing the Mess Orderly's cat and for humane reasons was slaughtered.

P.P.S. Lord Woolton [Minister of Food] is my wife's first cousin once removed.

Re P.S. Our Adjutant was an MFH.[48]

Colonel Wood may not have seen the following document, because it wasn't released until the period of secrecy was ended in 1999. I think he would have been amused.

Tailpiece to events of 1943:

Station XII's Christmas Porker.

The Camp Commandant wrote to the O/C Station XII that it had at last been possible to obtain a licence to kill a pig for Christmas for the

Officers' Mess. The Camp Commandant had first been referred to the Hertford Rural District Food Office, then to the Agricultural Officer ECD, then to the Herts and Bucks Area Bacon Officer, then to the Command Catering Officer and lastly to the Agricultural Officer Eastern Command.

The pig had been slaughtered at 1100 hrs on 11 December. Before the slaughter took place, however, the Hitchin Bacon Factory had telephoned to say the pig had arrived but they must refuse to kill it as the licence only permitted this to be done in the area of the camp. After ringing the War Office, at Command's instructions, special permission was obtained, following a call to the Ministry of Food, Colwyn Bay, from the County Pig Allocation Officer who had finally endorsed the licence and declared that everything was in order.[49]

Colonel Wood continued:

I know of one lovely incident where my sergeant-major was useful to me. I got one awful contingent of what was known as the Pioneer Corps – they were about medical grade C4, poor chaps and they were a curious lot. We started to miss things, hardware, like fighting knives and revolvers and things. They were working in the stores, you see. So I said to the sergeant-major, 'We must do something about this.' He said, 'Oh, easy sir, I'll tell their sergeant to march them into this corral and then, sir, ask you to appear.' So he marched them in and they all stood wondering what was going to happen next. He said, 'I'd like the order to come from you, sir, just order them "Remove gaiters".' There was hesitation and the sergeant-major said, 'You heard what the commanding officer said.' They removed their gaiters. It sounded like an ironmonger's shop being turned upside down! They had them inside their trousers, these armaments, and of course with their gaiters removed they all fell out. But I thought the lesson was good enough. I didn't take it further.

We were once asked to produce the noise of a simulated raid – that was a very clever idea of somebody's, not ours. Sinclair Munro was responsible for producing it and he went on one of the RAF bombers to drop it, I remember. 'Tail-end Charlie', he called himself, or something, anyway he was very excited. We made for them all the noises of a complete raid, to be dropped about twenty miles further along the coast from where the real raid was going to be. And it had small-arms fire, machine-gun fire and mortar fire, which is what you would carry on a raid, you see, you wouldn't go any bigger than that. They were just fireworks all mounted on boards and timed to go off, you know, brrr-r-r and individual pop-pop-pop, etc. etc. – and it worked marvellously.

The Germans weren't very clever – but were we? I wrote a paper on the defence of Great Britain against sabotage before the war. And after the war started they were still leaving milk on the Prime Minister's doorstep. It could have been poisoned, easily.

Towards the end of the war there was a demand for a large quantity of limpets.

The Limpet Mine was an explosive charge obviously designed for underwater use. A frogman could easily secure it to the hull of a ship using its six magnetic feet. The fuse was an acetone time delay device. Ampoules of acetone were supplied in different colours with an instruction sheet. Time was calculated taking into consideration the water temperature. A violet ampoule would delay the explosion for up to eight and a half days.

The Limpet Mk 6 became the standard maritime sabotage device for the latter part of the war, some 35,000 being produced by Aston House. Arguably the most spectacular and effective use of the Mark 6 Limpet was Operation Jaywick, a sabotage raid on Japanese shipping at anchor in Singapore Harbour. On 2 September 1943 a team of SOE saboteurs sailed from Australia in a captured Japanese fishing boat to a lying-up point near their target, whence three two-man canoes launched their attack on the night of 26/27 September. Limpets were attached to several vessels, with the result that 30,000 tons of enemy shipping was sunk. The mission achieved a successful conclusion, with the entire party returning safely to Australia a fortnight later. Tragically a repeat attempt was made a year later. Operation Rimau proved a disaster, with the entire party killed in engagements with the Japanese forces or executed after capture. The Junk and Sleeping Beauties [submersible canoes produced at Aston House] were scuttled.[50]

The Clam was a smaller version of the Limpet. This could be used with either a Time Pencil or an L Delay Fuse inserted in a pocket in the body of the device. It could not be used underwater. They were easy to conceal and would fit in the pocket. Some 68,000 Clams were made under supervision at Aston House.[51]

Colonel Wood continued:

I was posted to India in November 1943. I was Colonel Q to Force 136, built and became director of the Special Forces Development Centre, the equivalent of Aston House. When I left to go to my new appointment the mess gave me a very nice presentation, the usual silver cigarette box and so on and other things, and it was decreed that I ought to say farewell properly. Of course Sweetypie was longing for this and a formal parade was just his line of country, and why not? We had everything, all the transport was polished up, and the fire fighters there, and all the ATS. We had a rehearsal the day before and I remember Sweetypie saying to me, 'And here, sir, you dismount, I beg your pardon, de-bus.' He was desperately keen and very formal. All the officers paraded and the little parson [Revd Pugh] came along too and I had to inspect everything and so on. I gave them a final address, a few words of wisdom, I hope, and told them to get on with the war.

Valediction to Aston on being posted to India 1943

Dead and Bloody, Hand of Aston,
Dripping, clammy fingers see
As I vanish into exile
Clutching, clawing still at me.
It would seem the magic's potent
Never more shall I be free
Till the Dogs of War are muzzled
And we dance to V.V.V.
Shall we then again foregather
E/D., Products, Drawings, Stores,
Making whoopee in the ballroom
With others who have left our shores?
Yes, that Hand will surely garner
All the wearers of the Straws
Some are nameless ones – just numbers
But they have kept the 'SECRET' Laws.

Alma Mater, Ave! Vale!
Tyesules, cycles and A.C.s
May you keep on hitting Hitler
Till the *.............'s on his knees.

* Readers may here insert appropriate word to taste. But it *must* scan!

With the increase in the scope of activities in the South-East Asia Command and the corresponding increase of work thrown on clandestine organisations, it was apparent that Force 136, then known as GSI (K) would have to expand considerably. Late in 1943 Lieutenant-Colonel L.J.C. Wood together with Majors P.H. Moneypenny, (this surely must be where Ian Fleming found the name for his fictional secretary of 'Q' in the James Bond stories) and Munro, Captain Press and Lieutenants Rawson and Wampach of FANY left England to set up a Station in India which would serve Force 136 as:

A. Main Stores Depot.
B. Workshop and Development Centre.
C. Special Packing Centre.

In January 1944 the first Special Forces Development Centre (SFDC) personnel arrived at MEW (HQ) in Meerut and proceeded to classify all technical literature and drawings brought from Aston House. The development section was organised in January 1944 to undertake the adoption of standard stores for Force 136. The section was laid out to cater for the general directive of SFDC and in fact was a small edition of Aston House.[52]

A plan showing explosive filling shops with blast walls, incendiary stores and incendiary packing shop, static fire tanks and the outer security fence bears a strong resemblance to the Aston House ground plan.

Colonel Wood was given special powers and financial authority to place local contracts for building work on behalf of HMG and to pay for such contracts from funds made available to him. SFDC was set up at Poona for research, development and camouflage for Special Forces. The training school for Force 136 was along the lines of those constructed at Shanghai, Lochailort and Arisaig in Scotland.[53]

Colonel Wood and his party toured India investigating possible sites for such a station, and it was finally decided to set up in the Poona area. (Near Kirkee). The arrival of FANYs at SFDC gave rise to awkward questions as this women's Corps was practically unknown in India.[54]

Major P.H. Moneypenny seems to have been Colonel Wood's PA. In a long alphabetic listing of the India personnel their identification numbers are adjacent, 680 and 681.[55]

Colonel Wood continued:

I went to do a certain job and I built a large station out of nothing and without any priorities, by all manner of wicked contrivances and mass stratagems. I was told never to go back to India because I'd had very bad dysentery there, but I went back and did this job. I managed to build a large station in a very short time to serve Force 136. We had large numbers of FANYs to house, for each of our brave chaps behind the enemy lines had his own sending radio set and had to be monitored twenty-four hours a day.

Unfortunately I became ill and kept myself going with opium pills for the last six months. Eventually when I got home – I had already had amoebic dysentery, which they thought they had cured in hospital there. Anyway, I recovered from that and then I got sprue and then I got hookworm and all manner of things and finally I got home again. I was pronounced reasonably fit, and felt well, got over all my troubles and my tummy had settled down, so I applied to go back. They said, 'You can't, you have just been invalided home from India.' I said, 'I've helped to plan everything and the big fun is starting, and I don't see why I should miss it.' They said, 'Well, you'll have to have a medical.' They sent me to Millbank.

This sounds impossible but it's absolutely true. When you have had amoebic dysentery they want to make sure it's dead. Because if the amoeba germ is alive still, it gets into your liver, and you finish up dead, I believe. So I went in to see the old boy who was the amoebic dysentery expert, an elderly colonel. I said, 'Ah, we meet again.' He looked puzzled and obviously didn't know me. I had to strip and bend over, and they've got a bloody great thing they stick up your stern like a telescope, because amoebic dysentery leaves scars in your lower bowel and if they're fully healed and show no signs of starting up again you're all right. So he proceeded to shove this thing into my stern, and the next thing I heard was 'Ah, it's Colonel Wood!' He didn't recognise faces, they meant nothing to him, but obviously the interior of your arsehole did, because he knew at once who I was. He remembered because I'd been examined there before, you see.

Poor old chap, I couldn't help but pull his leg, because later on he said, 'You'll find it easier, Wood, if you open your mouth.' And I said, 'Oh, my dear chap, surely you don't want to come right through do you?' He didn't like it at all, he'd no sense of humour.

Anyway, I always used to commemorate amusing things, in doggerel rhyme – you've got all my rhymes of Aston House. I remember I sent this to the old boy:

> With his protoscope
> Like a telescope
> He gazes on ancient scars,
> Sometimes inspecting Uranus
> And sometimes even Mars.

He didn't reply, so whether he liked it or not, I don't really know.

After the Second World War Colonel Wood returned to Bestobell, at Slough, where he remained until 1966. Sadly Colonel Wood died in 1990 after a long, long illness. He was 92. Two of Leslie's own poems were read at his Service of Thanksgiving at the parish church of St James, Weybridge, on 17 October 1990.[56]

> *Stoke House*
>
> In the old hall – nearby the stair
> Stands a carved and ancient chair,
> Looking from the topmost stair,
> Someone's often seated there,
> But when, unthinking, I descend,
> He has gone, my unknown friend.
> We never speak, I never meet
> The shadow in that ancient seat.
>
> I know full well, some unwarned day,
> My friend will not have gone away,

But when I reach the lowest stair,
I shall find Him waiting there,
And I shall gaze, without surprise
Into kindly, quiet eyes,
Take His hand, without a sigh,
Waiting not to say 'goodbye',
I shall go most cheerfully
With the Friend who has waited so long for me.

L.J.C.W. Stoke House.

The Pilgrim Road to Badrinath
(with apologies to James Elroy Flecker)

The dawn flares crimson in the eastern sky;
I wrap my blanket close and shroud my head,
(It is not good to breathe the morning air).
I take the pilgrim road to Badrinath.

I've held the Tail, the waters wet my feet,
I've paid the priests and said the Words ordained,
Now Hardwa and its filth are left behind;
I take the pilgrim road to Badrinath.

The small green parrots fly to greet the dawn,
A jackal slinks away to seek the shade,
The shadows shorten on the dusty road;
I take the pilgrim road to Badrinath.

The road grows hot beneath my sandalled feet
But with each step the hills, the hills draw near.
And, far beyond, the goal of my desire.
I take the pilgrim road to Badrinath.
Across the Saswa and the Song I pass;
Clear streams that flow to keep their secret tryst.
The jungle closes, greener grows the way.
I take the pilgrim road to Badrinath.

I shall not sleep within the town tonight.
There is a hut, high on the river bank

Whence I can watch the sunset and the dawn.
I take the pilgrim road to Badrinath.

L.J.C.W.

Notes

1. Foot, M.R.D., *SOE The Special Operations Executive 1940–1946*, pp. 4–5.
2. Philby, Kim, *My Silent War*.
3. PRO HS 7/27.
4. *Ibid*.
5. *Ibid*.
6. *Ibid*.
7. *Ibid*.
8. *Ibid*.
9. PRO HS 2/224.
10. Messenger, Charles, *The Commandos 1940–1946*, p. 47.
11. PRO HS 2/224.
12. Dugan, Sally, *Commando, The Elite Forces of the Second World War*, p. 54.
13. PRO HS 2/224.
14. Stafford, David, *Secret Agent: The True Story of the Special Operations Executive*, p. 27.
15. Foot, M.R.D., *SOE The Special Operations Executive 1940–1946*, p. 123.
16. *World War II* Magazine, pp. 1841–2.
17. Parker, John, *SBS: Inside Story of the Special Boat Service*, p. 99.
18. *Ibid*., pp. 35–6.
19. Stafford, David, *Secret Agent: The True Story of the Special Operations Executive*, pp. 28–9.
20. Dear, Ian, *Sabotage and Subversion: Stories from the Files of the SOE and OSS*, p. 24.
21. Warwicker, John, *With Britain in Mortal Danger: Britain's Most Secret Army of WWII*, p. 80.
22. Personal correspondence with Colonel L.J.C. Wood.
23. Personal correspondence with Mr Peter Robins.
24. Willock, Colin, *Shooting Times and Country Life*, October 25/31 1984.
25. PRO HS 7/49.
26. *Ibid*.
27. PRO HS 7/27.

28. *Ibid*.

29. Lampe, David, *The Last Ditch*.

30. *World War II* Magazine, p. 1033.

31. PRO HS 7/27.

32. Personal correspondence with Mr Michael Summers.

33. Memories of Ralph Howard White, farmer and Aston parish councillor, as recorded on tape 7 May 1993 by John D. Amess and transcribed by Mrs Margaret Bowyer, Mr White's daughter.

34. PRO HS 7/27.

35. Boyce, Fredric and Everett, Douglas, *SOE: The Scientific Secrets*, pp. 42–3.

36. *Ibid*., pp. 63–4.

37. Seaman, Mark, *Secret Agent's Handbook of Special Devices*, p. 22.

38. Personal communication with Clive Bassett.

39. Seaman, Mark, *Secret Agent's Handbook of Special Devices*, p. 23.

40. Wilkinson, Peter, *Foreign Fields*.

41. MacDonald, Callum, *The Killing of SS Obergruppenführer Reinhard Heydrich*.

42. Colonel L.J.C. Wood's personal files.

43. Dugan, Sally, *Commando: The Elite Forces of the Second World War*, pp. 66–136.

44. Foot, M.R.D., *SOE The Special Operations Executive 1940–1946*, p. 45.

45. *World War II* Magazine, p. 1825.

46. Dugan, Sally, *Commando: The Elite Forces of the Second World War*, p. 285.

47. *World War II* Magazine, p. 1825.

48. Colonel L.J.C. Wood's personal files.

49. PRO HS7/287 SOE War Diaries – Miscellaneous.

50. *Secret Agent's Handbook of Special Devices*, p. 18.

51. Boyce, Fredric and Everett, Douglas, *SOE: The Scientific Secrets*, p. 49–50.

52. PRO HS 7/117.

53. Colonel L.J.C. Wood's personal files. Correspondence between Peter Robins and Colonel Wood 1989.

54. PRO HS 7/117.

55. PRO HS 7/179.

56. Colonel L.J.C. Wood's poems by permission of Patricia Crampton.

The Scientific Officer's Story

Colin Alfred Meek was born in Bristol on 4 July 1909, the son of a clergyman. When he was five his mother contracted multiple sclerosis, and so he was brought up in Manchester where his grandfather specially adapted the house for his invalid daughter. This involved the creation of hoists for bed and bath and the provision of reading tables and other devices, and all this ingenuity may well have influenced young Colin in the practical use of gadgets which became of lifelong interest. He was educated at Manchester Preparatory School, Manchester Grammar School and Manchester University for which he played lacrosse. He graduated in 1931 with a BSc (Hons) in physics and the following year received an MSc degree for his thesis on the 'Electrical Properties and Structure of Certain Zeolites'. (Zeolites are minerals, natural or artificial.)

During the mid-1930s Colin married Mamie and they had a daughter named Jill. His first employer was Imperial Chemical Industries at their Frodsham, Cheshire, factory and then in 1938 he was engaged as a scientific officer by Dr Drane at Woolwich Arsenal to work for the War Office on the development of plastic explosive. With the imminent outbreak of war with Germany his work became of 'national importance' and he was seconded to Section D of the Secret Intelligence Service. There was a general theory that, no matter how good your defences, the German bomber aircraft would always get through. Therefore all government departments were allocated stately homes out in the countryside to which they would evacuate if London were heavily bombed.

The MI6 wartime home was Bletchley Park, Bucks. It was coded DX Section: D for Destruction and X for Explosives. Dr Drane (D/X) and Meek (D/X1) began work there on 15 June 1939 and were joined by Capt. C.R. Bailey (D/X2), Capt. L.J.C. Wood (D/D1) and another. Mr E. Norman acted in a part-time capacity. Mr G. Doe and B.S.M. Stalton were laboratory assistants.

They occupied an office in the house, a workshop in the stables and a small magazine for explosives and incendiaries where full-scale experiments with weapons could begin.[1]

Before the war little was known about the principles, methods or weapons required to wage a successful sabotage campaign. Here they initiated a study on the time pencil fuse, pocket incendiaries and explosives. The work involved test explosions in remote parts of the Bletchley Park estate.

When the war began, some MI6 staff moved in and complained about the bangs. And when the code-breakers arrived they said they lost concentration with each explosion, so Meek and his colleagues had to depart. In November 1939 they moved to Aston House. Here, not only was there a large house and country estate where nobody complained about the bangs, but a chalk pit quarry as well, known to the locals as 'The Dell Hole' where, until then, children often played.

For security reasons the establishment was at first called 'Signals Development Branch, Depot No. 4, War Department' and accordingly time fuses were designated 'Signals Relays', incendiary bombs were 'Signal Flares' demolition charges were 'Sound Signals' and so on.[2]

Colin stated:

The 'signals' cover persisted until 12 May 1941 when it became 'Experimental Station 6 War Department' – E.S.6. (WD) although it was still known to SOE as Station 12. The name Inter-Services Research Bureau (ISRB) was also used as a cover identification. The civilian staff were given notional military ranks. The initial strength was about seven officers, five other ranks and a few secretaries.

Further details appear in the official records:

Dr F.A. Freeth and Mr Norman joined on a permanent basis in early 1940. Captain E. Ramsay Green (D/D2), Mr D.A. Barnsley (D/X1a), Captain O.J. Walker (D/X2) were appointed and shortly afterwards Lieutenant C.V. Clarke (D/DP) joined the section. During 1940 Captain F. Davis (D/DS) was appointed Stores Officer.

Section D/D was concerned with research and development problems of an engineering nature and also with small mechanisms. In addition, it dealt with the production and supply of devices.

Some of the earliest development work on 'Shaped Charges' was undertaken at Aston House. Apart from being concerned with research and production of sabotage devices, Aston House was also very largely responsible during this period for the training of saboteurs, with Lieutenant C.V. Clarke in charge. The Dell was used for training demonstrations and also for experimental work on explosives and incendiaries.

Machine and carpenters' shops were installed at Aston House, and stores for incendiaries and explosives were erected. A filling factory on a miniature scale was set up at Aston House, where high explosive demolition charges could be made up and packed with all the necessary precautions and in accordance with magazine regulations. It was not long before the storehouses and magazines at Aston House were holding a floating stock of several tons of high explosive incendiaries and other devices. Numerous delay, explosive and incendiary devices were under development during the period up to the end of 1940 . . .

Equipment was coming in fast from contractors and there were many problems because not everything worked. So the Aston House scientists spent more and more of their time on inspection of production samples. Progress on the new devices slowed down. Then Prof D.M. Newitt was appointed as Director of Scientific Research and he decreed that scientists should do science and that all the scientists should be in one place. So in July 1941 the research section moved to The Frythe, Welwyn, Herts. (designated Station IX), where a Radio Section was already established.

Aston House then became responsible for Design, Testing, Production, Inspection, Packing and Dispatch of Stores and Administration.

The Design Department at Aston House under Captain (later Major) E. Ramsay Green, RE, comprised a drawing office and a development workshop, staffed by civilians. Their functions were to take the sketch drawings and/or prototypes from the Research Section and work them up into a state suitable for production. It was also their duty to find contractors to undertake the work, and to place the initial contracts. In view of the increasing number of devices then beginning to come forward, and the greater volume of current production, it had become necessary to form a separate Production Section under Mr W.H.B. Billinghurst, to take over the control of all outside contracts. This included the placing and progressing of orders, and also inspection of stores at the manufacturers' works, assisted by the Testing Laboratory which carried out Routine Testing at the Station. Towards the end of 1941, this Section was taken over by Captain (later Major) W. Moreland Fox, RE.[3]

This separation of responsibilities was good in theory but in practice, due most probably to the urgent demand for new devices, neither establishment kept rigidly to this divide. Aston House undertook some research where necessary and equally The Frythe embarked on small batch production such as the Welman one-man submarine. The important result of all this was that the two stations worked closely together as a team, each able to support the other with ideas and solutions. The boffins moved around between the two establishments, which were fortunately in close proximity to each other, no doubt seeking as well as offering advice. All the personnel at both stations deserve the utmost credit for what they achieved in creating the devices for the special forces and the resistance organisations, enabling them to carry the war to the enemy.

Colin stated:

The Welman, a one-man submarine, was developed and made by the engineering group under the aptly named Lieutenant-Colonel John Robert Vernon Dolphin, the CO at The Frythe.

The Welman was a tiny submarine, nineteen feet long, steered by a joystick, powered by a 2.5 hp electric motor, which carried a large bomb – 255 kg of explosive – at its forward end, but it does not appear to have sunk anything.[4]

The Frythe was also responsible for the Welfreighter, a three-man submersible stores carrier which could run up on a beach. There was also the Sleeping Beauty driven by a man in a wet suit. The Sleeping Beauty was designed and produced by Aston House.

Colin stated:

A large charge was made for the Welman to attach to the German battleship *Tirpitz*. The Services provided the details of the systems for the *Tirpitz* but the attack did not take place. ISRB was given a floating dock (Laksevaag) near Bergen as an alternative target (Operation Barbara). Unluckily, when the four Welmans were deployed, the Germans were carrying out a major exercise in the fjord and the craft had to be abandoned.

The entire front end of the Welman craft was the explosive charge. This meant that all the fusing and safety mechanisms had to go through a hole in a centrally placed connecting screw. The front end of the charge was clamped to the target, and the Welman unscrewed itself from the charge.

The charge itself was difficult to design. It had to be neutrally buoyant and positioned at the top for the explosives to be effective, but this tended to roll the boat over. So the explosive became a 'semi-shaped charge' at the centre of gravity. For correct attachment, a hold-fast system was devised with many magnets and a series of equalising springs pushing the charge away from the boat. This seemed unlikely, but it worked. The system was tried in the Shetlands, and the engineers reported it as useless. Major Critchley was sent there and found that, as suspected, the engineers had reversed the springs. He quietly corrected this (on a gale-swept open quay!) and then asked the engineers to demonstrate this 'useless' fixing system. Sure enough they fixed it to a metal plate with a resounding clunk. He then said, 'now take it off' and went for a walk! The point was made and the design validated.

A few engineers gathered at the test tank at The Frythe to witness the floating of one of the first Welfreighters. As the water bore its whole weight it showed a very marked list. Colin Meek, who was merely an onlooker and had nothing to do with the submersibles, measured the angle with his eye, noted its width and other features, proceeded with some verbal mental arithmetic, at the end of which he put a foot on the craft and said something like, 'If you put 700 lb of ballast three feet below my foot, it will come upright.' The quiet-mannered Meek proved right and with the rearrangement of various components, this Welfreighter floated upright.[5]

Colin continued:

Dr Paul Haas of the Physiological Section supported the Welfreighter project by devising methods of disposal of bodily waste. He also introduced psychological and physiological tests for personnel to ascertain who was suitable for manning such a weapon.

He was in touch with Porton Down, the Chemical and Biological Defence Centre, the Medical Research Council and with Dr Roach Lynch, the government pathologist. Haas also worked on secret inks and on problems such as removing nicotine stains from the fingers of agents whose cover was that of a non-smoker. He also dealt with drugs and poisons.

To many, Dr Haas was the archetypal scientist. He was almost totally bald and wore steel-rimmed spectacles, a forbidding character at first meeting, but a mild, soft-spoken and kind person. Born in 1871, he had been a reader in Plant Chemistry at University College, London, and a lecturer in Physics and Chemistry at the Royal Botanic Gardens at Kew. He had an encyclopaedic knowledge of plant and medical chemistry.[6]

Colin stated:

Dr Haas's successor Dr K. Callow, a RAF squadron leader, once had to test a stone bottle of gin that was suspected of being doped by the enemy. He proposed an 'Organoleptic Test' – let's get a couple of glasses! It was eventually declared to be safe – but the owner demanded the bottle back – full!

The Arms Section under Eric Norman made the Welgun and the Welrod which was eventually produced by BSA [Birmingham Small Arms].

The Welgun was an effective 9mm machine carbine and though it did well in field trials it was rejected in favour of the cheaper Sten. The Welrod is a small hand gun made in two calibres, 0.32in and 9mm, with a built-in silencer that is extremely effective. The stock and the barrel can be taken apart and so are easy to conceal, usually by hanging on a cord inside loose-fitting trousers. This weapon is perfect for assassination attacks. Surprisingly, it is still used today for special British covert operations – in the Gulf War, for instance, as Chris Ryan has recorded:

We asked for silenced weapons and in particular for the make invented during the Second World War for SOE. Although fairly primitive, these have never been surpassed for sheer quietness. They come in two parts – the silenced barrel (a fat tube) and the pistol grip, which is also the magazine – and part of the secret is that they have so few working parts. They fire single shots only, and have to be reloaded manually, by undoing and pulling back a screw which lifts the next round into the breech; but the quietness of the report is uncanny – no more than a *pffft* – and at close range the 9-mm slug is deadly. The other two squadrons had such weapons and as things turned out there were several moments during my escape when I could have done with one.[7]

The Welbum, or Motorised Swimmer, was designed to give mechanised assistance to agents dropped in water, so that they could reach the shore. It was agreed that since droppings into water were limited there was no general SOE requirement for the Welbum and that none be ordered (29 June 1943).[8]

Colin stated:

All standard military explosive store items are given categories, and there are strict rules to prevent the mixing of categories. The experimental explosive stores at Aston House did not have enough separate storage buildings to comply with those rules. A serious fire in January 1942 persuaded SOE to build more storage facilities and apply the necessary safety procedures. Other buildings were also included in the expansion, a routine test laboratory, an explosives packing shed, a NAAFI and an entertainments hall, plus the acquisition of a piece of land for the safe burning and destruction of unwanted devices.

Activities in Africa and later in the Far East revealed problems with packing for tropical conditions, so Aston House set up a packing research section in conjunction with the Arc Manufacturing Company. Aston House developed a method of sealing PVC sheet by RF [radio frequency] welding. Maybe Aston pioneered this technique and should be credited with the invention?

Polythene bags are sealed by a simple heated strip, but this does not work for PVC. So to seal two sheets of PVC together, to make a bag or seal a package, the sheets are placed between two metal plates and radio waves are sent in which heat up the plastic and form a seal.[9]

Colin stated:

The explosives research section and radio research section were moved to The Frythe at Welwyn and placed under the control of Lieutenant-Colonel E. Schroter. He went horse-riding, allegedly to get ideas, which his two assistants Lane and Halliwell then toiled to put into practice.

Schroter had a patch over one eye and was nicknamed 'Dead-Eye Dick'.[10]

Colin stated:

The components of section DX at The Frythe were: explosives and incendiaries; drugs and medical; general chemistry (for example corrosion); small arms and fuses.

Charles Erwood was in the fuses section. He came from Spillers Shapes [dog biscuit products] after they were blitzed. He was later accidentally injured by the explosion of 'a nasty Polish device'. [It is not clear if this occurred at Aston House or at The Frythe.] He received much help and encouragement from Major E. Ramsay Green who lost both his hands in World War I.

The first major task undertaken at The Frythe was to support Operation Clairvoyant. This required a device for cutting penstock pipelines at the power plant at Vemork, in the Norwegian province of Telemark, where the Germans were producing heavy water and threatening to develop the atomic bomb, so this had to be stopped.

The pipes were made of an unusual non-brittle alloy to overcome water hammer, a problem caused by water flowing fast along a pipe that is suddenly closed off by a valve.

A sample of pipe was eventually obtained from a steel works and sent to Army Sappers for explosive experiments. They thought the task would be easy and set up a trial. I sent Captain C.R. Bailey along as an observer who took with him a very early development of the shaped charge. The formal trial proceeded using gun-cotton slabs placed on the test pipes, which were 9 feet in diameter by 14 feet long, and filled with water. The explosives were fired and all the pipes were slightly crimped, but none was cut. The Sappers pondered their next move. Bailey asked permission to 'try a little experiment'. There was some amusement as he produced a tiny shaped charge from his pocket, but the derision soon ceased as the charge was fired and water gushed from the severed pipe.

The charges for the raid on the heavy water [plant] were made up of six-inch lengths of V-shaped explosives, joined together with a belt and packed in zigzag fashion in a tall rucksack. There was also a rope sling to throw over the pipes, and clasps to pull the explosive assembly strip tight round the pipes which then acted as a cutting charge when fired.

I can find no evidence that Operation Clairvoyant took place. A plan of the site shows the area of the twelve penstock pipes situated on a very steep mountainside protected by a minefield. Was it abandoned, or could it have been the plan of attack for the airborne troops that took off from Wick in Scotland on the night of 19 November 1942?

One aircraft and both gliders crashed on the south-west coast of Norway about 100 miles from the target. The survivors from the gliders were captured and shot by the Germans in spite of the fact that they were in uniform. The British lost thirty-four specially trained men on this operation. The Germans were now aware of the target and strengthened its defences. The difficulties of attack had been multiplied. German interrogation of the airborne troop survivors had enabled them to guess the operational objective. The Rjukan garrison was again increased, the area combed for saboteurs, and many loyal and innocent Norwegians were arrested.

Immediately the news of the disaster to the glider operation became known, SOE requested permission of the Chiefs of Staff to attempt another operation, as it felt there was a chance of success using clandestine methods. So the Operation Gunnerside party was formed and training began. With Professor Tronstad, the Norwegian scientist, as adviser, the training was carried out by British officers, who were also responsible for the complete planning and equipping of the party. Our technical services tried to foresee every possible necessity and provide the necessary tools and training; a model of the special concentration plant was meticulously prepared.

The Germans no doubt considered that Vemork was so well protected by nature that it would be difficult for attackers to reach it. The works lie like an eagle's eyrie high up on the mountainside. In front the way is completely barred by a deep and sheer ravine. Its waters have carved a perpendicular-sided crack in the bottom of the valley. Across this crack, the Germans thought, no one could make his way. A narrow suspension bridge, about 75 feet long, crosses the ravine at one point, and this was kept under constant close guard. From the bridge a steep, narrow path leads up to the factory. At the back of the buildings the hill is very steep, and was usually covered with rough ice, the only way down it being a long flight of steps beside the pipeline. To be able to resist an attack in the dark the Germans had machine-guns and searchlights on top of the factory. They could illuminate the whole area and at the same time floodlight the pipeline.

A Special Force advance party operating under the code-name 'Swallow' and consisting of two officers and two NCOs of the Royal Norwegian Army's British-trained 'Linge Company', was dropped by parachute on 18 October 1942, and six Norwegian soldiers from Special Forces, operating under the code-name 'Gunnerside', were dropped by parachute on the frozen surface of Lake Skryken, 30 miles north-west of 'Swallow' on 16 February 1943.[11]

The attack that took place on 28 February 1943 is well documented. Without doubt it was one of the most daring and challenging ever undertaken by SOE. These men knew the mountain terrain and how to survive in the arctic conditions. They also had the expertise and determination to ensure a successful conclusion to the raid. They were aided by the collection of accurate intelligence regarding the target and its defences which enabled them to enter the factory gates and find their way into the high concentration plant. The models on which they had practised in England were exact duplicates of the real plant and the explosive charges were made to measure and fitted like a glove. They lit two 30-second fuses and left. The explosion, though confined to the basement, was cataclysmic and drew the sentry from the main gate, which left the way clear for their retreat without a shot being fired.

General von Falkenhorst, Germany's military commander-in-chief in Norway, visited Vemork immediately after the disaster and described the attack as 'an obvious military operation, the best job he had ever seen'. The saboteurs all managed to avoid capture in the massive search that followed the raid. Eight British and nine Norwegian military decorations were awarded to those eleven heroic men.

The prewar explosive TNT was cast in hard solid blocks. Plastic explosive is made of finely powdered RDX or PETN in a waxy binder, and handles much like plasticine. It can be moulded, poked into gaps or wrapped round targets, you just tear off the amount you need. It is ideal for clandestine use. 'Semtex', developed since the war by the Czech Republic and used effectively by the IRA, is plastic explosive.[12]

Colin stated:

Special explosive devices were required to attack targets such as radio masts and power line gantries. The attack on Radio Paris was very successful, using standard explosive blocks held in place by rubber bands. Various mast designs were studied to ascertain the minimum amounts of explosive needed and how the structure would fall. A standard charge was needed that would tackle all these tasks.

At this time my group's cover identity was MO1(SP), using War Office Room 055A as an address.

A major study was the Limpet Mine. There were many problems to overcome. The first limpet was designed at MIR, the rival organisation at Whitchurch under Major M.R. Jefferis.

The MIR design was essentially a tin hat shaped container filled with blasting gelignite. It needed a soluble delay fuse and for the first model aniseed balls were used. The device was tested at Bletchley Park and successfully blew a hole in a barge. The next step was to try it on a moving vessel. A dummy limpet was fixed with magnets to a police launch on the Thames but it fell off! Obviously the magnetic fixing system needed to be improved. The mine was retrieved by Colin Meek but unfortunately he lost his spectacles during the recovery operation.

The first mine design resulted in a ring of one-inch horseshoe shaped magnets set in bitumen forming a tunnel around the limpet mine, but if the target surface was uneven not all the magnets were in contact, as the mine was too rigid. Experts on magnets and water wake problems were consulted and further experiments were conducted in a test water tank. This led to a design with a large limpet mine and six newly invented Alcomax magnets, powerful for their size, attached to a flexible frame.

Another problem was to determine the right amount of explosive needed to blow a hole in a ship's side. The Royal Navy gave the section permission to try out some small charges in their depth charge test facility at Portsmouth. These not only successfully blew holes in the test plates but also in the test box itself! Not a popular result! But it revealed that with the limpet charge actually in contact with the target, only a small hole need be made, as the inrush of water would enlarge it. Hence the size of the charge was reduced. The wake experts advised that the flow along a ship's hull is turbulent, so there was no point in streamlining the shape of the mine. This reasoning had to be defended repeatedly during the course of the war, as the idea kept being suggested.

So many parties were involved in the design that it was impossible to get it agreed and frozen. This was eventually managed only by the expedient of sending a new junior officer along to the meeting who got up and said, 'Right, that's settled then.' It was such a shock, nobody thought to challenge him!

By 1943, with the limpet mine design agreed, there was now a shortage of explosive and a problem with the priority allocations. The main UK explosive was RDX/TNT. Woolwich invented RDX and this was preferred to the rival PETN. Canada was sending over quantities of PETN/TNT which nobody seemed to want, but it turned out to be satisfactory for limpets and so it was readily used. The metal containers for the charges were made by an engineer called Bill Green in London who, of course, had no idea these were for a limpet mine. The complete units were manufactured by a company based in Welwyn Garden City.

Towards the end of the war there was an increasing demand for large quantities of limpets. A search for likely contractors revealed an agency factory at Elstow, Bedfordshire, that was an experimental filling unit and had no work. The problem then was how to use the unit but not their current workforce. It was eventually agreed that Aston House staff would run the plant and five or six soldiers were permanently installed there until the factory closed after VE-Day in 1945. They were billeted in the local firemen's accommodation, advised to be on their very best behaviour and not to upset the local workers. This went well until their quarters were inspected and it was found that they had much better housekeeping and bed-making services.

The official history states:

With the commencement of preparations for 'D' Day, the demand for special demolition stores for raiding parties almost ceased, and Operational Supplies Department became employed more and more on production work which it had not been possible to place with ordnance factories, for instance 87,000 – 1.5 lb standard charges were made in 10 months, and 5,000 rail charges in three months. During 1943 it was decided that rigid explosive containers should be filled with cast explosive, and 25/75 Pentolite was adopted as a filling for MD1 Clams, Limpets, MSC charges, Spigot Bomb heads and a variety of special-purpose charges. In order to carry out this work, permission was obtained from the Royal Ordnance Factory at Elstow to use their experimental shop for poured fillings. A very high standard of filling was quickly acquired, and was maintained throughout.[13]

Colin stated:

The limpet was a successful design and had a long life. Similar underwater devices were made for cutting chains and attacking floating bridges.

The incendiary group noted with grim interest the rapidity with which Japanese homes burned. Their studies led to the design of a 'flash incendiary'. This device projected a very short but intense flash and instantly set fire to the thin skin of an entire wooden structure. With slower build-up fires, the heat is conducted away from the skin of the building. This flash phenomenon is well known to firefighters. A building suddenly igniting can place firemen in danger of becoming trapped.

The new flash incendiary was tested at a derelict ordnance factory at Dalbeattie, Scotland. Several wooden buildings were successfully ignited. In one of the structures the team of observers had to make a hasty retreat when the wooden access corridor they were using flashed over. The Germans used a similar 500lb oil mist incendiary towards the end of the blitz on London. It was very effective in causing fires, probably more successful than the Germans ever realised.

Dr David Malan, a research chemist at The Frythe, worked with David W. King under Dr C.H. Bamford conducting experiments with an incendiary bomb that would set fire to a Japanese house. He describes it as a fearsome weapon. The war ended before it was manufactured, although the Air Council ordered a million of them. Dr Malan would not like it on his conscience if the device was ever used or got into the wrong hands, hence I make no reference here to the materials or to the source document.

Colin explained:

The Building Research Establishment constructed three beautifully made Japanese houses side by side and absolutely correct in every detail – a sacred tree in the corner, tatami mats made out of rushes and squashed down to the right size, slats and paper windows were all perfect. A group of American representatives were lost in admiration for the work of these British carpenters. It seemed a terrible shame to damage the houses at all. We were competing against two other bombs, an American one based on petrol gel and a British J-bomb which was a cylinder that shot a jet of flame along the floor which worked well in a western house but not in a Japanese one devoid of furniture. The Frythe bomb won but the bombs were not dropped or fired from above but set off statically in the middle of the room and thus bore little relation to reality.

A mock-up of a German attic with heavy oak beams was also made for experimentation. This work was undertaken to solve bombing problems for the Air Council and was not part of the SOE remit. Experiments were also undertaken to discover an efficient method of setting fire to Chinese junks which at that time were carrying war material for the Japanese.[14]

Dr Malan also remembers being shown a development of a flat pistol that could be fired from the chest with both hands raised in the conventional surrender position.

Colin remembered:

Prime Minister Winston Churchill was so inspired by a popular novel he had read about the Norwegian resistance, titled *The Moon is Down*, that he called for a massive instantaneous uprising all over Europe by flooding the occupied people with masses of simple, easy to use lethal devices. This was to be called Operation Moon, but was later changed to Operation Braddock. Three new devices emerged, one, called a 'Liberator pistol', was an 0.45 calibre American handgun, very rough and dangerous to fire. Two other devices were produced by SOE: a general purpose explosive, called the 'moon charge', of which thousands were made, and the 'pocket block incendiary'. This was a wax incendiary composition in a clear, celluloid case. Later a metal version was developed. The plan was to parachute these devices into Europe individually for the finder to use against the occupying enemy forces. Studies were undertaken to investigate air-dropping techniques and the design of miniature parachutes, but the whole plan was abandoned. The explosive 'moon charges' and thousands of the Liberator Pistols were stored at Aston House for a time and the 'pocket block incendiaries' were sent to a store in Yorkshire where somebody managed to set fire to the whole stock!

Soon after D-Day there was a major problem reopening the French Channel ports such as Cherbourg. The Germans had laid many under-water mines close to the quays, some with unusual time delay fuses. Not only were they sinking our ships but they were also putting the quay out of action. The naval mine clearance experts at Havant had no immediate solution to the problem, but thought that it might be possible to disrupt the time clock fuse mechanisms without actually detonating the mines. The idea was to produce a long, thin underwater charge that would set off right across the harbour. They tried loading their own 1.5lb charges, shaped like an elongated jam jar, inside a hosepipe, and then detonating it. This failed because the explosion didn't propagate along the complete length of the hose. SOE was consulted and decided it would be an ideal way of disposing of the unwanted moon charges. Each charge had its own CE [Composition Exploding] pellet, so the detonation was likely to hand on successfully. Moreover, each charge had a hole right through for a detonator. By threading cordtex fuse through the entire length, it would ensure complete detonation. This proved to be so successful when tested at Hayling Island that it then became the standard naval line charge.

Another underwater problem was the cutting of chains and cables. This resulted in a design known as the 'Shepherd's Crook' which was a pair of charges producing a chopping action when fired.

Composition Exploding is also called Tetryl. A detonator will not always completely detonate plastic explosive so CE, which detonates more easily, is placed in between. The CE pellet is shaped like a miniature cotton reel and fits round the detonator and thus hands on to the main explosive charge.[15]

The official history states:

A few weeks before D-Day, one of the last large orders for special purpose charges was completed. It comprised special assault demolition charges for use by Commandos on the initial landings, and a similar batch of charges was prepared a little later for use in the operation against Walcheren Island. A letter of appreciation for this work was received from Major-General Sturgess, GOC Special Service Group.[16]

Colin stated:

SOE became involved in supporting Operation PLUTO [Pipe Line Under the Ocean], a pipeline under the Channel desperately needed to supply petrol to the Allied forces after D-Day.

The pipe was made of malleable steel in 72-yard lengths each weighing 15 tons. They were made at Gravesend and were welded together at Littlestone where a special technique enabled them to withstand the enormous pressure of the water. These continuous 3-inch diameter pipes, by then about 30 miles long, were wound on massive drums known as 'Conundrums' and towed out to sea by tugs.

The pipe was positioned on the seabed using cable-laying techniques. It was foreseen that if the pipe-laying vessel came under air attack and needed to take evasive action, the pipe would be damaged, so a special explosive charge was needed to sever the pipe instantly. This was supplied in the form of a V-shaped explosive cutter through which the pipe passed as it was laid. Later the PLUTO designers decided that the pipe would need to be sealed at the same time as it was cut, to prevent contamination by sand, seaweed and sea creatures, etc. This was less easy. However, SOE had already perfected, but never deployed, an explosive device that could sever a railway line and also bend it into a curved shape, similar to points, to ensure derailment. The system they had designed was the forerunner of the platter charge – a shaped charge that projected a piece of metal at high speed, but without shattering it, against the line. The system was adapted for the PLUTO task and neatly flattened the severed pipe end, just like the bottom of a toothpaste tube. Luckily Allied air cover was so good that the pipe layers remained unmolested and the explosive cutter was never used.

Top Secret installations were established at Dungeness, Kent, and Sandown Bay on the Isle of Wight. In order not to arouse suspicion, harmless-looking 'Holiday Bungalows' were built to conceal some of the pumping plant, while high pressure pumps which maintained the supply were hidden in the sand dunes at Dungeness. By the end of the war 172 million gallons had been supplied to the armies on the continent.[17]

Colin noted:

Research was then begun in earnest on charges specifically for cutting metal, to discover the best angle of the V-shape relative to the thickness of the steel plate. Extra plates of mild steel were used as witnesses, as the side flash from the explosion left a diagnostic signature.

The original time pencil fuse used an aqueous solution of cupric chloride that would activate the charge too quickly for many timing purposes. Glycerine was added in two different concentrations to give a total of three timings, short, medium and long. Commander Langley predicted that operators would forget which was which, so they were identified as red, white and blue. Later two more intermediate timings between white and blue were introduced, so these were identified by the remaining primary colours, green and yellow. Later a special short-time fuse was required, which became popular with the training units as they didn't have to wait too long for the bang. This was identified as black, because black is not a colour and is also used to mark training store items. Later a low temperature fuse was made and colour-coded brown, but this did not go into general use.

Another amusing nomenclature problem arose over a flare, a simple incendiary in a cardboard box, made by Brock Fireworks. There were three sizes, small, medium and large. Then there was a requirement for an intermediate size, which became the medium-large flare (ML Flare). Subsequently a smaller version was introduced, so the small-medium-large flare (SML Flare) was born!

Colin Meek's most memorable characteristic was a boyish enthusiasm for work, combined with a delight in clever mechanisms. He never seemed to give orders, but just swept others along with his eagerness. He was close to the action (unlike many defence scientists) and could foresee what was needed in action. He concentrated on the safety of his own people and reckoned that his devices were safer to handle than those produced by MI(R).

The time pencil was a British invention, not German or Polish. Twenty-five were given to the Poles just before the war. Within three years an identical 'Soviet' invention appeared. Meek comments 'Even a design weakness of ours, later corrected, had been copied!'[18] He also remembered:

As resistance groups expanded in occupied Europe, demand increased for these devices. The time pencil capsules were made by Boots and British Drug Houses; the spring snouts, to hold the detonators, by Stephens Pens; the piano wire by a steel company and the complete fuse was assembled by Joseph Lucas Ltd, Birmingham.

A pair of freestanding tall radio transmitting masts, near Bordeaux in southern France, were broadcasting low frequency messages to German U-boats and became a target for SOE. The appearance of the masts was similar to that of the Eiffel Tower. To ensure a successful attack the lower section of the target was modelled in Juneiro, a kind of Meccano, to identify the points of overstress on which to place the explosives. Then a full-size wooden mock-up was made for practice in climbing and placing the heavy charges in the dark. The target tower was made up of girders shaped like a box with one side open. A special 'prayer book' charge was designed, in the shape of a book with hinges. These were to be inserted in the box girders and then opened up. The operation didn't take place because bracken, on the selected landing strip, seemingly flat, was in fact hiding sawn-off tree stumps!

By June 1945, the total staff at Aston House was 524. There were 20 officers and 324 other ranks, 2 ATS officers and 109 ATS other ranks, and 59 civilians.

When the war ended in Europe, SOE at Aston House continued to support the campaign against Japan. Another major undertaking was the safe disposal of unwanted European explosive stores. Eventually after VJ-Day all contracts were cancelled. Aston House staff was reduced. However, it was decided to return the explosives research to Aston House from The Frythe. The move took place in July 1946. The Frythe was then sold to ICI and became its advanced research institute. Aston House was identified as MO1(SP), and the War Office handed it on to the Ministry of Supply. Colin Meek was placed in charge and Aston House became a secure area for the safe disposal of all the unwanted devices from other SOE stations, some arriving from as far afield as Australia, Cairo and Ceylon.

More stations were absorbed into Aston House, including Station VI (Small Arms) from Bride Hall near Ayot St Lawrence, Herts, Station XV (Camouflage) from The Thatched Barn, Borehamwood, Herts, Station VII (Radio) from Watford, Herts, and Wembley, Middlesex, and XVII (Training) from Brickendonbury, Herts, and also the SOE Exhibition Room from the Natural History Museum in South Kensington. There was also a series of unfinished projects to complete and write up. Moving all the equipment from The Frythe to Aston House was a huge task, especially the big environmental test cabinets.

At this time Aston House appeared to be the favoured station for carrying on the work into the future. However, with everything in place, the War Department then decided to close down Aston House when all the disposals were completed. The decision was influenced by an announcement by the Ministry of Town and Country Planning that the countryside adjacent to Station 12 was to become Stevenage New Town.

Prefabs were built in Aston House Park to provide homes for the first architects and the ATS billets housed the initial group of Irish labourers who were to build the new town. Aston House was demolished and eventually the magazine area became part of Stevenage Golf and Conference Centre. With hindsight Aston

House could have served as a prestigious golf clubhouse, perhaps even housing a small SOE museum.

Colin stated:

It took fifty men three weeks to clear the Dell chalk pit and the adjacent burning ground of explosive debris and by March 1948 Aston House was released from military service.

After the war Colin moved to the Explosives Research and Development Establishment at Waltham Abbey, working for the Ministry of Supply. This became the Ministry of Aviation, then Technology, and finally Defence. Colin retired in 1971. He moved with his wife Mamie to Wadebridge in Cornwall. Sadly Mamie died in 1975. Colin married Margaret, a widow, in 1977. Colonel Leslie Wood described him as a 'brilliant young scientist'. Colin received the BEM from King George VI for his enormous contribution to the research and development of explosives and devices required by our special forces. Sadly, Colin died of cancer at Wadebridge in Cornwall on 26 April 1993, aged 83.

There were glowing tributes from the Wadebridge community where Colin had served as a town councillor and mayor, 'the most modest and self-effacing of men, dedicated and gentle, always willing to assist and advise. In other words, the perfect gentleman.'

Notes

1. PRO HS 7/27.
2. *Ibid*.
3. *Ibid*.
4. Foot, M.R.D., *SOE The Special Operations Executive 1940–1946*, p. 111.
5. Boyce, Fredric and Everett, Douglas, *SOE: The Scientific Secrets*, p. 144.
6. *Ibid*., p. 37.
7. Ryan, Chris, *The One That Got Away*, p. 18.
8. PRO HS 8/199.
9. Personal communication with Dr John H. Vernon.
10. Boyce, Fredric and Everett, Douglas, *SOE: The Scientific Secrets*, p. 206.
11. PRO HS 7/175.
12. Personal communication with Dr John H. Vernon.

13. PRO HS 7/27.
14. Personal communication with Dr David Malan.
15. Personal communication with Dr John H. Vernon.
16. PRO HS 7/27.
17. Ogley, Bob, *Kent at War*, p. 200.
18. Personal communication with Dr John H. Vernon.

The Laboratory Assistant's Story

Born on 14 March 1921 in Cobridge, Staffordshire, one of a family of seven, Arthur Christie grew up in the nearby Potteries town of Burslem, Stoke on Trent, where his main interests in life were the Chapel and Boys' Brigade. He left school at fourteen and worked as a 'wheeler' at the Sneyd Brick Company but at sixteen he became a coal miner and attended college in order to specialise in the blasting of coal and learn how to handle explosives and detonators at the coal-face. He also gave up the BB in favour of the Territorial Army and was assigned to a searchlight battery in the 5th North Staffordshire Royal Engineers. In June 1939 he enlisted in the regular army and joined the Loyal (North Lancashire) Regiment but was soon transferred to the Royal Army Medical Corps (RAMC) and trained as a medic. Unusually, his entry to Aston House was via a summons to the War Office in Whitehall.

Arthur explained:

Soon after the outbreak of war I teamed up in Leeds with a Lancashire Fusilier named Douglas Doe – there was a group of about 100 of us who were sent to open a training depot for the RAMC. Many of us weren't keen to become medics, we were infantry and wanted to return to our regiments, or for that matter any infantry unit that would have us. My friend Douglas, or Doug as I called him, was a gentle giant of a man, six feet plus tall with broad shoulders, one of the world's real gentlemen. He didn't start trouble but if there was a barney, then Doug was the man to have on your side. We tried all kinds of dodges to get ourselves posted to another unit but all failed.

However, Doug eventually got his posting and some time later I received instructions to report to Room 124 of the War Office in London. Boy, that put the fear of God into me I can tell you! Me, just a private, to report to the holiest of holies! I could not understand what I had done to merit being sent there. I set off in full marching gear, kitbag, rifle, the lot. On arrival I reported to the master at arms and left my kitbag by his desk. He led me up flights of stairs that seemed to go on for ever until finally we stopped at a door with a polished brass plate, upon which was engraved the name Brigadier J.G. Jaw.

I was told to wait. The brigadier finally appeared. I tried to jump to attention and present arms. 'At ease, hello old chap, relax, we don't go in for that sort of thing.' He turned to the master at arms and said, 'I say Alf, this lad has travelled a long way, get him a cup of tea and a wad and look after him until his transport arrives.' Three cups of tea and two sticky buns later a lance-corporal, RASC [Royal Army Service Corps] arrived. 'Come with me,' he said, 'I'm Tich.' He led me to a large black American Buick parked outside and drove me to King's Cross Station, gave me a travel warrant to Knebworth Station and told me that I would be met on arrival. I stood in the station square at Knebworth with all my kit and waited for an army vehicle to pick me up. Then a little green MG appeared with two smashing girls. One of them said, 'Mr Christie, how nice, jump in, we'll soon have you there.' I couldn't believe my luck. I thought, please don't let me wake up until this is all over.

It was an unusual day, full of surprises. The girls drove me to a remote village with a large country house, set back from the road and fairly well hidden in the trees. There were a few military huts on one side. A high security wire fence surrounded the whole site, with an inner fence around the house. I wondered what was inside. I expected to report to the guardroom but we passed that and halted in a courtyard. A company sergeant-major of the Royal Artillery approached. 'Hello, I'm George, I'll show you to your quarters. First dump your kit, we'll get you something to eat. I bet you could do with some decent food inside you, follow me.' We went into the house via the back door, to the servants' dining room. I sat down at a table and was waited on by civilian maids.

Then I was taken to a large back yard that led to a building with two entrances. I went through the door on the right and up the stairs. Apparently this used to be the gardener's rooms, but would now be my home for a few months. The door on the left led to the packaging rooms, previously the stable. I bedded down for the night, went out like a light and allowed the day's events to unfold in my dreams. This was my rather eventful introduction to Aston House, on 21 April 1940.

I was awakened rather suddenly by a loud bang that really made me jump. I hurried out of bed and found a very welcome bowl of hot water and a towel on the dresser with a note that said all would be collected later. I shaved and dressed, went downstairs, and found my way back to the room where I'd enjoyed dinner the night before. Here I was astonished to find a full English breakfast: bacon, sausage, eggs, fried bread, toast, butter, jam and tea, delicious!

There was yet another surprise in store for me: the first person I met was my good friend Doug Doe, looking quite mature now. Doug introduced me to Alfred Burrows, a fellow in the Kents. We all sat down and Doug explained that he had arranged for my transfer to Aston House. He said, 'This war is going to get very nasty, and I thought to myself who can I help to get out of it? We were old pals, so I set about fixing it for you.' Amazingly, Doug had arranged my previous day's adventures.

Alf was courting a local farmer's daughter, Jenny Gray, whom he later married, so he was away at every opportunity doing his squiring bit around the village. Doug introduced me to all the staff that we met as he showed me round. A naval lieutenant-commander appeared when we were in the packing room, 'Hello,' he said, 'you must be Christie, welcome to the firm, I need you to come with me and sign the Official Secrets Act.' I followed him through into his office and signed my life away. After lunch I was to see this man again; he was none other than the commanding officer of Station 12, Lieutenant-Commander John Langley, Royal Navy.

He explained to me that I was now a member of MI6(R) and as such would play a role in secret intelligence work. My duties were to assist with experimental work on explosives, arms, and various ways of waging war in the field of sabotage. I had been an explosives man at the coal-face, had attended college once a week and been taught how to place charges, so blowing things up came naturally to me, I wouldn't have any problem with that. However, I was not at all prepared for what was to come.

Doug and Alf were billeted in Aston village in a cottage called 'The Beehive', behind the local pub. I was invited to share a large attic room with them. The couple living in this attractive thatched cottage made us feel at home, her home cooking was a delight, and her husband was an agricultural worker on one of the nearby farms. We discovered an old BSA motorbike in the garden shed. Doug said, 'This could provide a means of transport to get us into town.' Alf talked the owner into selling the bike for £3. We decided that it needed a sidecar to enable the three of us to use it. The frame was attached, but no sidecar, so Doug persuaded the carpenters at Aston House to make us a suitable box containing a seat.

Doug and Alf couldn't wait to try it out and dashed off with Doug on the bike and Alf in the sidecar. Doug told me the result of the trial, 'We shot down the hill towards Stevenage, past the Roebuck Inn, turned left onto the Great North Road, whizzed round the bend and I had to swerve to avoid an oncoming car. Bang, clang, the bike went over one hedge and Alf in the sidecar over another. He was thrown into the air, landed on his feet and just kept running, I've never seen Alf run so bloody fast in my life!'

One night, while I was on duty, Major Freeth, one of our boffins, came in and said 'I've got an idea that I would like to try.' We obtained several rounds of 0.303 ammunition and he asked me to remove the explosive from each one. This I did by placing the end of each brass cartridge case into a vice, gently removing the lead bullet with a pair of pliers and emptying the explosive contents into a box.

Major Freeth set about hack-sawing half an inch off a No. 27 detonator and inserting that into the empty brass cartridge with the open end towards the firing cap. I re-fitted the lead bullet into the case, pushing it up to the detonator. The two parts were then reassembled and looked just like the normal 0.303 cartridge. We repeated this procedure several times.

The following morning we prepared to test the modified round. We did this by placing one of them into the breech of a rifle and fixing it on a stand. A piece of string was attached to the trigger and we retreated to a safe distance. When the trigger was pulled – BANG, the rifle shattered into several pieces. Freeth's idea was to place modified bullets in among the enemy's rounds.

I left the lab and went for my midday meal in the servants' dining room. I met Alf who had just come back from a night on a binge and told him what we had done. His reply was, 'If I'd had to cut the end off a detonator in my state, you'd be looking at a corpse. As it is, I feel like one.' I had to agree he didn't look too good.

The laboratory was in one of the outbuildings of Aston House, next door to the garage with a glass porch. We usually started work around 8.00 a.m. I remember helping Captain Robin Bailey, the inventor of the Bailey Bridge, during the formulation of his idea.[1] We worked for almost three days cutting out thousands of pieces of balsa wood and gluing them together to produce an accurate demonstration model of his bridge. When it was finished we suspended it on wires and hung it up in the window of the lab.

Another task was collecting the biggest lumps of coal that I could find in the storeroom and taking them to the lab. I had no idea what they wanted them for; it was seldom explained to me and, when it was, it was often as clear as mud.

My instructions were to try to drill a large hole in each piece of coal without shattering it. I tried with a brace and a six-inch long tube that had a serrated end. I found that, if too much pressure was applied, the coal would disintegrate. I thought, I wonder what the hell they want this for? Don't ask, just do it, and I did manage to drill three lumps of coal.

I placed the drilled coal on the table of the MI room and set off for the officers' dining room to inform the CO that I had been successful. I was told to insert about a quarter of a pound of PE and a detonator into the hole and glue the coal dust back over it. The mud in my brain now began to clear. The lump of coal could be placed in the coal tender of a locomotive and find its way into the firebox, or perhaps into the furnace of a factory. Later the PE was dyed black, which was better than using coal dust and glue. This idea led to plastic explosive being moulded into a multitude of objects and colours to fool the enemy.

A reliable timer capable of working under water was needed for the limpet mine. The boffins came up with a sweet answer: multi-coloured 'gob stoppers'. It was discovered that a boiled sweet immersed in water dissolves at a constant rate and so serves as an ideal timing device. I'm told that the gob stopper was eventually replaced by an aniseed ball.

Colonel Stuart Macrae confirms the aniseed ball story:

We needed a spring-loaded striker, maintained in the cocked position by a pellet soluble in water. When the pellet dissolved, the striker would be released to hit a cap to initiate a detonator that exploded a primer to explode the main charge. Finding a suitable pellet was difficult and chemists were called in to find the answer, but all failed. One day a pellet would dissolve at an alarming rate and next day a similar one might take several hours.[2]

The use of aniseed balls was therefore no joke and nor was the use of condoms, mentioned elsewhere. Colonel Macrae was based for a time at Whitchurch where experimental and design work on explosive devices was also undertaken. He was responsible for the mass production of their devices. There seems to have been a degree of rivalry between the different establishments, which makes one wonder how much duplication there may have been in the design of weapons. They probably did not reveal their secrets and ideas to each other.

So it seems that experiments on aniseed balls were being duplicated at Aston House. Perhaps Sweetypie Barratt was the undercover link, as his sweet company was also supplying them to Whitchurch! This 'feathering your own nest' attitude probably prevailed throughout SOE. Colonel Wood was no exception, having engaged his pre-war company Bestobell to make the light 'Camoflet Set'. (This was the production of boring equipment used to produce a hole to insert a 'TV' switch to blow up railway lines – TV probably stood for train vibration.) So they used their own companies where possible. The organisation was, by its highly secret nature, a bit of an old boys' network. You engaged people well known to you, whom you knew you could trust and rely on *implicitly*.

Because of the timer problem Nobby Clarke, Aston's last hope, was engaged. His arrival was, to say the least, unconventional. Before describing his arrival it is necessary to be aware of some of the Aston House conventions at the time Arthur Christie was there.

Colonel Macrae continued:

Commander Langley was a wonderful organiser, aided by his second-in-command Colonel Wood, and a large staff at Aston House. Commander

Langley had surrounded his establishment with wire and sentry boxes complete with armed soldiers. It was most impressive when I arrived in uniform in my appropriated general's car but it took half an hour to gain admission to Aston House. The guard rang the officer of the guard who arrived by Jeep and frisked me for concealed weapons and solemnly escorted me into the house.

Commander Langley got upset if anyone tried to vary this drill. I received a furious note when I sent an enterprising officer to Aston House to collect some high explosive. He decided that as previously it had taken an hour to gain admission, he would make out an order on the appropriate War Office form and just walk in. 'Did I not realise,' said Commander Langley, 'that such actions could completely destroy his security screen?'

I apologised, and then more trouble. I sent Nobby Clarke, who was an Admiralty designer, to solve the limpet problems at Aston House. Nobby, after waiting five minutes at the guard post, contrived to avoid security measures and get to Commander Langley. Nobby relished this exercise and specialised in it when he joined SOE at Aston House and later as CO of Brickendonbury. I received a note from Commander Langley deploring this conduct. In future, he said, would I send an officer with some sense of responsibility. Captain Clarke might be admitted to the grounds to work on testing limpets but would not be allowed inside the house, nor would he be served meals. Later Commander Langley resigned and Nobby got into the house – in fact he lived there for several months, having been taken on by Commander Langley's successor, Colonel L.J.C. Wood.

Security made Aston House look vitally important and Commander Langley had introduced other useful formalities. He ran the mess on shipboard lines, his officers dressing for dinner every evening. Rules were faithfully observed, including proposing the health of His Majesty King George and passing the port the right way round. This was a place to which one could invite VIPs from the PM downwards.

One of Nobby Clarke's children solved the Limpet problem. We upset its bag of aniseed balls and I tried one which took a long time to dissolve in my mouth. After trying a couple Nobby agreed this might be the answer, so we commandeered the whole supply and began to experiment by rigging up some igniters with these aniseed balls in place and trying them out under various conditions. They behaved perfectly, so we bought up all the aniseed balls in Bedford. Eventually we acquired our supplies from Messrs Bassett.

The aniseed ball part of the device had to be protected from damp. Again we found what we needed in the local shops – condoms! We bought up the entire stocks. Eventually the design was refined and the aniseed ball was replaced by an 'L' delay fuse.[3]

The AC (Acetone Cellulose) 'L' delay fuse was activated by the softening and eventual breaking of a cellulose acetate tension bar holding back a spring loaded striker. The solvent – a mixture of acetone and amyl acetate – that caused the action was contained in a glass ampoule which was crushed by a thumbscrew, operated through a watertight gland. The ampoules were coloured to denote the time delay variation, e.g. Orange 4.5 hours to Violet 5.5 days. As with the Time Pencil the problems of design, the specification of the amyl acetate and strict quality control involved close collaboration between Aston House and The Frythe.[4]

Colonel Macrae continued:

General Gubbins transferred Nobby Clarke to Station XVII at Brickendonbury where he was made the CO and entrusted with the training of saboteurs. This enabled him to become even more of a menace. He had no security guards on the gates of his magnificent estate. One just drove in and then found the vehicle being battered by rounds fired from spigot mortars set off by trip wires. Nobby emerged smiling and pointed out that if they had been live rounds the occupants of the vehicle would no longer be with us. But that was of little consolation to the driver who had to explain how the bodywork of his vehicle had been badly bashed.[5]

Arthur Christie also worked with his friend Douglas Doe in the magazine area, as he explained:

It was fenced and wired all round to prevent adventurous types from getting in. We were trusted with the only keys to the explosives stores; we first entered the 'dirty room', where we changed our boots and put on felt slippers thus avoiding generating static electricity. This was part of the safety procedure, otherwise it might have been highly 'uplifting'. We then entered the 'clean room', where we prepared the charges. I say prepared: our most common conversation was, 'I think that's enough,' followed by, 'Are you sure?' I had a bench with two machines – one I used to cut fuses. There were three types, one coloured orange was 'instantaneous' but in truth had a delay of some three seconds. Another was black; it had a longer delay, timed in minutes according to length. For instance, two inches equalled half a minute. We used to demonstrate this by taping both these fuses together, lighting them, and throwing them down with the instruction, 'Don't go near until you think it's gone off.' The short fuse exploded, the thrower thought it was safe, but seconds later the other fuse would go off – a lesson in trust and timing.

Arthur Christie was involved with the training programme at Aston House and among his students were some prominent people such as Colonel Stirling of the SAS and possibly two spies, both French, a man and a woman, who ended up working for Britain on a former French merchant ship that was converted into a kind of Q-ship, or undercover warship. He was Claude Peri, she Madeleine Bayard, but they changed their names to Jack Langlais and Madeleine Barclay. Also on the ship in its early days in spring 1941 was Albert Marie Guérisse, who became better known under his nom-de-guerre Pat O'Leary. It is also almost certain that he did some training at Aston.[6]

Arthur continued:

We also used plastic explosive code-named PE3. This was new and had not been issued to the regular army. It had a very fast burning rate: half an ounce blew a hole through a railway line, so we needed to be careful with it, though it could be moulded and shaped like putty and thrown against a wall, no problem. We boiled our kettle with a few ounces placed between two stones: lighted with a match, it boiled the water in three seconds flat!

We had to keep an eye on gun cotton; as long as it was damp it was stable, but if it dried out, just rubbing it would set it off. It was stored in boxes with a removable plug to allow you to test its condition with your finger. If dry we would pour in some water.

When our work was completed we locked up the explosive stores securely, knowing that if that lot went up so would most of Aston

House with us inside. We informed the nearby sentry 'All Clear' and left the site.

Across the field was a clump of trees with a shallow dip in which were four large tanks mounted on concrete blocks. The tanks contained a mixture of petrol and paraffin used for making 'Molotov cocktails', such was our varied arsenal.

Shortly after Dunkirk, the 'Arms to Britain' campaign started in America. This was a gesture of support to help us with the war effort. As a result of this, we received boxes and boxes of arms. There were all kinds of rifles, revolvers, pistols, automatics, submachine guns, and a Colt machine gun that had last seen action in the Cuban/American War. Alf and I had to unpack them all and of course try them out!

We used one of the guns for our own air defence. It was mounted on the verandah of Aston House just above the CO's office and outside the FANY girls' quarters. We were cleaning it one day when one of the girls asked us how it worked. Of course we were only too pleased to show her but as we were leaving she sat down behind the gun and pulled the trigger – BANG, off went a shell in the direction of the village. We hadn't set the safety catch. The CO was fuming and stormed up the stairs shouting, 'What the hell is going on?' We never did find out where the shell landed but we certainly knew the repercussions. The gun was removed at once and taken to a six-foot trench in the field and mounted on an old gas pipe which raised it about three feet above the parapet. When the air-raid sirens sounded this was to be our defence if attacked. Then it disappeared and surfaced on the roof of the War Office in Whitehall. Trust the Colonel Blimps to steal something that was useful to us!

It was quite a leisurely job at Aston House at first until someone foresaw the pending defeat of our Allied forces and British Expeditionary Force and decided that we should busy ourselves building up secret caches of explosives in France and Belgium. France fell on 22 June 1940. Security was tightened up for us, no leave, no days off, and of course no letters. We were given extra pay, sixpence a day danger money plus sixpence a day special duty. This meant my pay was equivalent to a full corporal's. I was well off but couldn't get out to spend it!

In July 1940 Mr Churchill evidently decided that he did not like the complacency that had set in among a lot of people who still thought the war would be over quickly. We were told that, in future, all our work would be answerable to him and the War Cabinet and the less anyone knew about us the better. I did not know it but that was when I became a member of Special Operations Executive – SOE.

We went into full swing, things became hectic, supplying sabotage materials and training the operators; it was general mayhem. New fuses, new incendiary devices, and many new weapons were devised.

One was the ST (Sticky Tank) Grenade, which was covered in a sticky substance that would attach itself to the side of a tank or alternatively to a wooden surface. We demonstrated this sticky bomb by throwing it against a wall of Aston House that was covered in ivy. The device broke open, spilling its phosphorus contents. When this hit the wet ivy and the wet soil, it ignited! We then spent some six hours ripping down the ivy, washing and digging up the soil until every bit had been safely dispersed.

I wonder how many members of the Home Guard remember the anti-tank weapon that we devised? It was a plate of metal with a rifle bolt welded in the centre, which fired a rocket type bomb. Very Heath Robinson I know, but it worked. We made it! We tried it! It was the forerunner of the anti-tank rocket.

We tested the strip mine and dozens of other lethal weapons for the first time. They all came from the minds of men who said 'Nothing is impossible'. For example: Dr Francis A. Freeth. He devised the hollow charge principle of the anti-tank bomb and the spigot mortar. Problem was, we didn't have a tank to try it out on at that time, all the armour we had was too valuable to us. We were on the way to the demonstration range when Dr Francis spotted a large farm roller in a field. 'That looks like a tank', he decided, 'and will make an ideal target.' 'Stop, Christie,' he said. We got out of the car and set up the spigot mortar at a range of about 100 yards. I aimed it in the direction of the roller and BANG, it disappeared in a cloud of smoke. All he could say was, 'Damn good show, perfect.' This wouldn't have been too bad on the official range but here we were on private land without permission.

The police did not accept our explanation, no matter what we said; we were frog-marched into the local police cells still trying to explain without giving away too much information. Mind you, looking at it from their point of view, I suppose it's not every day that someone blows up a useful thing like a roller. It required War Office clearance eventually to get us out of there for us to reach our destination and give the proper demonstration.

One of the nearby SOE stations started to train operatives to go into France. Most were men but I was told there was also a woman. Our job was to supply them with special explosives and weapons, now known as gadgets, but to us they were tools of the trade. We didn't stay long enough to get to know any of the operatives, but we always wished them luck.

The Free French needed a training film on 'How to blow up a Power Pylon'. I knew nothing about filming but was given the job. I set off with a crazy scientist and while he fixed the ring main charges on a real electricity pylon, I filmed him. A special police constable approached, stuck his nose in, and asked what we were up to. Without pausing the captain said, 'Good show officer, you can use the camera and allow my assistant to help me, and we will be able to do the job twice as quickly.' The constable accepted and carried on with the filming and all went well until we were about to light the fuse, when once again we were both 'invited' to take up residence in the local police cells. I was beginning to get used to this as again the War Office obtained our release.

The Army officers were all scientists and given the nickname 'boffins'. They were civilians in uniform and couldn't care less about military discipline. They just wanted to get on with the work in hand without interference from anyone. They are unsung heroes to whom this country owes a great deal.

Aston House was often visited by various officials from government and other departments. One such visitor was Clement Attlee, the Deputy Prime Minister. He was being shown around on a chilly day and asked for an overcoat. Major Johnny Johnston took me to one side and said, 'Fetch me a British Warm.' This was a type of overcoat worn by British officers in the First World War, fawn pink in colour and shorter than the normal Army issue. 'Make sure that it has a few surprises in it!' Following the orders of Major Johnston, I really went to town on that coat! If I had used live explosives, Britain would not have had Attlee as Labour Prime Minister in 1945. [Christie wouldn't reveal just what he did to the coat.]

Sir Alfred Clark-Kerr [later Lord Inverchapel] arrived on another occasion. This man had experienced many attempts on his life in

China, including being machine-gunned from the air by the Japanese in 1937, and being badly wounded. Once again we were given the job to demonstrate what we could do at Aston House. This time we decided to 'fix' his car which proved to be a little awkward because his personal driver-guard would not leave the damn car. But with a few loud bangs, etc., we were able to distract him long enough to attach a couple of limpet mines and time fuses to its petrol tank. Unfortunately the car left quickly before the mines could be revealed and removed. This led to a high-speed chase along country lanes, eventually catching him up at Station IX, The Frythe. Boy! The expression on his face and the driver's, when they saw us remove the live limpets from his fuel tank! I think his driver received a different type of rocket.

Duff-Cooper [Minister of Information] had just returned from reporting to the War Cabinet on the situation in Malaya and wanted to be shown around Aston House. He also received the treatment, for unorthodoxy was the by-word at Aston House and nobody was too sacred. One of our favourite tricks was to rub gelignite around the inside band of the hat of anyone visiting our explosive stores at an inopportune moment or who did not approve of our type of warfare. When perspiration mixes with gelignite it has the effect of the worst hangover ever experienced.

Many special operations were successful thanks to weapons from Aston House. We seemed to think up all the craziest ideas, and then put them into practice. One such attack, known as the Keyes Raid, was on Rommel's HQ on the North African coast, using explosives and devices made at Aston House.

The raid that Christie refers to was led by Lieutenant-Colonel Geoffrey Keyes, whose father, Admiral Sir Roger Keyes, was head of Combined Operations in London. This was part of Operation Crusader, an offensive in late 1941 by the Eighth Army in North Africa designed to regain ground lost to Rommel.

The raid was a daring, mad idea to infiltrate behind enemy lines to cause maximum confusion on the eve of the launch of Crusader. The plan was to assassinate General Erwin Rommel in his villa, 190 miles inside enemy territory, to hit the German HQ, destroy its communication installations, blow up the Italian HQ and the

Italian Intelligence Centre and to launch a secondary diversionary attack on the same night using Colonel Stirling's L Detachment SAS to attack five enemy airstrips destroying bombers and fighters. This was the first-ever raid by the fledgling SAS. The Commandos were disembarked from two submarines. They transferred to canoes and dinghies of the SBS. The sea was rough and prevented eighteen of the raiding party from landing.

The raid on the villa was led by Lieutenant-Colonel Keyes, who was shot and died soon after entering the villa. The Commandos could not get back to the submarine as their boats had been washed away. Only two of the party made it back to British lines after a long trek on foot through hostile countryside and desert.

Keyes was posthumously awarded the Victoria Cross for his leadership and bravery. The raid had been a costly failure; the advance intelligence had been dreadful. The house had never been used by Rommel and in fact he was not even in North Africa at the time.

The second diversionary raid was also a fiasco, due to bad weather. David Stirling's men were divided into five groups. Each group had sixty incendiary and explosive bombs for the attack, undoubtedly all supplied by Aston House. Winds gusting at 45 mph blew the parachutists miles off target out in the desert. Lessons were learned. Colonel Stirling later expanded the SAS most effectively but was subsequently betrayed and captured and spent the rest of the war in Colditz Castle. He and his older brother Bill were cousins of Lord Lovat who owned the Inverailort estate on the shores of Loch Ailort in the Scottish Highlands – which became the main training base for Commandos, and was originally Major Bill Stirling's idea.[7]

Arthur recalled:

We were also involved with Colonel David Stirling and the formation of the SAS and the Long Range Desert Group. I was introduced to him when he came to Aston House from Palestine for training on some of our new arms and explosives.

There was much resentment from the old die-hard Colonel Blimps in the War Office of our many new and untried methods of ungentlemanly warfare. They gave us the name 'Dirty Tricks Department', a name that we relished. We were kicked out of Room 055A at the War Department, our last home there.

Towards the end of 1940, we were sent to London to set up an office near Baker Street Station, next to a confectioner's. We occupied the first, second and third floors. It became the meeting place of the 'Baker Street Irregulars' [SOE staff]. I also visited Station IX at Old Welwyn and the forgery section, Station XIV, at Briggens near Roydon and Station VIII at the Queen Mary Reservoir, Staines and also Winchester and Henley-on-Thames.

SOE was expanding fast. Doug, Alf and myself were now assisting in the packing rooms loading lorries with arms, explosives and other items. We worked to a list and packed the items in boxes that we then stencilled with the various addresses. Most of them were destined for the Arisaig and Inverailort House training camps in Scotland, where live explosives and ammunition were used to create realistic battle conditions.

Regularly, once a month, we drove our 3-ton lorry (it looked a bit like a furniture removal van) to the Bryant and May [match] factory in London to collect 'Fuzees' [officially – Catalogue No. F 29, Matches Fuzee, Non Flaming] These were special matches, about twenty to a box; they burned slowly, igniting the core. There were also 'lighter fuel flasks', about 3 feet long and about 1 inch wide, fitted with tapered ends and covered with phosphorus, which exploded when struck.

Lucas supplied us with silver tubes about 2 inches long with a detonator fitted in one end. The tubes were then filled with plastic explosive and resembled normal pipe work, and so could be placed next to hot surfaces that would eventually explode them.

Doug came to me one morning and said, 'Collect some plastic explosive from the store, we've been ordered to go to the Woolwich Arsenal to try something.' I picked up several pounds of PE3 and some fuses, as I thought we might need them, loaded them into a car and we drove to north London. On arrival we were asked to pack some PE3 into a large empty shell case. I said, 'What about the fuse?' expecting to be told to shove it in the end, but no. The shell was taken from me, reassembled and loaded into a 15-inch gun [*sic*] which was wheeled onto their test firing range set out with block markers to record the shell's range. The gun was fired by remote control – BOOM: the shell, gun and most of our hearing were instantly removed! Doug and I burst out laughing. Not surprisingly, PE3 was never used again to fire a shell.

Winston Churchill was present at a demonstration given by paratroopers in a field near Aston. It had been arranged to try out the new 'static line' idea for releasing parachutes at the right time when exiting an aircraft. The crazy Polish airborne troops refused to jump from above 500 feet. They didn't want to be floating in the air for too long and become easy targets to ground fire and while hanging about up there they couldn't kill any Germans. Accidents had been caused by parachutes snagging on the aircraft when released too soon or not opening in time when close to the ground. When Winston Churchill was told about this problem he suggested, 'Why not have some form of attachment inside the plane connected to the pull system on the chute so that when the paratrooper has left the plane and dropped a certain distance the chute will open automatically?' This led to the 'static line' system being introduced for all airborne troops.

Our contribution to this same demonstration was a new mine, but it very nearly killed Churchill. We had acquired an old car to show off the effect of this device. The plan to roll the car gently onto a 'strip mine' worked perfectly, then – BANG, the vehicle whizzed through the air and landed quite near to him. He didn't even miss a puff on his cigar!

Shortly after Dunkirk, at the beginning of autumn, we were in the explosive stores preparing a number of special charges. We moulded plastic explosive into old waterproof gun cotton and placed it inside a black bag. The bag was then tied with gun-cotton primer, linked to a length of detonator primer cord and pressed into the charge. The fuse was taped to the bag with its end coiled into the top section of the bag with a specific time detonator tied into the upper part of the bag which was then pulled together by the drawstrings at the top.

We fastened two-pound incendiary bombs and a fuse to wooden frames that we made and were designed to float. We did not know what all this was for but within twenty-four hours of it being collected we had news of the very first commando raid at Lofoten Island, off the coast of Norway, where our charges and incendiary devices had done a first-class job.

One morning we were working in the explosives store when suddenly there was a BOOM, BOOM, BOOM. The explosions came from across the road at the back of Aston church. We ran out and up the path round the side and to the back of the church. By then there were several villagers peering at several craters in the nearby field and at the cows in the next one that had had a lucky escape. We didn't see the plane that bombed us.

Another event I recall was Doug and myself being sent to Harrods to purchase two canoes. We brought them back, unpacked and assembled them and confirmed that they were what was wanted, and then re-packed them. These were required to mount a surveillance operation in the Channel Islands. The two canoes were duly delivered to the Navy at Portsmouth Dockyard where two operatives were waiting for them and loaded them on board a submarine. It set sail for the islands and at the prearranged time and place the two canoes were brought out on deck. There was only one problem: the canoes were still in their kit form. The operatives asked the submarine commander, 'How do we fix them up?' to which the submarine commander replied, 'I sail boats, not build them.' Eventually the canoes were fixed up; the operatives reached shore, climbed the cliff face, and dropped into a slit trench full of Germans!

I performed the duty of courier, taking messages to the underground bunker in Whitehall where Churchill had his HQ. I reported to the duty officer with my pouch and inside that another pouch, not unlike a Russian doll, containing the documents or letters. On one occasion I was kept waiting so I had a quick look around, something I was told I should not have done, but I was naturally nosey. I had been told 'If there is anything of interest, look at it,' so I suppose I was doing just that! I wandered down the main corridor. To the right was out of bounds, but on the left was a row of doors. I walked on and saw a secret memo regarding the possible Japanese take-over of French Indo-China and the likely consequences. Churchill had advance warning of what might happen and subsequently did happen in Singapore. [Coincidentally, Arthur was there to experience it first-hand.]

Around April 1941, I was approached by Major Jim Gavin who had learned that I had made the explosives for the Lofoten raid that had proved to be such a success. He wanted me to go with his group on a special SOE mission. He didn't tell me the destination, only that the mission's code name was 'Puma', later changed to 'Scapula'.

The destination turned out to be Singapore. The knowledge and experience gained at Aston House made Arthur Christie a prime candidate for this task. So he left to take part in Operation Scapula, leaving the safe posting that his friend Douglas Doe had arranged for him to keep him out of a very nasty war. Arthur was involved with the formation of Special Training School 101 in Singapore, with the specific task of training Chinese and others to infiltrate behind Japanese lines, 'stay-behind parties' they were to be called. Christie's job was to teach them to use explosives, fireworks of the demolishing kind, time fuses, plastic explosive and anything that came to hand, just so long as it had the desired effect. Bits of bamboo cane stuffed full of explosive strewn across the road; dead rats also stuffed with explosive that ultimately might be thrown into a fire. But all was not as it should be, as Christie soon realised, much to his chagrin, that Singapore was not properly defended.

They tested the readiness of military units all over Singapore including the naval base and Fort Canning and found them to be completely open to attack; they could have walked in and destroyed them in no time at all, including places that were considered to be secure.

Arthur found that the Singapore British elite's only thoughts were about 'tiffin' and 'dressing for dinner' – the war was on another planet. The prime occupation was making money from war materials such as rubber, tin and bauxite. Everyone in the military upper echelons knew that Singapore could *not* be defended and so it proved to be. The Singapore garrison, its back to the wall, was in no position to defend itself against an attack through Malaya and on 15 February 1942 the British surrendered unconditionally. Lance-Corporal Arthur Christie was captured and spent the rest of the war in a Japanese prisoner of war camp. In his words, 'We were too damn late.'

He managed to keep his clandestine mission a secret from the Japanese. If they had found out he would have been executed by the sword. Subsequently two members of his group were beheaded in this manner. The remainder of his story is one of survival up to the time of his repatriation. Amazingly, when he regained his fitness, he decided to continue with his Army career, serving in Germany, Hong Kong and in Korea, after that war ended, with the United Nations peace force.

Sadly, Arthur Christie died on 22 August 2003. He is survived by his wife and three children.

Notes

1. The Bailey Bridge was in fact invented by Donald, later Sir Donald, Bailey. Possibly Captain Robin Bailey was involved in developing the idea.
2. Macrea, R. Stuart, *Winston Churchill's Toyshop*.
3. *Ibid*.
4. Boyce, Fredric and Everett, Douglas, *SOE: The Scientific Secrets*, p. 59.
5. Macrea, R. Stuart, *Winston Churchill's Toyshop*.
6. Personal communication with Edward Marriott.
7. Parker, John, SBS: *The Inside Story of the Special Boat Service*.

The First Aid Nursing Yeomanry Story

In June 1940, Colonel Gubbins, Officer Commanding Auxiliary Units, asked Phyllis Bingham if she and another volunteer would carry out a special job in the country. The matter was discussed with Commandant Gamwell at FANY headquarters and the two volunteers, Bingham and Peggy Minchin, left for Aston House and were employed in packing weapons and explosive devices safely for distribution to the Auxiliary Units. Later during the summer, Volunteer Bingham took over the running of the officers' mess and the number of FANY at Aston House increased to about six.

This work continued for six months, and from this start, FANY were gradually taken on, in very small numbers, as orderlies and cooks. The experiment of using Bingham and Minchin established the success of the system of using FANY as housekeepers at the stations. Bingham was promoted lieutenant and was in charge of the FANY unit of SOE, doing the interviewing and selecting. She later attained the rank of commander. The unit was known as Bingham's. It was entirely due to her great drive and personality that the growth of the SOE FANY unit was so extremely rapid and successful. She expected all recruits to turn their hand to anything. She is reported to have said 'I want girls who have been taught to do as they are told!'

Towards the end of 1941 Captain Peggy Minchin was requested by SOE to train FANYs as wireless operators. She had already agreed to train coders to encypher and decypher signals traffic and she had also been a dispatcher of FANY agents who dropped into France. She undertook parachute training with them. Later she went out to Mola, Italy, to become second-in-command of all FANYs in the Mediterranean area.[1]

Originally no pay other than living expenses was rendered and members provided their own uniforms! Later members were paid by SOE according to recognised military rates for tradeswomen, officers, WOs and NCOs. Some became secret agents; fifty-four women died in different theatres of the war, twelve met their death in German concentration camps after having been parachuted into enemy-occupied territory as secret agents to serve the allies by aiding resistance movements. Some were tortured after capture in the hope of extracting information; some were shot; some died in gas chambers. Three of these courageous women – Odette Hallowes, Violette Szabo and Noor Inayat Khan – were awarded the George Cross, the latter two posthumously.[2]

FANY HQ was St Paul's church vicarage, Wilton Place, Knightsbridge. A tablet commemorates the sacrifice of the FANY victims.[3]

The First Aid Nursing Yeomanry was founded in 1907 by Captain E.C. Baker, sometime a cavalry Sergeant-Major. The experience of being wounded in the Sudan with the Kitchener expedition led him to create a small unit of nurses on horseback. They were to provide a link between the fighting units and the Front and the Field Hospitals. At the outbreak of the World War One, the services of the corps were turned down by the War Office, but were quickly accepted by both the Belgian and French Armies. The first FANY reported for duty in Antwerp in September 1914.

During the First World War the FANYs ran Field Hospitals, drove ambulances, set up soup kitchens and were often in great danger. At the end of the War the Corps received decorations from the French, the Belgians and the British: 17 Military Medals, including the first awarded to a woman, 1 Légion d'Honneur, 27 Croix de Guerre, 1 Ordre de Couronne and 2 Ordre de Léopold Chevalier, as well as 11 Mentions in Dispatches.

Between the Wars, the emphasis in training shifted from nursing to motorised transport and the Corps became known as The Women's Transport Service (FANY) in response to the Army Council's recognition of it as a 'voluntary reserve transport unit . . . for service in any national emergency'. It was this specialisation which enabled the Corps to provide 3,000 driver/mechanics that formed the nucleus of the newly-formed Motor Driver Companies of the ATS.

However, the FANY spirit of independence burned on and led the Corps down another avenue, to that of SOE in World War Two. FANYs were allowed to carry small arms, unlike the ATS and other women's services. Most of the female agents sent to France by SOE were FANYs. Three of these women won the George Cross, two posthumously. Some 2,000 other FANYs provided the backbone of SOE, working in cyphers and signals, as agent-conducting officers, administering the Special Training Schools and among others the Jedburgh teams, Massingham and Forces 136 and 139. One section of FANY was attached to the Polish Army in Britain for the duration of the War.[4]

Sadly I was unable to locate any members of FANY who had served at Aston House, but nevertheless I did find two ladies, June Mecredy and Ishbel Mackenzie, who joined FANY after working at Aston House as civilian shorthand typists. They were young teenagers and it was their first job out of college. Naturally at that age they soon felt stifled by office work in a remote country house and decided to join the Wrens (WRNS: Women's Royal Naval Service). They were taken aback on being told that this was not permitted because they were part of SOE and as such had knowledge of its secrets. However, it was all right if they applied to join FANY, which they did, and were soon enjoying adventures overseas.

June Mecredy took up the story:

My friend Ishbel Mackenzie and I were civilians. We were billeted in private houses at Knebworth and we cycled to and from Aston House every day. At Aston House I worked for Major Robert Flowerdew. We had to work on Sundays and I remember we were taken for a meal at the Clock House Hotel at Welwyn because the cook at Aston House had that day off. There were so few of us at Aston House at that time. I can remember things exploding, being tested for a big raid. It was just a fascinating job at Aston but I knew I was going on to other things. You can imagine how interesting it was being in North Africa and all through Italy so that's why the memories of Aston House have become blurred. I was there for less than a year.

I was sent to North Africa about April 1944 so therefore I must have been at Aston House in 1943 and then joined FANY. My close friend Ishbel and I came from the same secretarial college. All I can remember is cycling off in the morning and that the place was all very hush-hush. I didn't even tell the people I lived with what I was doing. There was no question of ever telling anybody, my parents, or anyone. They had no idea what I did, just a secretarial job outside London. I can remember trying to write up the results of experiments on explosives and equipment and what have you. A lot of the technical terms were quite difficult, we just had to learn them. Some of the devices were absolutely crazy but I'm sorry I can't talk about them, not even now. They are probably the sort of things my husband John Wilmers would have taken with him. He was a captain in the 2nd SAS. He parachuted into France in 1943, I think, and got out by boat at Dieppe. Then at the end of 1944 he parachuted behind the lines into Italy, he jumped into mountains near La Spezia. We met in Italy in 1944. My being a member of FANY meant that I was able to keep in touch with him and send him letters and clean socks etc. because I had access to the packing station near Florence. He spent that awful winter of 1944/45 holed up in the mountain village of Rossano. The villagers gave their lives to help escaped prisoners of war and the SAS troops who were there. After the war a scholarship scheme 'The San Martino Trust' was set up for the young children of Rossano and other villages and a large memorial erected to commemorate their families' bravery in the war. The children are able to visit England each year as part of the scheme. When the allied advance moved up beyond Bologna my husband was relieved by the incoming British forces. He had been organising resistance in the mountains. When the war was over we emptied our minds of it. We never told the children or anyone about it until it was revealed in his obituary.

My work with FANY was assisting SOE, first with the maquis in southern France and Algiers, then I was moved to Bari in southern Italy working with the Italian resistance. I think we were trustworthy, reasonably well educated, but we only had secretarial skills, though my French and German shorthand was useful. Ishbel and I were only eighteen or nineteen; it was ridiculous, we were far too young to be sent abroad, the whole thing is almost unbelievable now. We had to work extremely hard and the conditions were quite difficult. We were housed in a very basic place in Bari and it was very, very cold in Florence in the winter because they have those high ceilings, and in Siena I was billeted on an Italian family and it was bitterly cold!

We were called 'cadet ensigns' which was half-and-half. It was half being an officer but without the pay. Our uniforms were ordinary khaki much the same as the ATS.

June has three children and six grandchildren and keeps busy with voluntary work teaching English language to the wives of officers who are in England for a year's course from countries such as Colombia, the Czech Republic, France, South Korea, Norway, Romania and Turkey.

Ishbel Mackenzie was recruited by Aston House from the Kerr-Sander secretarial college which had been evacuated from London to Stanway House near Cheltenham. SOE established a connection with the college and any secretaries the college thought might be useful were sent for interview at the ISRB office in Baker Street.

Ishbel took up the story:

If accepted you were told not to talk to anybody about where you were going to be working or anything about what you would be doing. The college girls came trickling through to Aston House, I think I was the first in 1943. Three or more came later including June Mecredy who arrived a few weeks after me. We were both in the design office with the engineers and closely connected to the prototype room and tool room where they made the tools for producing the prototypes. I remember Major Ramsay Green, an RE officer, was in charge of us all. There was also a drawing office with three or four staff and three secretaries.

I typed highly technical reports at Aston House. They were designing these mysterious gadgets and things. It didn't register with me what they were, quite honestly, I was a keen eighteen-year-old who could only just about type. I remember they were very proud of the spigot mortar, I just thought it was very noisy, there were always lots of explosions.

Aston House needed lots of technical supplies from companies like ICI who thought they were dealing with a War Office department E.S.6. (WD) in London. We couldn't reveal the Aston House address, so when someone at ICI telephoned and said, 'Look I'm going to be in London this morning can I pop in and see you, at E.S.6. (WD)?' We had to say, 'Well I'm sorry but major so and so is terribly busy this morning, perhaps in a day or two, may I ring you back?' Then you waited until our representative hurtled up to our room at the War Office in London to meet them and act out the pretence of working there permanently. No outside business people were allowed to visit Aston House.

June and I thought we ought to join up with something as it was rather boring sitting in the middle of the countryside and so we said, 'We think we'd like to leave now thank you and join the Wrens.' They said, 'No way, you're in SOE and the only service you can join is the FANYs' and we said, 'FANYs, what are they?' We didn't know anything about FANYs. We joined them in 1944 and went to Algiers for a few months and then were sent to Rome so it was probably a lot more fun than the Wrens might have been. I did secretarial work and my French was useful. At my young age, whatever they said do, you did it. I have very vivid memories of it all.

I was in 'Bingham's Unit'. I could well have been interviewed by her. When I was in England I had the rank of sergeant, that was what we secretaries were, it was a strange organisation. But once we were sent abroad we were given a phony officer rank of 'cadet ensign' except we weren't really officers – it was a FANY officer rank. That meant we could go into officers' clubs and things which was all a bit snooty really because the ATS sergeants wouldn't have been allowed through the door.

I arrived in Algiers where I worked with agents who were sent into France. We were closely connected with the landings in the south of France about the same time as D-Day, which most people didn't realise were happening. The people I worked with were all SOE, recruited from every force imaginable. My immediate boss was Lieutenant Francis Brooks Richards, RNVR, head of SOE's political section, who later became Sir Francis Brooks Richards.[5] Later I worked for a man in the Argyll and Sutherland Highlanders who was seconded to SOE and was soon posted to Rome. He said, 'I expect I will need a secretary in Rome, why don't you come along?' I said 'What a good idea!' We were in Rome very soon after it was liberated and I stayed for about a year.

FANYs did a lot for the agents, looked after their domestic needs at the holding house and their training before they were sent off to remote corners of Europe. Here I met Charles Orme, my future husband. He had been in the North African desert for five years thoroughly immersed in the Desert War. He was in the Territorial Army and went straight out there in 1939. He was a captain when I met him but he had been promoted through every rank from private through to company sergeant-major to a commission.

I was a refugee in England, my family was in Jersey in the Channel Islands in June 1940 and we were told the Germans would be arriving in three or four days so if we wanted to get out we should go now. So we all left and arrived in Cheltenham.

I am a founder member of the Special Forces Club; we began it in 1946. There is still a good solid membership including people from Holland, France and Italy.

I suppose FANY helped me to grow up really because we were all very young for our age in those days, we left school at seventeen or eighteen and lived pretty sheltered lives. Even at Aston we were billeted in private homes with almost stand-in mothers and fathers to look after us. And then suddenly you were in the great big world learning more about life generally. We weren't strictly drilled or controlled like the other services were. We were a sort of sheltered army, were the FANYs.

Ishbel lives near Lymington in Hampshire. She has two children and five grandchildren.

The former Women's Transport Service WTS (FANY) is currently based at the Duke of York's Headquarters, Chelsea, London, and has been officially renamed the Princess Royal's Volunteer Corps. It is now known as FANY (PRVC).[6] It remains an all-women volunteer organisation. FANYs now specialise in communications for the Army and the City of London Police. Corps members are trained in radio communications, paramedical skills, map reading, navigation and orienteering, shooting, self-defence and survival techniques, advanced driving and casualty bureau documentation.

Notes

1. PRO HS 7/7 and Pawley, Margaret, *In Obedience to Instructions: FANY with the SOE in the Mediterranean*, pp. 6–8, 10, 17, 126.
2. PRO HS 7/7 and The First Aid Nursing Yeomanry (FANY) website: <www. reserve-forces-london.org.uk> 16 December 2003.
3. *Ibid*.

4. The First Aid Nursing Yeomanry (FANY) website:
   <www.royalsignals.army.org.uk/museum> 22 November 1999.

5. Obituary, *Daily Telegraph*, 14 September 2002. Author unknown.

6. The First Aid Nursing Yeomanry (FANY) website:
   <www.reserve-forces-london.org.uk> 16 December 2003.

The Secretary's Story

Cicely 'Scottie' Hales (Scott was her maiden name) was born in Kensington on 25 March 1920. She was educated at the County Secondary School in Bermondsey and her first job was with David Grieg's, a grocery chain; she was in the accounts department and responsible for checking the daily banking and cash transactions made by the various branches. A couple of years later she moved into the printing trade and studied at the London School of Printing, qualifying with high grades in costing and clerical studies. She did the costing for the Old Bailey Press until it was flattened by German bombing.

The managing director of *The Engineer*, a well known publication for industry, then recruited her as his personal secretary; she excelled in this role and her boss, in an attempt to keep her, wrote to the call-up review board praising her abilities and requested that she be made exempt from the services. Unfortunately the request had the opposite effect and the board took this to be a fine recommendation for the ATS.

Scottie became secretary to the purchasing officer at Aston House and has a clear memory of the materials that were required to make the many varied clandestine devices. However, she was disappointed to discover that she had lost a treasured photograph of the entire Aston House ATS contingent including the officers – a print that was so long it had to be rolled up! Nevertheless she did locate two genuine SOE artifacts that more than made up for the missing photograph.

When the war ended Scottie left Aston House and returned to her former job with the Old Bailey Press in its newly acquired London premises. She married in 1945 and has two daughters.

When the children had reached a suitable age to allow Scottie to seek employment again she began working for the Citizens Advice Bureau and continued there until her retirement in 2003.

Scottie recalls the 'numerous' letters that her boss at *The Engineer* wrote describing how valuable she was:

He insisted that I was doing my bit for the war effort, but they didn't see it that way and I was called up and assigned to the ATS.

I had to take some rather unusual intelligence tests and I did very well apparently on the electrical paper. Therefore my knowledge of electricity was assumed to be very good. Which surprised me considerably because I really didn't know one end of a light bulb from the other! So the system was rather hit or miss. I passed the intelligence test with flying colours and I finished up at Aldermaston before my feet could touch the ground.

I did three weeks basic training there. Mary Churchill [the Prime Minister's daughter] had just been there and I think Princess Elizabeth also had passed the course so it was paramount that we all did as well as they had done.

From there I did another three weeks training at Mill Hill and was then instructed to report to Dunstable. I wasn't very tall and was struggling along a road with a kitbag nearly as big as myself. It was a *very* hot day in the middle of July and I was so green that I thumbed a flagged car for a lift! A flag on the bonnet of a car indicates a high-ranking occupant so this was about the biggest sin I could ever commit. Fortunately it didn't stop – nor did anyone else for that matter – and I eventually arrived at my destination. They gave me tea, but I had to provide my own mug which of course was at the bottom of my kitbag. I then returned to Welwyn Garden City and caught a train to Knebworth. I was told to locate the stationmaster and ask him to direct me. I wasn't allowed to know my destination or what I would be doing. He knew, he knew much more than I did. I tapped on the glass partition and announced my arrival. He said, 'Oh yes, somebody will pick you up in a minute.' A car duly arrived and the driver, Bob Batting, said, 'You'll love it here.' I said, 'I won't.' 'Yes,' he said, 'you will.' He delivered me to a country house. I was ushered into what I think would originally have been the billiard room. I sat down at one end of a beautiful huge refectory table about eighteen feet long. A tray was brought in with a pot of tea, hot water, sandwiches and cake. I thought, 'If this is the Army it's not so bad, I rather like this.' Later a Major Barratt entered with papers and I had to sign the Official Secrets Act, and suffer a fate worse than death if I revealed to anybody what went on at Aston House. I was then taken to the head gardener's quaint little cottage and introduced to Mrs Winifred Félicie Asher, the head gardener's wife, with whom I was to be billeted. Here I could really relax, she was French and the most lovely lady you could ever imagine. The cottage was charming and stood just outside the military security fencing on the edge of the Aston House estate.

There was no landing upstairs so Grandfather Frederick Asher, aged 90, had to pass through my bedroom to get to his. It was arranged that he should go to bed early and get up late to avoid any likely embarrassment. There was no hut available for me, it was early 1942 and they were still being built. I was one of the first ATS to arrive and so saw the whole place build up.

The officers were billeted in Aston House. It was always my hope that I would stay at the cottage where I was so comfortable but it wasn't to be. I was eventually moved into the first hut to be completed.

The job allocated to me was secretary to the purchasing officer, Mr Cecil Lake, a civilian. I took the place of a civilian secretary, Miss Spurgeon, who returned to Whitehall – she hated being at Aston. I was the only Army personnel secretary there. They were all civilians but it was thought that I could do the job. In fact I did more than Miss Spurgeon; I also did the costing. She would have been on a very good salary compared with my Army pay of nine shillings a week. My day started sharp at 9 o'clock and ended about 5.30 p.m.

Major Ramsay Green was in command of the section. My boss Cecil Lake was told what materials were needed – lots were in short supply – so he would go out and purchase whatever he could, as did Mr Max Hill, his assistant, who resided in the village and was often out and about buying stuff locally. Also, very often, I had to search around for materials by telephone.

I remember there were all manner of steels, molybdenum, stainless steel, mild steel and piano wire. Very heavy canvas was another material. I think they made two-man canoes from that, which they tested in the Firth of Forth. I only ordered for our REME workshops on site. I didn't order for the other sections, no explosives, that was someone else's responsibility.

I remember seeing big parachute containers being packaged at Aston House. I didn't order the contents for those which varied from explosives to Welbikes, scissors and even sweets.

The Welbike was given the prefix 'Wel' for Welwyn. In other words identified with The Frythe, Station IX, which was also a country house in nearby Old Welwyn. There was a feeling, always, that we did more of the design of the Welbike than did The Frythe. I used to see the completed bikes being loaded into containers and overheard Cecil Lake and Max Hill saying that we had done more than The Frythe but they had claimed the credit. I am not sure where the containers were destined prior to dropping but it was probably RAF Tempsford. They certainly took our leaflets there. I think the rollers for the leaflet drops in the Halifax bombers were also made at Aston House.

Amazingly, Scottie still has in her possession a silver-plated rectal/ vaginal secret message container that was made at Aston House. This particular one was fortunately converted into a cigarette lighter in the REME workshops, thus ensuring its survival. It was designed so that the two aluminium halves could be unscrewed at the centre and secret messages placed inside.

Typewritten messages were photographed on 35mm film sent undeveloped in specially designed containers, for example the handle of a shaving brush which if examined by the police, would spring open and expose the film to light, destroying the message. Later these (rectal/vaginal) containers were used.[1]

Scottie didn't know how many of the containers were made. She remembers Aston House as a small research and development prototype REME workshop. What Scottie didn't know and didn't need to know was that the small numbers of gadgets being perfected from the materials that she and her department had scoured the country for were then being mass-produced elsewhere and were passing through the quality assurance and stores at Aston House unnoticed. It demonstrates just how well the security aspect at Aston

House was controlled. People only knew about their immediate
area and regarded anything else as none of their business.
Scottie recalled:

Most times we didn't see the end product. Everybody had a little bit
to do and that was that. You seldom knew what the whole set-up
would be. Nobody ever spoke about the job or discussed what they'd
been doing all day. Someone might say, 'I'm bloody well fed up with
it today'. It hadn't gone right you see but nobody said what they had
been doing all day. There were twelve of us in our hut; we kept to our
own hut and made friends in our own hut. At the end of the working
day the first girl back would light the coke-fired stove.

If you wanted different company you visited the NAAFI. The ATS
girls came from all over the place; my friend Mary Wardrope was from
Scotland, another came from Ireland.

Lots of them worked all through the night on dangerous explosives.
If a special raid was on, the work would have to be done by a
specific time.

Mary Wardrope, Dora Circuit and I were asked by, I think Lieutenant
Wordsworth, were we interested in applying for a transfer to Station
X at Bletchley Park to help with their work, but by that time Mary was
engaged to her boss Ernie Welch and I was going out with Herbert
Hales. So we declined but Dora accepted. How she fared there I
never knew.

Scottie then produced more Aston House souvenirs – two powerful
horseshoe-shaped magnets. She explained that these were used
to secure the limpet mines to ships' hulls and also to secure little
black bags of explosive on either side of a railway line.

I think all our ATS owned a black sponge bag made from the black
rubberised cotton sheet that I bought for making the bags for
explosives. It was waterproof and didn't show up in the dark. Of course
there was always a bit over so the girls in the workshop used it to make
the sponge bags for their friends. The magnets survived because I kept
my paperclips and pins attached to them in the office at Aston House!

Cecil Lake's drawer always contained masses of aniseed balls, and
masses of condoms. He explained to me that the aniseed balls dissolved

at a constant rate and were used as a timer to set off explosives. The condoms were used in conjunction with the aniseed ball timers to keep them dry. Mr Hill used to visit the condom manufacturers Durex, who weren't too far away, and purchased various sizes and thicknesses. I think they must have imagined that he was a dirty old man, but he wasn't, he was buying them for the War Office! Of course he couldn't tell them that; they wouldn't have believed him anyway.

Scottie remembered a weapon referred to as a tin fish:

It was a small torpedo, about two feet long, powered by a small motor. Plasticine was placed inside as ballast to keep it at a certain depth below the surface of the water. The expert on those was Mr Bowman. He was seconded from Smiths Clocks.

The tin fish weapon that Scottie mentions was seen by another Aston House veteran who prefers to remain anonymous, who reported that these small torpedoes were used during the disastrous Dieppe raid. They were intended to blow up beach obstacles in advance of the landings but were not a great success, probably due to the sea's heavy swell at the time. This weapon may have been the Baby Mobile Mine or Welmine which was eighteen inches long and was driven by an electric motor that powered a two-bladed propeller. Aston House worked closely with The Frythe in producing these and other versions.[2]

Scottie also remembered ordering white cotton-covered trip and trap wire. This was to be placed in the snow on a special operation in Norway.

She explained:

I had to lose a day of my weekend to await delivery of that wire. It was finally delivered on the Saturday by dispatch riders and was obviously needed urgently to trigger some explosives somewhere. I remember an officer known as Buzz Bomb Barnett – an Army captain I think. I didn't know much about him except that he was extremely clever in handling explosives and defusing bombs.

The Redrup twins were close friends of mine. Lucy and Gertie were both drivers. They took the officers to wherever they needed to go. They also made frequent sorties to London to deliver and collect different material or documents, etc. from Whitehall and Baker Street. Aston House was top secret so all collections and deliveries could only be made by the military.

I mentioned to Scottie that an army driver told me that he delivered a miniature submarine to Aston House. She confirmed that there was a water tank there large enough to test a small submarine but she was not aware of it being done.

However, she did remember the spigot mortar because she did the costing for it. She explained:

The men filled in time sheets and delivered them to me at the end of each week. All the projects were allocated job numbers: the spigot mortar was M 37. If someone couldn't account for a half an hour somewhere – 'Oh well, I'll put it down to the spigot mortar.' So the spigot mortar must have been very, very expensive in the end; it didn't really take as long as we said it did.

Scottie revealed that Aston House was mentioned on a German propaganda radio broadcast by Lord Haw-Haw. His voice had a distinct nasal sound that was quite funny. He began with 'Jarmany calling, Jarmany calling' and then tried to alarm the British population with knowledge of secret bases and other military information obviously gained through German intelligence networks.

Scottie was away at the time of the broadcast but when she returned the camp was buzzing with the story. Lord Haw-Haw was supposed to have said that he knew what went on at Aston House and he mentioned Colonel Wood by name and it was hinted that they would get him. It certainly caused great excitement and the personnel felt that the broadcast had put them on the map. So far from terrifying everyone as was intended they were all rather flattered to be mentioned.

Lord Haw-Haw was William Joyce. Born in America of Irish parents, he was a devotee of British fascist Oswald Mosley. He arrived in Germany in 1939 on a British passport and happily broadcast pro-German propaganda to Britain throughout the war. His messages were treated as comical. After the war he was arrested, tried for treason and executed.[3]

ATS officer Lieutenant Wordsworth was the ATS commandant, Scottie liked her and stated:

She was nice, I had to report to her on one occasion because Major Barratt had put me on a charge for not saluting him. She said 'Well, it was very serious,' but let me off.

I was working with civilians so I didn't experience much military discipline at Aston House, and if there was anything undesirable to be done in the ranks I would say, 'Well Mr Lake my boss says I can't be spared, I have got to work overtime.' So I avoided the parades and all the other unpleasant chores that some of them had to do.

I also avoided the 'passion wagon', a lorry which, every other week, took Army personnel to local dances including the Town Hall in Stevenage. It took them there and brought them back. I enjoyed the dances held in our own NAAFI and I enjoyed my time at Aston from 1942 to 1946 and got to know the area well. I was able to go home to Lewisham virtually every weekend. I would cycle to Knebworth Station and catch the train.

We visited the local pubs, so enjoyed contact with the villagers. Our own security people were always present listening to conversations to check if anybody was talking out of turn. Making sure that the beer or spirits didn't loosen the tongue.

Some villagers, of course, would indulge in scandal and spread rumours about us. On one such occasion a group of us ATS girls ate the remains of some salmon that must have been unfit for human consumption. We all got food poisoning and about a dozen of us were whisked off to hospital. The locals jumped to the conclusion that we were pregnant and had gone off to the Lister to have our offspring. I suppose there was hanky-panky going on – there was certainly plenty of opportunity in the surrounding fields and woods, but this time it was sickness and diarrhoea!

Reverend Pugh was the vicar at Aston. We called him Pug-H. At the end of the war we were all asked to contribute towards a carillon for Aston church tower that was duly installed but unfortunately the church suffered an arson attack in 1958 when the carillon, church bells and part of the tower were destroyed in the ensuing fire. Sadly the carillon wasn't replaced but the brass plaque remains recording station

E.S.6. (WD)'s gift to the village church. It stands close to what was once the main entrance gate to Aston House.

I was invited to a really nice party at the Clock Hotel, Welwyn, arranged for all REME personnel by Major Ramsay Green. I was guest of honour and so sat on his right, being the longest-serving member of REME at Aston House.

Scottie married Herbert Hales at Hitchin church on 29 December 1945. (Sadly Herbert died in 2005.) Scottie remembers that she was demobbed at Northampton in January 1946 and returned to her old job. She said she wouldn't have missed Aston House for the world. She felt she was doing something that was a bit different and special. So driver Bob Batting who picked up Scottie at Knebworth Station in the staff car on her very first day was right in what he predicted – she did love it there. Scottie died in March 2010 and is survived by two daughters, four grandchildren and one great-grandchild.

Notes

1. Haukelid, Knut, *Skis Against the Atom*.
2. PRO ADM 226/48.
3. Farrington, Karen, *Secret War: Spies, Traitors and Weapons of Doom*, p. 52.

The ATS Driver's Story

Just about everybody that was at Aston House remembers the attractive twin Redrup ATS girls, though maybe not their names, because they were so alike they were noticeable.

Lucy was twenty minutes older than her sister Gertrude. They were born on 17 January 1917. Home was Brighton Road, Watford. The family business was a butcher's shop that comfortably supported the eleven children. Lucy left Alexandra School at the age of fourteen and her first job was spraying the colour onto leather skins in a glove factory. After various other jobs she and her twin sister volunteered for military service. They both joined the ATS and both were assigned to the Royal Army Service Corps (RASC). They trained as drivers and arrived at Aston House in a lorry in the middle of the night. It was probably 1941. Their younger sister Gladys also joined them at Aston House in late 1942, having also trained as a driver. At that time eight of the family were serving their country. Happily all survived the war, including her six brothers, some of whom saw action in the battles of North Africa. Lucy met her future husband at Aston House. Of her brothers and four sisters Lucy had one younger sister and one younger brother alive and well in 2003. Lucy enjoyed a wonderful childhood within a loving family. She has two children and four grandchildren.

Lucy remembered:

I passed my Army driving test at the Hog's Back, Guildford. It's a very steep hill and I was driving a 3-ton lorry. I am short so I could hardly reach the foot pedals and at times I had to lean right out the side and hold on to the steering wheel at the same time. It was difficult for me getting in and out but I passed my test first time. I drove everywhere when I arrived at Aston House including frequent trips to our HQ in

London's Baker Street. It wasn't easy because all the signposts and street signs had been removed and at night the headlights on your vehicle were fitted with covers that almost blacked out the lights completely so it was very difficult to see where you were going. You called that driving in those days, it was nothing like it is now. I remember driving home in thick fog with my eyes streaming, it was so difficult but by travelling slowly I could just find my way and when I finally got back to Aston House totally exhausted, the NAAFI was shut so I couldn't get anything to eat or drink.

When I first arrived at Aston House I was assigned to driving big lorries in convoys but later transferred to cars chauffeuring the officers around to wherever they needed to go.

There was a large garage and many differing types of vehicle including motorbikes and sidecars which I really enjoyed riding round the compound. I have a rare photograph of some of the vehicles lined up with the drivers including my sister and me. Most of the drivers were men; my two sisters and I were the only girls but the boys were all very nice to us. Our younger sister Gladys joined us after we had been there for a while – she had been driving ambulances before she joined the ATS. It was lovely to be together and all in the same hut, so for us Aston House was a very good posting.

I remember Colonel Wood and Major Barratt, I used to drive the latter to his sweet factory at Wood Green, or Greenford, it was Bassetts Liquorice Allsorts or something like that. He used to go in and do a bit of business I suppose but he never offered me any sweets.

I was very well treated by ATS Captain Taylor. She was very kind when I was given compassionate leave to visit my family at Watford. She visited us there to make sure that we were managing allright.

I met my future husband at a NAAFI dance at Aston House, Andrew Holdaway, he was in REME and worked as a toolmaker in the workshops. We went to dances once or twice a week and could walk the lanes and meadows as our evenings were free, unless I had to take a late journey out with the car.

Because my twin and I were so alike we could play games with people. I well remember one evening we were being taken out to a dance in a lorry, Andrew sat with my twin sister thinking that she was me. And if I was driving an officer and lost my way, even though I had done the journey several times, I would say 'Sorry, I've never done this journey before, my sister usually drives you.'

I was driving out of Aston House one day and saw a hen nesting in the hedge and as I passed it stood up and walked away so I stopped to see if there were any eggs. And sure enough there was just one so I reached in and picked it up. You have to realise that an egg for breakfast was a real luxury in wartime and it was so delicious. Naturally I did this for several weeks until one of the fellers spotted me. After that he used to beat me to it so that was the end of that amusing interlude.

Another treat unexpectedly came my way when I drove an officer to an airfield, probably RAF Tempsford. He said, 'Have you ever had a flight in a plane?' I said, 'No sir, I haven't.' He said 'Would you like a trip?' I said, 'Oh, yes, I would!' And it was such a nice experience to fly in this Halifax bomber, I thought am I doing the right thing because it was all unofficial, anyway we came down safely.

Lucy married in August 1945 and now lives in Norwich. Sadly her husband, twin sister and younger sister have died but she was thrilled to visit Aston in 2004 with her own family and recall those happy ATS days.

The Workshop Engineer's Story

Johnny Riches was born on 11 June 1923, at Blaydon-on-Tyne, County Durham, on the opposite side of the river to Newcastle. He was one of a family of nine children, with four brothers and four sisters. His father was an excellent musician and taught drums and various instruments and naturally wanted to hand down this skill to his sons. Johnny thinks he was his dad's last hope, so he took to playing the clarinet and was taught by the bandmaster of the town's military band of the 4th Battalion the Royal Northumberland Fusiliers. What Johnny didn't realise was that by joining the town band he was also joining the Territorial Army! He remembers going to an army camp with the band but the penny dropped when he and his father, a French horn player, were both immediately called up when war was declared in 1939. Within weeks they both had to report to the drill hall and shortly after that the battalion was shipped abroad, but it departed without Johnny. He was released and allowed to continue his apprenticeship with Vickers Armstrong. He was enjoying quite a good income for a young fellow, but when he reached the age of eighteen, with his apprenticeship still not completed, he found himself back in the Army. Vickers Armstrong's protestations were ignored. He was doing a useful job there, at the huge Scotswood works, working as a fitter and turner on centre lathes, helping to produce 3.7-inch anti-aircraft guns and battle tanks.

Johnny found himself back in the Royal Northumberland Fusiliers, and was sent to Letchworth, Herts, to complete a course on instrument work, and then transferred to the Royal Electrical and Mechanical Engineers (REME) and sent to Woolwich Barracks.

Johnny remembered:

We used to hear little rumours at Woolwich about a magical place where we might be posted if very lucky. About a dozen of us struck lucky and were each given a pass to Knebworth Railway Station. We had no idea where we were going except for the coded address E.S.6. Our leader was told to knock on the hatch at the ticket office and say 'E.S.6.' This he did and soon afterwards a 3-ton army lorry appeared and we jumped aboard. It was a bit disheartening as we were driven seemingly for miles into remote countryside. We arrived at Aston House right out in the wilds. It was about February 1942.

We were gathered together to sign the secrecy act. One chap was cuter than the rest of us and refused to sign, said it was against his principles. He was gone within a couple of days or so.

We were taken to the camp huts in a field behind the war memorial. It was so muddy we walked on duck-boards – if you stepped off you could be up to your knees. It was terribly depressing and I think all of us who arrived that day wished ourselves somewhere else.

Aston was a very small village, though it did have three pubs. but it took a while to get used to being stuck there. There was nothing but open countryside between the village and old Stevenage, no new town then, but in the end we did get used to it.

The fairly big main workshop was divided into various sections. The whole of the northern bay was a large machine shop where I worked for most of the time. Centre lathes were installed along the north wall with larger lathes positioned down the middle of the floor. A grinder was in the north-east corner. The fitting and assembly shop was on the east side of the centre bay with automatic machines occupying the remainder. I remember these machines because for a time I looked after the ATS girls who worked on them producing fair quantities of components on turret lathes, etc. The south bay contained a paint shop, a sheet metal shop and a sewing machine shop where they made up webbing and canvas bags, etc.

I worked on a small bench type centre lathe producing parts in small quantities, maybe a dozen to twenty or so at a time. Small batch production, but they did keep repeating the batch orders. I made component parts for the limpet mines, one of the biggest products of Aston House.

The official history describes the workshop as follows:

In September 1942, a much enlarged workshop had been built and equipped, thus providing a comprehensive workshop with its own raw material and tool stores, in addition to the small-scale prototype and gauge-making facilities which had previously existed. The new shops were staffed from the outset with REME personnel and were conducted like a static REME workshop. The original layout was found to be unsatisfactory and was changed, the machines being regrouped and new machines being introduced. By the middle of 1943, under Major C.F. Moore, REME, the reorganisation of the workshops was complete, and the capacity considerably increased.

Towards the end of 1943, owing to the piecemeal addition of machines, considerable trouble was experienced in balancing the electric power load across the 3-phase system; in addition, there was no system of inspection of electrical installations, and a deal of the early work was unsafe. A small separate section was, therefore, set up to be responsible for all electrical installations throughout the Station, which functions were later extended to include the main boilers. Early in 1944 the sub-station capacity was increased to 400 KVA and a plating plant of 1,000 amp capacity was added at the beginning of 1945. Captain J.N. Barnett, RE, the officer-in-charge of the section, was also responsible for the design of a number of electrical devices which were produced for special purposes.

In April 1944, on the departure of Major E. Ramsay Green for the USA, the Design Department ceased to have a separate existence, its functions being divided between Quality Control and Workshops; the drawing office and the design function were absorbed by Quality Control, whilst the Tool Room and Prototype Shop were taken over by Workshops, which enabled more extensive tooling to be carried out, and made the workshop facilities as a whole much more flexible. Therefore all development work was undertaken by Workshops.

The transfer of the Drawing Office to Quality Control ensured that the negatives of all manufacturing drawings could not be altered unless approved by the various parties concerned, i.e. the designer, the Trials Committee and the Designs Department. The fusion also afforded more direct control by QC over the design of gauges and test rigs required for manufacturers and CIA [an Army quality control inspectorate]. Provision was made to carry out the inspection of articles produced in Workshops, other than work for Operational Supplies and for Stations VII, IX, etc., which carried out their own inspection on receipt of the goods, and the filing of all technical correspondence and the registration and issue of all drawings, specifications, gauges, jigs and test rigs, were perfected.

By January 1944 the workshops were beginning to engage in production runs not only for Aston House, but also for other sections of the organisation, especially the Radio Section, and it was not uncommon to put in hand orders for 10,000 on capstans, whilst the sheet metal shop produced some 50,000 boxes of various types per annum. A very high class of workmanship was produced, and all the production tools were designed and made on the premises. The workshops also undertook an increasing share of the development work, and were responsible for bringing a number of devices to the production stage and for several original designs. Captain (later Major) E.C. Kelly, REME, became officer-in-charge in September 1944.[1]

Johnny continued:

There were stores for machine-tools and materials, steel, copper, brass, sheet metal. I remember a chap called Livingstone, he worked with Captain Kelly in laboratories set up in the old Aston House stables. They did development work there and often required me to make them special little bits and pieces. I was aware that there were many young officers billeted in Aston House, quite young officers – they never entered the workshops, had no connection with what we were doing whatsoever. There must have been many other secret projects that they were engaged in, but for which they will never receive credit.

Occasionally I had to go into the officers' mess to put up the window shutters to comply with blackout regulations. Sometimes the officers would object as they were still enjoying the remains of the evening light. One of them stopped me and said he would do it later, but that put me in the awkward position of disobeying orders. He was a young officer and I didn't know his name.

I remember one of Captain Kelly's gadgets, the nail-gun. It was a small simple device that fired a nail into armour plating on which to hang an explosive device. I made the prototype nails that were shaped like a rocket with a conical shaped nose, tapered body and a flange around the base. They were about two inches long, made of special hardened tungsten steel.

I also made Perspex containers for the conveyance of microfilm messages by secret agents. These were for concealment in the anal and vaginal orifices of the human body. This is now quite a common practice in drug smuggling but in wartime it was thought to be quite clever and innovative. The two halves were compressed together. Each end was tapered, radiused and polished. The drawing stated 'Important – No Sharp Edges' which caused some amusement among the lads in the workshop. I believe the containers were quite successful.

A gun, with the appearance of a genuine fountain pen, was made by Sergeant Evans on a small lathe next to mine. It fired a single 0.22-inch bullet and was probably issued to officers. It gave them a chance of ending their lives or a one-shot chance to escape and survive. They were not made in large quantities.

I often used to see the Welbikes being tested around Aston House – the lads had fun riding them. I think we co-operated with The Frythe in the development stage of this small motorbike. It wasn't often that we received any feedback on our products but one day we were assembled outside the workshops and told that a British platoon was surrounded by Germans on one of the battlefronts. To get them out we air-dropped a supply of Welbikes overnight which enabled them all to escape *en masse*.

This news cheered us up because, without knowing what happened to the devices that we made, the job could become a bit tedious at times, especially when I thought of the lads that served an apprenticeship with me at Vickers Armstrong who were all earning damn good money and here was I in the Army receiving eight shillings [40p] a day. It's a pity they didn't enlighten us a little bit more about events in the field.

A regular occupation of mine was the fitting of silencers to revolvers for agents in the field, quite a simple task, nothing secret or clever about it. They arrived in pairs wrapped in waxed paper and packed in several crates. I put each silencer in the chuck of a lathe and enlarged the bore with a tapered reamer to a fixed depth, tested it on the revolver barrel until a good push fit was obtained, and then rewrapped it and placed it back into the crate.

Another device we made was a very simple rack of rollers. Each roller was about two inches in diameter and about three feet long. I understood that these were to be fitted to the floor of Wellington bombers to make a continuous track upon which bales or sacks of leaflets could be trundled and released into the air over Germany. Incidentally a Wellington bomber crashed about a mile away, just outside Aston, near the crossroads on the way to Benington. It got into difficulties and made an emergency landing. It wasn't shot down but may have suffered battle damage and was on its way back to base.

I think the local pubs were never so popular as when the Army took over Aston. In the evenings when we finished work we used to walk across the fields to Shephall [a nearby hamlet, now part of Stevenage New Town] to the Red Lion. We found it more sociable than Aston's Rose and Crown. There was also our own NAAFI Nissen hut where we could get a cup of tea.

Several concert groups of ENSA [Entertainment National Service Association] came along to entertain us. I remember a small trio or quartet played classical music. It didn't go down very well with the majority. The comedian Tommy Trinder joked that ENSA was 'Every Night Something Awful!' The organisers would say to us that they hoped that we would turn out and appreciate what these people were trying to do for us.

I met my future wife, Christine Spicer, at one of the camp dances – our own band was playing there. The first time I asked her for a date she didn't turn up because she didn't understand my Geordie accent and when we visited my family near Newcastle she couldn't join in the conversation, she said it was like a foreign language. Christine is three years younger than me and was about seventeen or eighteen when we met. She had to be home by half past ten or her father would come after her and she wasn't allowed to marry until she reached the age of twenty-one.

I played quite a lot of hockey for the 'Workshop A' team while I was at Aston House. The team was made up of a close group of friends: I remember Bradshaw, he was a Welsh lad, he actually visited Aston with his wife one day long after the war. Then there was a Harvey,

Steve Long, Charlie Nurser, Sergeant Wilf Evans, and a civilian Evans-Watts, he loved hockey. It was never clear to us what his secret job was, but he certainly spent a long time in the workshops. George Hoyle, Harry Walters, he chopped his fingers off in a press at Aston House. Frank Woods, he was a great friend of mine and we kept in touch for a while after the war with Christmas cards and visits to each other. The hockey team played against Knebworth, RAF barrage balloon sites and other similar small military establishments that had formed teams.

Aston was a good posting, we were lucky to be there. We knew that our soldiers were fighting and being killed and injured every day. We didn't have a great deal of military discipline. It's true we did wear uniform including hats and we did march every day from the workshops, out of the front gate, past the church down the road to the NAAFI and after the meal we used to fall-in and march back to the workshops. I think we did our best to keep in time, we used to laugh and joke on the way and I remember my pals pointing to the churchyard and saying, 'Johnny Riches will be over there one of these days.' They knew I was courting a local girl and would probably settle in Aston.

We were all moved out quite quickly after VJ-Day as the job we had been doing wasn't required any more. I was sent to Cairo to work at an Army experimental station, not SOE. I was there for a very interesting twelve months developing special tank tracks. We were widening the tracks on various types of vehicles to try and get them across the Qattara depression without sinking. A lot of German tanks had stalled there during the North African campaign. It is a dried up inland sea with a thick salt crust but is soft underneath.

I eventually returned to Aston in 1948 to marry Christine and have lived in the village ever since. Regrettably I saw Aston House reduced to rubble. The Stevenage Development Corporation considered it uneconomic to maintain after they had used it as their headquarters. A lot of valuable items such as the chandeliers and the fireplaces were looted. It was a great shame that the house was demolished. It was deliberately set on fire and then bulldozed.

Johnny played an active part in Aston village life and was the parish council clerk for some twelve years. He joined the scientific instrument company Hilgar and Watts and later moved to ADC

(Analytical Development Company), which specialised in gas analysis and control equipment. He became its sales manager and travelled to many countries including Canada, the USA and Russia. Sadly he died in 2005 and is survived by his wife and two children.

I think for Johnny, Aston did become that 'magical' place that started out as just a little rumour at Woolwich in 1942.

Note

1.   PRO HS 7/27.

The Storeman's Story

I interviewed Richard Bignell several times by telephone and we finally met in June 2003 at Aston, when he and his wife Brenda returned for a mini-reunion that I arranged for a few of the Aston House veterans. Richard was born on 27 March 1917 in Marylebone. He attended the Kilburn Building Polytechnic when just fourteen and was taught the building trades, including design, which prepared him well for his first job as a draughtsman with the shop-fitting firm Hickman's at Cricklewood. Here he was able to continue training in the carpenters' shop and the metal workshops. Unfortunately the slump in 1932 caused most of the workforce, including Richard, to lose their jobs.

Fortunately he soon found other employment with the Kodak Company in its advertising department and after three and a half years he was invited to transfer to the finished film division which he enjoyed until 1941 when he was called up to serve his country.

He joined the Royal Army Ordnance Corps (RAOC) and completed his basic training at Chepstow and was then moved to Worksop, No. 24 ASD (Ammunition Sub-Depot), Nottinghamshire, to train as an ammunition examiner. He was taught to blow up bridges and railway lines with plastic explosive and to dismantle hand grenades and bombs and inspect them. He said to himself, 'Goodness me! I might be under attack in the front line just sitting there checking ammunition, surrounded by all manner of explosives – what *have* I let myself in for?' Fortunately he was rescued from that fate by Major Duke who was searching for recruits to take charge of the Aston House stores and found him ideal for the task.

Richard described how he later came to be selected for Aston House:

It was October 1942 and I was stationed at a Nottingham ammunition dump when we were suddenly visited by a War Office major who explained that he was seeking six recruits. My turn came for the interview. 'Name, number and army experience? Where do you live? What are your hobbies and favourite sports?' etc. I answered all his questions; my hobby was photography and my sport was cycling. He was interested to know that I had passed the course for 'Ammunition Examiner' and had a good knowledge of explosives. Eventually he said 'Righty ho, you wouldn't mind being posted near your home, would you?' I said 'No, I certainly wouldn't, sir.' He said 'Report to me in six weeks time.'

But for this lucky intervention by the major I might well have gone on to bomb disposal. I didn't see much future in that. As Bob Hope said 'Death can ruin your career'. He selected about seven others and together we travelled to Knebworth Station, transferred to a lorry and were driven along the A1 which is also the Great North Road, turned into the narrow, long Broadwater Lane and arrived at the very remote Aston House.

The engagement of stores personnel is confirmed in the official history:

Aston House needed additional personnel to cope with increasing demands for materiel.

The stores section was having to meet many of them at very short notice, and in April 1942 an order was placed for 1,200 standard dump units ('S' Shipments), comprising mixed explosive and incendiary stores for infiltration into Norway.

The introduction of RAOC personnel under Captain (later Major) D.S. Duke, RAOC, resulted in a proper system of stores accounts being set up. These were based upon normal ordnance procedure, but the regular system had to be modified to meet the special needs of the organisation. Furthermore, steps were immediately taken to complete segregation of the various stores into their explosive groups and to arrange for storage at proper safety distances, in accordance with magazine regulations. Up to this time it had been the practice to send out all stores in plain or commercial cover packages, but in July 1942 official classifications from the Explosive Storage and Transport Committee were obtained for all SOE devices, which were thereafter sent out with their proper explosive group labels. All the packing cases required were constructed in the carpenters' shop on the station. The activities of enemy aircraft had led to some dispersal of stocks as early as 1941, but in July 1942 a substantial allocation of storage was obtained at 84 Command AD at Sandy, Bedfordshire.

To meet the requirements of a new Quality Control department a 'Bond Store' was established at Aston House into which all goods received were first delivered. Samples were then taken by QC department and tested, after which release or rejection notes were issued and the goods were either transferred to bulk stores or returned to the manufacturers.[1]

Richard revealed to me what was held in his store:

It was all secret stuff, so I had to sign the Official Secrets Act and have my signature witnessed by an officer and a sergeant-major. This procedure was repeated again when I was demobbed. I was told not to mention anything whatsoever about my work and I kept to that rule. I didn't tell anybody anything. If I was asked what did I do in the war I answered, 'Well I was in the RAOC and it was all hush-hush.'

However, sixty years have passed and I am now 86. During my time at Aston House I knew nothing about SOE or Bletchley Park and the Enigma decoding machine. That has all been revealed now so it seems that telling you about my store will do no harm.

It contained many things that I didn't fully understand. There were some unusual guns, for instance. I opened one of the boxes, just being nosey. I made sure that nobody knew, for the officers would come round at different times to inspect everything and check that all was in order. There were thousands of these handguns, it was an odd thing really, a one-shot 0.45-inch calibre pistol, the breech broke open like a shotgun; it wasn't rifled so it wouldn't have been very accurate. After discharge you poked out the spent cartridge with a little stick that was supplied in the box along with five cartridges.

Richard couldn't remember this weapon's identity, but from his very accurate description it must have been an American OSS Liberator pistol complete with a piece of wooden dowel to eject the spent cartridge case. Over one million were made.

Richard continued:

The Welbike, a small motorcycle intended for use by paratroopers, was in my store. It had a bump-start 99cc two-stroke engine and was made commercially after the war and renamed the 'Corgi'. I tested these Welbikes by riding them over ploughed fields. I'm tall so I had my knees up in my armpits! One threw me off and I landed in a heap. It was designed to fit snugly inside a large parachute container that I also stored. Everything needed for fighting a war was packed in those containers – guns, ammunition, etc. They were dropped in Burma and Holland, etc. A lot of our stuff was dropped down at Arnhem, for Operation Market Garden.

I well remember an occasion when everybody, even the officers and sergeants, was called upon to help load a dozen whacking great big lorries that arrived about five o'clock one evening. It was quite a difficult job because the tailboards were high and you had to lift the containers up and throw them in. It took about an hour, resulting in many cut and bruised hands. Two weeks later we heard about the drop over Arnhem.

The Yanks also came into our depot with a fleet of three or four lorries. I don't know what they collected or what it was for. I had a chat with one or two of the drivers and then off they went with their vehicles fully loaded.

Other items held in my store were pressure switches, compression switches, trip switches, all that sort of thing, pencil fuses, 120-feet long alpine ropes, limpet mines. I don't know what was in the adjacent stores, only what was in mine. Everything was packed in boxes with identification numbers.

My first job at Aston House during the winter of 1942/3 was to pack and load what were called 'Dumps'. I filled big A 12 ammunition boxes, they're not very deep inside, with explosives, booby-traps, a small rifle, plastic explosive, Colt revolvers, fuses, pressure switches, and ammunition, etc. My colleagues and I made up loads of them. Two or three lorries were coming in every day to collect them. These caches of weapons were to be hidden in secret underground dumps around the country to provide arms for the Home Army [Auxiliary Units] civilian volunteers in the south of England who would act as a British resistance movement after a German invasion and occupation. After about three weeks of this activity I was moved to another store with a protective blast wall all round it.

Richard checked through an official list of weapons and kit supplied at the time for a typical dump and confirmed it was what he packed: 5lb gelignite, 3 Mills bombs, 2 magnesium incendiary bombs, box of detonators, instantaneous HE fuse, fast burning fuse, slow burning fuse, a selection of time pencil delay switches ranging from 10 minutes to 2 weeks, pressure switches, trip switches, coils of trip wire, a crimping tool, sticky tape.[2]

Richard was also able to identify from photographs some SOE weapons he had seen at Aston House. One that immediately jogged his memory was the 'Tyreburster', a device designed to explode under pressure and small enough to be concealed inside a camouflaged object such as a stone, a lump of mud or an animal dropping.

Richard continued:

Aston House had its own fleet of lorries so there was obviously a lot of activity with goods in and out all the time; some arrived via the local railway station. Our stores were quite big buildings and always absolutely full. Packages arrived from many different firms and different places, a lot in wooden boxes that we knocked apart and distributed the contents to the appropriate Army-issue metal containers. All would be unloaded at the receiving area. That was a building opposite my store. The corporal in charge signed everything in and ensured that it was passed to the store appertaining to that particular product.

Richard recalled a special consignment of explosives arriving from the USA packaged in beautiful American white wood crates. These were fine for shipping but no use for delivery to a front-line battle area. He stated:

I broke open the crates and transferred the contents to the usual metal containers. We were told that the devices were smoke bombs. We called them 'Flowerpots'; eighteen of them would just fit inside a big cylindrical shaped container. The pile of white wood was supposed to be burned but I have to confess that we all found a use for it. I took a lot home in the pannier bags of my tandem! It was beautiful wood and nothing was wasted, there was just two holes in the ends of each piece where panel pins had held them together. You must understand that you couldn't buy wood in this country at that time.

Richard's description of the 'Flowerpot' device suggests that this was in fact a 'Firepot'. This was an incendiary device similar in shape to the Tyreburster, but with a magnesium case, and much larger, weighing nearly 2lb.

Richard continued:

There were three big magazines built underground for blast protection with a road sloping down very steeply to each entrance and then up the other side. Lorries were loaded and/or unloaded out of sight below ground surface level so one never knew what was going on there. All the ammunition and high explosive supplies were stored and dispatched from there. They were situated in a very secure isolated magazine area with an inner security wire fence and gate. Although the explosive store was part of my section and we all worked together in various packing areas I had nothing to do with the storing of explosives.

There were a few Nissen huts in the magazine area where work was done on explosive material, for instance assembly shops built in isolation right down at the very end of the stores where the field sloped down towards the Dell.

There was a big old army tank full of holes in the Dell, used for trials and experiments with live ammunition and explosives.

Old ammunition is dangerous stuff to handle – it could be inert or it could be twice the power. TNT high explosive has a shelf life of about ten years and is then destroyed. This is achieved by burning it! Small lumps are placed on a large steel platform, oil is poured over it and it is set on fire using a fuse. It should burn slowly but it can explode, so there is a blast wall to stand behind and get safely out of the way. I knew a couple of fellows at Aston House who were assigned to dispose of explosives, They would set the fuse going, stand behind the blast wall and hope everything was all right. But on this particular occasion, one got behind the wall and the other didn't, it went off and killed him. I don't remember his name – he wasn't in my section.

There was also another tragedy – a good friend of mine who rode with me on the back of my tandem. He had a terrible pain and attended the hospital at Hitchin for treatment. It had no effect so he regularly reported to our medical orderly who gave him aspirin but the pain became much worse, in fact so intense that he went down to the gun store where he worked, placed a few cartridges in a revolver and killed himself. It was discovered afterwards that his medical records had been lost in the hospital – he had a duodenal ulcer and was receiving the wrong treatment, the aspirin was just making the pain worse.

One of the fellows who worked in the goods receiving hut came to me with a camera. He said, 'You know something about these, don't you? What's this worth?' He knew I had worked for Kodak. I said, 'Yes, that's a Leica, the body alone is worth £53.' He said, 'There's five of them with all the accessories.' I said, 'Let me have a look.' He brought them over, there were different lenses, holders and goodness knows what. He said, 'I'm packing them up, they're to be sent out to Burma.'

The package arrived in Burma allright but when it was opened up it contained bricks and stones! A couple of years later – we were all demobbed by then – I was reading a daily paper and spotted his name. He'd been sent to prison for stealing so I've a pretty good idea who had those five cameras!

I cycled home on my tandem to Harrow in Middlesex twice a week, a 23-mile each way journey. I picked up my weekend pass and departed at about half past twelve on Saturday and arrived back in camp at 8.00 a.m. on the following Monday.

Les Carter was a really good pal at Aston House. He liked cycling and would come out with me on my tandem – he said they were the happiest days of his life. I was amazed when he said that. The tandem gave us complete freedom during the evenings. We'd even go as far as Cambridge and back. He said to me, 'I'll never forget the first time I saw you, we were sitting in the mess.' I remembered him because he looked so miserable. He said, 'I remember you smiled at me and we got chatting.' He hated the Army. He was always saying, 'Roll on death,' as he worked on packaging in the stores.

I have an amusing story about Les. One day there was a knock on his front door at home and a couple of red-caps [Military Police] were standing there. They had called to arrest him for desertion before he had even joined up! Unbeknown to him his call-up papers had been delivered but his mother, who didn't want him to join the Army, had thrown them away! Anyhow he overcame that problem, I suppose he got a bit of a warning. But not long afterwards Les was at the front in France with the expeditionary force and was ordered to retreat with his unit to Dunkirk. He was on that beach for three days, but he survived the constant air attacks and managed to get aboard a big ship for home. Unfortunately a shell went right through it and he landed in the water again. He was then rescued by another ship and brought back safely to England. The Army then required him to pay for the loss of his rifle! He'd abandoned it in the sand, it was no good to him, he'd got no ammunition!

I think it was all resolved sensibly in the end because a driver had lost his lorry! Les was fortunate to survive Dunkirk and be posted to what must have seemed to him, after being strafed at Dunkirk, a very tranquil Aston House. Sadly, he died about five years ago. He would have been absolutely thrilled to know that I am talking to you in Aston after all these years.

I took my cine camera with me on my cycling jaunts around Hertfordshire and used what was then rare – colour film. I dare not take it into the depot of course. But I do have two still photographs. One is of my 'Hut 29' with thirteen of the residents standing outside; I can only remember the names of six of them. The other is of Les and me sitting on the tandem at High Road, Aston. Everybody knew us, the camp personnel and most of the villagers because, I suppose, a tandem is noticeable.

Richard's girlfriend Brenda, now his wife, also remembered riding on the rear of the tandem. She said, 'I only used to see the back of him!' Richard recalled that when she had a week's holiday she would come to see him and lodge in the next village.

She was a nurse, we met in hospital. We both have happy memories of the fun in the entertainments hut at Aston House, the dances and ENSA shows, we remember enjoying comedians Arthur Haines and a marvellous show with Charlie Chester. [ATS girl Edna Jacobs also remembered Charlie Chester joking 'Aston is just three pubs and a graveyard.']

Our own lads put on shows there. A friend Danny and I joined in with our piano accordions, we played a duet at one concert. Someone else would sing a song. We also had our own camp band. I did play in it, just once. I was on stage playing this heavy piano accordion watching all the lads enjoying themselves dancing with the girls and I thought, 'I'm not doing this any more. It's more fun down there than playing up here in this band!'

I remember being very impressed by the lovely Bechstein grand piano in the officers' mess. There was a duty roster that came round every six months or so that gave each of us a chance to go into Aston House. It was to place the blackout boards in the windows and then take them down the next morning. I also noticed the lovely armchairs in the room.

I made wooden toys. Even Colonel Wood bought a fire engine from me! I also made model tanks. It was just something to do, there was plenty of wood and plenty of time. Many of the lads had young brothers, children, cousins or grandchildren. I was trained in carpentry, so I knew how to use the tools you see. One of the sheds in my store area was a carpenters' shop with just a couple of soldiers working there and nearer Aston House was another building with mainly civvy carpenters making the parachute containers. That's where I made the wheels for my fire engines.

Richard recalled the names of certain people that he had known at Aston House:

I remember Colonel Watts, Watkins, Major Bunt, Major Duke, Lieutenant Turbofield, the adjutant Major Midson, Barratt was the name of the camp commandant, Mr Parsons, I think he was a draughtsman? I met him in 1936 on an outing at Kodak. Also Reg Parson, he lived at 1 Park Street, now demolished, Stratford-on-Avon. One poor chap received his call-up papers a fortnight before his 42nd birthday, you imagine that! He must have thought he'd got away with it; he was most annoyed. Two of the lads in the camp actually lived in Aston village – George Doe and Duggie Doe, I remember his wife Margaret (Daisy) Doe. I made her a handbag as I kept my tandem in their garden shed. Well, I couldn't leave anything at the camp, could I? I remember the Holdaway twins: on my very first day I went into the NAAFI and saw a few ATS girls sitting at a table, I joined them and we chatted away; they introduced themselves but didn't tell me that one of them had a twin sister at the camp. The next day I met her again and said hello but it was the twin sister and she completely ignored me. I thought that's nice! When I eventually saw the pair of them together they were absolutely identical, especially in uniform.

I once visited Bletchley Park to deliver a parcel. Major Bunt telephoned me and asked me to report to his office. I knocked on the door and entered. He handed me quite a heavy parcel and said, 'Now you don't let go of this, just hold on to it all the time. Go to the front drive of Aston House, there is a car waiting for you, the driver will take you to a destination, he knows where it is, and he will tell you where to go.' I also delivered a parcel to our head office in London, probably Baker Street. It was a sort of mansion, a block of flats. I was told to go up to the second floor, find a certain room and knock on the door. The door was opened by an officer, I couldn't see inside, he just opened it wide enough to see me and poked his arm through, snatched the parcel and slammed the door! He didn't even say thank you. I would love to know what was in those parcels, it was all secret stuff you see.

Our own REME workshops were also secret but I was allowed to go in and talk to the chaps working on the machines. I remember an officer who was designing the spigot mortar. He was always fiddling about. The spigot was screwed into a tree and then fired by a time fuse or trip wire. I don't know if anything came of it. There was a door with a notice 'Strictly Private – Keep Out' and behind this the scientists were at work, so obviously secret stuff was being developed in there.

Once I volunteered to try out some diving gear down the estate's sixty-foot deep well, but nothing came of it and the equipment was sent for testing elsewhere.

It was a marvellous posting. I spent three very happy years there; it was almost like a holiday camp. I didn't really want to leave after the war was over but there was no way I could stay on at Aston. I could have applied for demolition work because I knew how to blow things up but I decided against it.

Richard married his 'Little Nurse', Brenda Mary Brown, after VE-Day and was demobbed on 16 October 1945, when he was directed to work for the Ministry of Housing erecting 'prefabs' in Harlesden.

He and his team of men could assemble these temporary prefabricated homes at the rate of two a day. They were for families who had lost their homes in the blitz. Eventually, Richard managed to get back to his old job at Kodak in Harrow and retired in 1978. Richard and Brenda died at Bristol in 2007, they are survived by three children and six grandchildren.

Notes

1. PRO HS 7/27.
2. Seaman, Mark, *Secret Agent's Handbook of Special Devices*, p. 23.

The Craftsman's Story

Joe Wardle was born in Manchester on Boxing Day 1923, the youngest of a family of eight. He left school at the age of fourteen and was apprenticed as an engineer with Fairey Aviation, where the Swordfish and Barracuda aircraft were being produced for the Fleet Air Arm. At eighteen he tried to join the Merchant Navy and begin training as a junior engineer, but his employer, Fairey Aviation, refused to release him, so Joe, in his annoyance, decided not to go back there to work. He was ordered to appear before a civilian tribunal that opposed his wishes and directed him into the Army. He was very disappointed, as three of his friends had been accepted into the Merchant Navy as junior engineers. However, all subsequently perished, going down with their torpedoed ships, so that tribunal's decision to divert Joe from his original Merchant Navy ambition may well have saved his life.

In February 1943 Aston House needed engineers and sent out scouts to find them. Joe was located and interviewed by Captain Kelly at the Royal Artillery Barracks in Woolwich. About a fortnight later he was posted to Aston House and remained there until after VE-Day in 1945.

After the war Joe was promoted to sergeant and in 1947 married Doris Fisher, a Manchester girl whom he'd met on the dance floor before the war. Together they brought up a family of two boys and a girl who in turn have presented them with seven grandchildren.

He realises now that the war period was his education; all the varied experiences at Aston House were more beneficial than any grammar school could ever have been. After the war, a wiser and more confident Joe returned to Fairey Aviation determined to obtain the qualifications he needed, and began to study at home after work.

I arrived at Knebworth by train and a lorry picked me up [Joe recalled]. While waiting for the lorry I noticed the Station Hotel and thought: that looks inviting. It was my kind of haunt, so I made a mental note to visit it some time. And sure enough I did spend many Saturday nights there and enjoyed the dances at nearby Knebworth Hall.

My senior officer was Captain Kelly, later promoted to major. I was in the REME as a Craftsman II. I worked in the very well equipped workshops at Aston House, where we made all sorts of secret stuff, mainly for clandestine purposes. I did a bit of everything. To become a craftsman you have to pass trade tests in all types of machining, welding and bench work. At Aston House I made parts to specified detail drawings but without the assembly drawing I had no idea what the finished device might be. You could use your common sense, of course, and the buzz would get round, things were leaked out, so you would get bits of information from a close friend you worked with or socialised with. In my case it was members of the dance band, a regimental sergeant-major, and another pal, Harry Dent, an engineer, who like myself came from Manchester.

One large job I worked on was the first one-man submersible, Sleeping Beauty. It was tested at Luton Public Baths. I remember I had to go there twice to help deliver it, I think the Navy did all the tests.

I only remember the prototype, because we didn't do production on that type of thing. The prototype was assembled at Aston but parts were made elsewhere and delivered to the workshop. There were a lot of manufacturing processes that couldn't be undertaken at Aston House, like the argon arc welding of the aluminium casing which is quite a tricky job.

We made a lot of very complicated limpet mines. There was a particular one called a 'wreath mine', an Australian development. It was circular, torus shaped, the inner circle was about ten inches in diameter and the outer about twelve inches diameter. It was made from very thin brass sheet and in section was shaped like the letter 'W', and was filled with plastic explosive. Across the centre was a bar on which two magnets were mounted. When tested, the resulting explosion cut a hole in a steel sheet exactly the same diameter as the mine.

Joe was unaware that the wreath mine had been specifically devised to blow up the two big caissons that operated the St-Nazaire dock. They were connected to a ring main of cordtex. There were twelve wreaths for the interior faces of each wall of both caissons and others to blow holes in the internal decks. For the wet outer surfaces, twelve 18lb charges that looked like plum puddings were to be suspended 27 feet below the water level. Charges for blowing the lock gates, dockyard bridges, impeller pumps in the pump house, motors in the powerhouses, guns and the caissons were made up by Major David Wyatt at Aston House. Clams, limpets, firepots, tarbabies, Tyesule incendiaries and other items were also supplied for the raid.[1]

We tried the wreath mine on two old tanks in the Dell chalk quarry [Joe remembered]. I'm sure one was a Sherman and the other a Churchill. They were for demonstration purposes and for testing the effects of various devices. The wreath mine blew a hole in the half-inch thick tank body so neatly that it looked as if it had been cut out by a mechanical device.

On another occasion we fired a tree spigot mortar to test the effect on the Churchill tank. We located two trees in line with each other on opposite sides of a road and screwed a spigot mortar into each tree. The mortars were aimed and then connected with a booby-trap trip wire. When the tank pushed against the trip wire it was hit by the mortar bombs from both sides. It's the weakest part of a tank really, but there was no penetration, just two damn big dents. So the spigot mortar would then have to be improved until it worked more effectively. One or two things used to go adrift before they worked properly.

Tests on hand guns were carried out in a gun room, where they tried out various types of silencer. A silencer is a very simple device, just a tube filled with solid rubber fastened on the end of a gun, that's all it is. I was quite surprised. My job was to assemble them in the workshops.

The worst assembly job was the calthrop. I dreaded having to assemble those, because it was total repetition and we made them by the score. The material was pressed sheet metal with four angled spikes positioned so that, when thrown on the ground, one spike would always be vertical to penetrate a tyre that passed over it. They were dropped on the runways of enemy airfields.

Occasionally agents, both male and female, would come into the workshops. Their identities were never revealed. They would walk round, look at what we were doing, and ask technical questions. They were dressed in officer's style uniform, but devoid of any insignia or rank. Other visitors were naval officers who would appear in their full rig and be given a conducted tour to show them who was making their weapons.

I remember we made a prototype device at Aston House that would cause a V-1 flying bomb to explode on its ramp. Whether it ever got into production or not I don't know. The trigger for the flying bomb was the engine. When the engine cut out the bomb would glide downwards and would detonate just before it hit the ground.

Joe amazed me by identifying the device from my photographs. He exclaimed, 'That's it! Yes! We actually worked on those.' It was a German fuse that was copied and filled with explosive at Aston House.

An SOE 'Crossbow' committee was formed on 28 June 1944 under the chairmanship of Air Vice-Marshal A.P. Ritchie to counter the threat of the new German flying bomb and rocket weapons.

A plan was devised using information received on the procedures adopted by the Germans in the storage of aerial bombs. It was probable that the warheads of flying bombs would be stored complete with the fusing device or pistol screwed into the fuse pocket. In the case of bombs the gaines were not screwed into the fuses but were held separately as a safety measure and were introduced only immediately prior to the bombs being loaded into aircraft. It was therefore proposed to try and fit substitute impact fuses which, while being identical in appearance and weight to those fitted by the Germans, would cause a premature explosion during the process of launching, thus destroying the launching apparatus and possibly killing the crew.

With the assistance of bomb disposal, SOE was able to secure a specimen of the mechanical fuse normally operated on impact. On the basis of this sample, 100 counterfeit special fuses were prepared and arrangements were made to send these to the field, together with the necessary spanners and instructions for fitting them into warheads.

Experimental work was put in hand to produce a long-delay mechanism which could be inserted into the warheads during their transit to the large depot so as to cause explosion of the warheads in the depots themselves.

Sixty 'Fireflys' (a similar fuse device for the V-2 rocket) were also ordered, thirty standard and thirty modified to give short timings. Special spanners were also required for removing the caps from fuel tanks. Research was taking place into methods of destroying bulk stocks of hydrogen peroxide (used as a fuel in the V-2) in storage or during transit. One method under investigation was the use of incendiary ammunition with a metal alkyl filling. Penetration tests were carried out on replica liquid oxygen road and rail transport tanks. 0.303-inch ammunition was fired at the replica using a Bren gun at 30 yards range with some success. Attacks on replica hydrogen peroxide containers using a 2-inch mortar at 150 yards were also investigated, but were not accurate or powerful enough to achieve penetration.

Joe remembered seeing another device that mystified him. He recalled:

I was sent to Watford on a mission, our driver took us to a place making luminous paints. I noticed some flat discs that were painted with this stuff and imagined that people would wear them to identify themselves in the dark. I assumed it would be for some Commando raid. They were in open boxes, we didn't see them properly, just had a peep, nosey buggers we were!

What Joe and his friends had noticed were most likely the discs applied to parachute containers to help resistance groups find them after a drop in the dark.

A 2-inch diameter disc was visible for up to 100 yds and a 1-inch disc was visible at 25 to 50 yds. Staff at The Frythe were concerned about the possible danger to health if a person was in close contact with the highly radioactive luminous paint for any length of time.[2]

Joe continued:

Another Aston House invention that I remember was a tubular nail gun that drove a steel spigot into the side of a ship on which a mine could be hung. It was a very simple device, like a piece of tubing, easy to fire by pulling out a pin or something. There was a problem with magnetic limpet mines being shaken off by the explosion of a neighbouring limpet on the same hull – maybe this was a possible answer? I remember the steel nail going into steel, quite remarkable really.

Lots of special webbing equipment was made up in the sewing machine shop. This was needed by agents to conceal the weapons they were carrying, some of which could be taken apart.

I also remember lead-lined metal boxes containing all types of guns, weapons and armaments, but we didn't pack them; someone else did that. These were dropped just off shore for a resistance organisation to pick up. They became so efficient at this that they were bringing the empty boxes back and saying 'more please'. The Navy must have delivered them; a lot of stuff was transported in this manner, they were picked up fairly soon after the drop.

I also remember a Bailey Bridge being built for test purposes. But I may be confused about that. I also worked at Fairey Aviation in Manchester, where they were manufactured.

There were a lot of boffins at Aston House and hence a great deal of experimentation. Although it was not a production unit Joe agreed that Colonel Wood did more or less what he wanted and made a lot of devices of which few people would have been aware.

Joe continued:

He was a nice chap, I remember him because he put me on jankers.

You do some really foolish things when you're young. On Saturday nights about thirty of us would board a liberty truck that took us out regularly to dances at Knebworth and sometimes to Ware. At Ware I met a lovely young lady and after the dance she accepted my offer to escort her home. We did a bit of snuggling in the back garden and when I returned to board the liberty truck it was no longer there. It's quite a long walk from Ware to Aston so I thought I'll ring up and request a car to pick me up. I knew that my senior officer Major Kelly did this every Saturday evening when he returned from London. So I walked to the railway station and rang up for his car. I said, 'I, Major Kelly, require a car to pick me up at Ware Station.' Of course it was dispatched immediately. I decided to begin walking along the road to Aston and had reached the outskirts of the town when sure enough the car passed me en route to the station. When it came back I flagged it down and the driver said, 'I've been to pick up Major Kelly and he isn't there. I waited for a while but nobody's seen him.' I'd had a few beers and I thought I could trust him, he was a corporal and I knew him well, so I said, 'It was me, I just sort of impersonated him.' When we got back he put me in the guardhouse!

Next day I was marched in front of Colonel Wood in the big house; luckily he'd got a good sense of humour and had a good laugh about it. He said 'You've used a lot of initiative, but on the other hand you have committed a serious offence.'

He put me on a fizzer, I got seven days jankers – CB [confined to barracks]. I served it at Aston House performing extra duties, washing up the kitchen utensils and cleaning out the toilets and that sort of business. I was confined to camp and not allowed in the NAAFI.

I remember a beautiful theatre being built for us at Aston House. Prior to that all our dances and entertainment took place in the NAAFI. The new building was much bigger and well-equipped with a stage, etc. It meant that a few very famous people in ENSA could come and entertain us. I think Brian Rix was among them. We also produced our own plays and shows. I took part in some of them and also helped backstage. I was a member of a Hillbilly quartet and sang songs like 'She'll Be Coming Round the Mountain When She Comes'. We toured the local village halls with this form of entertainment and I also sang with our own dance band, so we gradually built up a good entertainment group.

The dance band also toured the local halls, we played at Stevenage Town Hall, Knebworth Village Hall, at Station IX The Frythe at Old Welwyn, and Station XV the Thatched Barn at Borehamwood.

Joe showed me a photograph of the band, taken in the new entertainments hut. He explained:

The music stands were made in the carpenters' shop and the background stage scenery was painted by the guitar player. I can't remember his name, he was quite artistic but had an unfortunate flatulence problem and used to stink out the hut to the extent that we all had to evacuate it!

Harry Walters from Somerset was the bass player and a former professional musician who had played in most of the top-class hotels in London, including the Grosvenor Hotel, Park Lane. Staff Sergeant Fletcher from Derby played the piano – he was in charge of the workshops. The drummer from Birmingham had played with the Ted Heath band in its early days. He married one of the ATS girls from the camp. George Hoyle was from Chorley near Halifax [*sic*] – he was the bandleader and played the saxophone. His favourite solos were 'Woodchopper's Ball' and 'Stardust'. During the day he was an expert machinist in the workshop.

We even played for our own officers at Aston House. Major Kelly organised the social activities in the officers' mess; he was a very smart, good-looking sociable chap. So much so that he kept plying us with drinks and we all got a little bit tight. George Hoyle, our leader, was normally quite strict with us but he couldn't object really with Major Kelly providing us with liquid refreshment. It didn't improve the playing so we did make a bit of a botch of it really by the end of the evening. It was absolutely crowded with people that we had never seen before. I think some of the guests were from The Frythe. The ballroom was much like the dining room in appearance. I was at the back of the house with doors that opened out onto the lawn. The band set up just outside the doors to make more room for the dancers.

We also did a couple of dances in Stevenage, at ESA [Educational Supplies Association]. The company is best known for producing school furniture but during the war it was converted to manufacture wooden assemblies for the de Havilland Mosquito aircraft.

I had a very nice girlfriend, Peggy, in those days. She lived near the Astonia cinema, Stevenage. She persuaded me to organise a couple of dances at the ESA factory.

The music was wonderful. I used to sing 'You'll Never Know', that was a great favourite, 'Who's Taking you Home Tonight' and 'Long Ago and Far Away': quite a few of them really. There were six or seven of us in the band and we received plenty of invitations to play at various functions. Local dances kept up morale – it was like going to a party. There were many dances that involved everyone like the Paul Jones, the Conga, the Palais Glide, Spreading Chestnut Tree and both lady's and gentleman's excuse me dances where you were permitted to cut in on another couple. I actually met my best sweetheart at an Aston dance. Unfortunately she was posted and so we were separated. Sadly I never saw her again.

When VE-Day arrived and the European conflict was over the plan was to ship us out to Fremantle and carry on with the work against the Japanese but the atom bomb put an abrupt end to that. Instead, we celebrated with a huge party for all the SOE units at the Seymour Hall in London. It was absolutely wonderful. The music was provided by Stanley Black and his orchestra. There was also another memorable party at The Frythe.

There was a strong ATS contingent at Aston House and I often wonder what happened to them all after the war. Some of the boys actually married local girls. There's no doubt that we had some good happy times. To be truthful it was a nice little enclave and we all worked well together. Aston House was my home for two years. I now live in Northendon, Manchester. I worked for British Airways as a licensed aircraft engineer superintendent at Heathrow for a good deal of my life. Whilst there I visited Aston a couple of times on sort of 'memory lane' trips and found that the whole lot had vanished. The house was gone, the camp gone, there was a modern house where the guardroom stood. All that remained was one little hut in a field and there seemed to be chickens or something in it. The Astonia cinema is now a snooker hall. The Publix cinema has long gone. The railway station has also vanished and a new one built for the new town. I could hardly believe that Station 12 ever existed.

Joe attended my little reunion at Aston, which brought Johnny Riches and him together again for the first time in forty years. His night-time studies after the war did bear fruit – he was promoted to flight shed foreman at Manchester's Ringway Airport where he corrected any problems found after each new aircraft had been flight-tested, prior to delivery to the customer. The aircraft were Barracudas and Fireflys Mks II to VI and the new Gannet. His team from Fairey Aviation embarked on HMS *Ark Royal* for sea trials and competed against rival manufacturer Blackburn in a timed competition to change an engine on their respective aircraft. Joe's team won and consequently Fairey Aviation was awarded the lucrative contract.

Joe passed the basic licensing examination for the Civil Aviation Authority and then trained on different aircraft for British European

Airways and gained aircraft type-licences for the Vickers Viscount, de Havilland Trident and de Havilland Comet, the world's first jet airliner. For British Overseas Aircraft Corporation he obtained licences for the Vickers VC10 and Boeing 707. At that time he held more aircraft licences than anyone else in the company. Some courses were nearly six months long and all were subject to CAA examination. That's not a bad achievement – and it all stemmed from the skills that Joe developed at Aston House.

Notes

1. Phillips, C.E. Lucas, *The Greatest Raid of All*, pp. 59–61.
2. Boyce, Fredric and Everett, Douglas, *SOE: The Scientific Secrets*, p. 185.

The Design Office Story

Mary Wardrope was a draughtswoman in the ATS and Ernie Welch was a civilian weapons designer. Sadly both have died without revealing the secrets of the Aston House design office. Ernie and Mary met at Station 12, fell in love and married and had a son named Jimmy and it was he who told this story for us:

My recollections will simply be anecdotes that my parents shared with me. My mother was born in 1921 and died in 1992. She was from Dalziel in the County of Lanarkshire and before the war worked as a draughtswoman for the Glasgow city architect's office. When she joined the ATS it made use of her skills and sent her to Aston House to continue as a draughtswoman but on rather different things. Father was born in 1913 and died in 1972. He was at Aston House from, I think, as early as 1941, and was still there at the end of the war. He initially intended to join the Navy, but his eyesight let him down and I think had he been accepted he would still have been directed into weapons design because of his particular talents. Before the war he worked for Shelvoke and Drury at Letchworth, designing vehicles including refuse lorries.

I know my father worked on the Welman midget submarine, the Sleeping Beauty submersible canoe, shaped explosive charges and clandestine weapons. He was really quite proud of the Sleeping Beauty, a motorised submersible canoe which was made of aluminium and I understand was being used right up to the time of the Suez crisis. The Sleeping Beauty could also be fitted with a sail to conserve power. It was designed for a frogman to approach enemy ships in harbour from a position very low in the water, with only his head above the surface until closing on the target when he would submerge and attach magnetic limpet mines to the hulls of the target vessels and sneak away.

The official history confirms the Aston House involvement:

A single item that absorbed a large proportion of the capacity of a number of officers in Contracts (formerly Production) and Quality Control Departments during the fifteen months starting in the Spring of 1944, was the construction of the MSC (Motorised Submersible Canoe, Sleeping Beauty). Although this device was made under Admiralty instructions by the Fairmile Marine Co. Ltd of Cobham, Station 12 was made entirely responsible for the technical control of the contract and for the inspection and testing of the craft. The testing station (Station VIII) at the Queen Mary Reservoir, Staines, Middlesex, came under the command of Station 12 in November 1944.

A very great deal of high pressure work had to be done to produce the requisite number of craft and the 'J' Containers in which they were to be transported by a mine-laying submarine, in time for shipment for Operation Hornbill. At one time, owing to a shortage of labour, it was necessary to transfer to Fairmile's some ten to fifteen personnel from the Aston House workshops to carry out assembly and inspection work. With the MSC, the responsibility for the provision of the necessary oxygen breathing apparatus and underwater clothing, together with the ancillary equipment, also fell upon Aston House. Over 200 craft were produced before the order was cancelled after 'VE' Day.[1]

Sleeping Beauty's general length was approx. 12 ft 8 in. Beam 27 in. Weight 600 lb complete with batteries, bottles and paddles, but not including pilot, oxygen apparatus gear and cargo.[2]

A courageous commando unit made up of British and Australians sabotaged Japanese shipping in Singapore harbour until the unit was wiped out in 1944. The men were taken there aboard a submarine. The raid, code-named 'Rimau', was to carry out their mission in 15 'Sleeping Beauties'.

However, they were spotted and were forced to scuttle their SB craft for fear the new technology would fall into the hands of the enemy. Nevertheless they continued their mission by paddling canoes into Singapore harbour and fixing limpet mines to anchored cargo ships. Relentlessly the Japanese army hunted them down. Out of the 23-man squad, 10 were captured, beheaded and their heads were impaled on spikes in the Singapore streets. Two bit on their cyanide pills when cornered. The rest died fighting, taking many of the enemy with them. The mission was branded 'a failure' despite the bravery of those involved and was kept secret for years after the end of the conflict.[3]

Of the 200 Sleeping Beauties that were produced, one survives in the Western Australia Maritime Museum collection. Jimmy continued:

My father was instructed to take an idea of Lord Cherwell's for a bicycle pump that would fire a poisoned dart. My father said 'There was no way that this could be done and the manner in which it was conceived would kill the person loading it!' He thought that Cherwell, Churchill's scientific adviser, did quite a bit for the German war effort and actually called him Lord Charleton.

Nevertheless the bicycle pump did become a weapon of sorts. It camouflaged a small bomb, filled with plastic explosive, which was initiated by means of a pull switch and detonator. Any person operating the pump would cause the pull switch to function. 138 of the pumps were made.

Method of use: The safety pin is removed prior to the prepared pump being placed on a bicycle in hostile services. To encourage the enemy to use the pump, one of the tyres may be deflated.[4]

Jimmy continued:

My parents never talked about the people who were trained at Aston House but they did tell me about the people they worked with on the permanent staff. One of those was Fairbairn, who was the Fairbairn half of the Fairbairn and Sykes partnership, designers of the commando knife. He was very fond of my mother and took her out once or twice before she and my father got together.

There was also a sergeant-major who liked my mother very much and had to endure a lot of stick from the female NCOs because he polished her shoes.

My father was very proud of a weapon that was one of the simplest he designed. It was a knife for the Naga headhunters, who were helping us fight the Japanese; he based it on a Saxon sax. It comprised two pieces of wood for the handle, a blade and a tang made of one piece of steel and all held together by two rivets. He brought the prototype home and used it for odd jobs but the blade was only mild steel so it effectively wore away. Another device that pleased him was the task of quickly waterproofing a torch – he sealed it in a condom!

I sorted through my father's effects after he died and found a letter from the War Office at the time of the Suez crisis requiring him to be available at short notice as his services might be needed. I have kept a few things like my mother's pay book, my father's ammunition area pass and his NAAFI pass, both bearing the E.S.6. (WD) rubber stamp of Aston House. There is also a German military diary – the writing inside it is my father's and it contains illustrations of German insignia. Some of the intriguing entries are:

Plastic Paddle for Captain Davey. Made of Halex.
There is a perfect hull at Teignmouth, Devon.
No. 4 RMPI Major Stewart.
500 fuses and 500 adapters in ten days, etc. etc. etc.

Amazingly my father brought home a lot of dangerous devices that I wasn't allowed to touch. He disposed of them all before he died.

I sorted through a series of photographs of SOE weapons with Jimmy and he was able to identify the following items as being part of his father's personal collection:

There were loads of pencil fuses and an amazing amount of different devices in boxes. He had some spring fuses (Release Switch No. 6). I presume they were for booby traps? They were wired shut.

Pocket Incendiaries. Mk IIB. PR 5s – four or five tins of those.

Detonator Bursters, Type 6 Mk 1 & 2.

Percussion Caps. Had lots of those, some of them with a sleeve on but most of them unprotected.

Pull Switch No. 4.

Pressure Switch No. 5.

Knives, Dagger, Jack DB. Yes, dad used to have one of the knives, not sure which type.

Rucksack, Gun Spigot, Tree type. Yes, we had a photograph of a chap wearing one of those.

Sight Gun Spigot B 117. We had a photograph of this so I assume my father had something to do with that; there may be records in the Patent Office under E.G.R. Welch. We had loads of photographs of shaped charges and the Tree Type Spigot, Catalogue No. 255.

Why did Jimmy's father collect all these devices, some of them quite dangerous, and take them home? I can only assume that he had designed them or been involved in the design of some or all of them and so they were part of his engineering career. At the end of the war they were being destroyed so I imagine he just rescued a few for posterity. Maybe he hoped that some day people would want to see what was made at Aston House and that he and his colleagues might then receive some recognition for what they had done. It must have been frustrating to carry out such important work successfully, receive no credit and be prevented from telling anyone because it was top secret. Jimmy continued:

After the war my father designed the Vincent Black Shadow motorcycle and when the company became Vincent HRD he was made chief designer. It was based in Stevenage Old Town. Later he transferred to Norton and designed some of their later racing motorcycles. Norton was taken over by AMC and he moved to BRM [British Racing Motors] as engine designer, having already worked with them on combustion chamber design while at Norton.

Jean Behra, the well-known French racing driver, had guested as a driver for BRM in 1958. In 1959, a few weeks before he was killed racing at Avus, Germany, he was in the UK talking to BRM about becoming a driver for their team, and incidentally fixed my train set for me.

Jimmy lives at Flitwick in Bedfordshire.

Notes

1. PRO HS 7/27.
2. PRO HS 7/28.
3. Farrington, Karen, *Secret War: Spies, Traitors and Weapons of Doom*, p. 14.
4. PRO HS 7/49.

Postscript

It has been extremely interesting discovering Station 12 secrets. This is not the whole story of course but I hope there are enough pieces of the jigsaw in place to provide the reader with an impression of the overall intriguing picture. It is extremely unlikely that we shall ever see the puzzle completed. The senior officers, civilian scientists and designers tended to be older and will have taken their secrets to the grave. Most of the documents that survived have now been released to the Public Record Office. Nevertheless, if there is anyone who can offer new information about Aston House, I would like to meet you.

It was a joy locating and meeting the veterans and recording their memories, talking to those interested in SOE, and visiting various wartime locations and museums, both at home and abroad. I have enjoyed reading many books on the subject and searching through documents, photographs and other items.

The veterans struggled at times to recall events that happened over sixty years ago, but their focused concentration squeezed out some memories that they probably thought they had forgotten. What these young men and women achieved at Aston House in so short a time, with so few personnel, is quite staggering. It is difficult to assess the overall effect that their joint endeavour in producing the many devices and explosives had on the outcome of the Second World War, but it must have been quite considerable.

When I realised that the research aspect of Aston House had moved out to The Frythe at Welwyn and Aston House became responsible for production, I thought at first, that can't be right because Colonel Wood didn't mention production, and gave me the impression that most of their time was spent on inventing new gadgets and weapons for special agents and special forces.

Coupled with that, the fact that the main workshop was too small to manufacture large quantities, the existence of a prototype workshop, a design drawing office and the small number of staff, all gave the impression that only small batch production was possible at this site.

However, as more documents came to light they revealed that Aston House had subcontracted its various designs to British industry which produced the bulk of the devices. Aston House still kept control of the orders, design, inspection, testing and quality control, so all the manufactured items must have passed through Aston House goods inwards and stores before onward dispatch to the services – no mean feat for this small unit. Appendix A provides a sample of facts and figures, including the production totals, but do bear in mind that this does not show the complete overall quantity. Prior to June 1941 Aston House staff do not seem to have kept many records, though Appendix B does give an indication of what they were working on in 1940. The first CO, who worked for SIS, said that, 'None of us had kept a diary nor retained a single copy of any memoranda we had written; we were all too conscious of security to retain records.'

It was also around mid-1941 that the split occurred and the research moved away to The Frythe, which no doubt caused administrative aspects to improve.

The subcontracting of production allowed Aston House the freedom to continue to innovate, research, design, make the prototypes and test new devices on site. I feel sure that producing the tailor-made weapons and their designs would not have been abandoned. The station's second CO did it on the q. t. and had no interest in production totals or records.

The thousands of explosives and incendiary devices produced were used in every theatre of the war. The Americans were given the British designs and also produced them in huge quantities for use by their own forces. The many resistance movements supported by SOE in occupied countries, and the Allies' own special forces, relied on Aston House to supply them with their needs: plastic explosive, igniters, booby trap devices, limpet mines, fuses and much else. These were required all the time and so became standard issue for blowing up the enemy's installations and infrastructure. SOE agents were engaged in acts of sabotage on factories producing war materials. Enemy supply lines were disrupted by blowing up trains, railway lines, bridges and power lines.

For instance, between June 1943 and May 1944, 1,822 locomotives and 8,000 goods trucks were damaged by the French resistance. Peugeot, Michelin and ninety other factories were put out of action.[1]

The Aston House staff designed and tailor-made weapons, tools and explosives for special one-off attacks on specific targets. The agents and the commandos who volunteered to carry out these extremely dangerous attacks were sent to Aston House for training on the equipment, some of it heavy and bulky, requiring special rucksacks to be designed and made. For example, for the raid on St-Nazaire, the average load of explosives carried by officers and men alike was 60lb per man and in some cases 90lb. This meant that the only weapon that each could carry to protect himself was a Colt pistol. They were introduced to the devices they were to handle for blowing up the caissons that operated the huge dock gates at St-Nazaire. Aston House had prepared ring mains of cordtex, the whole forming a firing circuit with some 1,000 feet of fuse and cord. These were to be placed quickly into position on the target, in the dark, under fire, without becoming hopelessly entangled. It needed not only a practised and steady hand, but also a cool nerve and unshakeable determination.[2]

Aston House did not stick rigidly to its production remit. It undertook its own research and was at least given some official recognition for control of the design, development, testing and manufacture of the 'Sleeping Beauty' submersible craft and its underwater breathing equipment. I do not believe the heads of SOE were aware of all the tailor-made weapons that Aston House produced. Colonel Wood kept this under wraps, concealed within his own E.S.6. (WD) disguise that allowed him to work without interference from above. Maybe this is why Aston House has received so little recognition. It was certainly a well-kept secret.

Surprisingly SOE came under MEW (Ministry of Economic Warfare) but was not controlled by it. I have purposely avoided the politics of SOE, its disputes with MI6, the early dismissal of Laurence Grand and changes in leadership, problems with the Admiralty, the Foreign Office, SIS and the Air Ministry, also with some branches of the War Office and Bomber Command. This is covered elsewhere by the SOE historians M.R.D. Foot, William Mackenzie and others.

Winston Churchill did not visit Aston House – Colonel Wood admired him but didn't want the work to be delayed by his interest and potential meddling. This probably cost him due recognition after the war but that did not bother him. He should have received a decoration and/or an honour for his leadership, initiative and achievements within the SOE organisation.

However, someone at the top did recognise his ability, gave him a blank cheque and sent him off to India to locate a suitable site, build a duplicate Aston House and operate it in double-quick time against the Japanese, which of course he did, but at the expense of his health. The plan of the Poona site resembles the ground plan at Aston, so he must have been well pleased with the way it had functioned.

The Frythe (Station IX), which I have mentioned only briefly, worked closely with Aston House and deserves equal credit. Like Aston House, The Frythe did not keep to its research remit either. It manufactured the Welman one-man submarine on site, made prototypes of the two or three-man Welfreighter submarine, and also produced the Welrod silenced pistol. It is incredible that this small team even contemplated starting such specialist engineering projects, let alone set out and made them. Such tasks were usually best left to the Admiralty or Royal Ordnance who were experts in the field, with years of experience and know-how. But The Frythe did make them, and made them very well.

Not a single wartime military building remains in Aston village. A footpath and a short piece of road are the only remaining evidence, proof that all the activity really did take place. I don't think the demolition of Aston House could happen today: it would be listed by English Heritage and protected. The fact that the house and all the buildings have vanished does not help the Aston House case to gain some credit for its wartime success, as there is nothing for TV companies to film or journalists to report on or photograph.

Aston House was built around 1700 and remodelled in the nineteenth century. It occupied a 46-acre estate. The coach house, which had stables incorporated, has survived as a dwelling and is most attractive, with alternating circular and oval windows on the upper floor and a central clock tower on the roof. At the time of wartime requisition the house was owned by Mrs Francis Elizabeth Goodall, who inherited it from her father, Arthur Richard Yeomans, when he died in 1938. HM Queen Elizabeth II visited Aston House on 20 April 1959 to inspect an exhibition of plans and models of the Stevenage New Town development.

I would have liked to locate more veterans to broaden the story. I regret that I have been unable to visit ATS driver Margaret Richards, née Allen, who met her late husband David at Aston House. He was a sergeant in the South Wales Borderers and worked in the orderly room. She remembers driving officers to London and getting caught in air-raids. Also Jim and Edna Edwards, née Jacobs, who met at Aston House, have been married 59 years and say life together has been wonderful! She fears that as physical training instructor she was the most hated person on the camp but was nevertheless proud of the crossed swords on her stripes. They remember comedian Charlie Chester visiting and joking about Aston, 'It's the only cemetery with a bus service.' Jim was a corporal in the carpenters' shop making parachute containers, lots of them.

It is heartening to find that so many met future husbands and wives at Aston House and have stayed together. Aston is so important to them and they think of it affectionately. They were in their prime and grew to love the surrounding countryside. They worked hard and enjoyed their leisure time. The music and words of the wartime songs were romantic, sentimental and optimistic about the future and have a special meaning for those who lived through the war. Seemingly everybody knew the words and community singing was never more popular. Aston was a small, quiet and remote village but not one person I interviewed ever mentioned being bored. And those who disliked it when they arrived, like the young ATS girl Mary Wardrope from Glasgow, who I'm told 'was in tears for days', grew to love it, and she too met her future husband there, so it all worked out right in the end. How different it would have been if Britain had been occupied by the Germans.

As for SOE, it was abolished in 1946. But that is not the end of the story. Research and development of special weapons continues in secret establishments. The work goes on, the technology will be of the new digital and microelectronic age but I doubt very much if the participants are having the same kind of schoolboyish fun creating it as their predecessors at Aston House.

Notes

1. Pattinson, Juliette, *Secret War: A Pictorial Record of SOE*, p. 142.
2. Phillips, C.E. Lucas, *The Greatest Raid of All*, pp. 59–61.

Appendix A:
Aston House Production

(a) <u>QUANTITIES PRODUCED OF CERTAIN STORES.</u>

Switch 4 – Pull	... ...	770,000
" 5 – Pressure	... ...	610,000
" 6 – Release	... ...	478,000
" 10 – Pencil Time Fuze (excluding U.S.A. production)..	...	12,800,000
Limpets, Type 6	... ...	38,500
A.C. Delays, Mk.I	... ...	133,500
Tape, Adhesive, $\frac{3}{4}$" (10 yd. coils)	... ...	2,150,000
Detonator Magazines, Mark II	... ...	2,285,500
Pocket Time Incendiaries	... ...	1,630,000
Incendiaries, 1$\frac{3}{4}$-lb. (Firepots)	... ...	733,000
Spades, Lightweight and Parachutist	... ...	39,750
Tyrebursters	... ...	1,500,000
Charges, G.P. Containers	... ...	1,113,000
" " Filled	... ...	717,700

(b) <u>TONNAGE ISSUED.</u>

	Tons
Year ended 30th June, 1942	400
" " 30th June, 1943	1,122
" " 30th June, 1944	2,460
" " 30th June, 1945	2,685
Total for 4 years	6,667

(c) <u>VALUE OF INVOICES PASSED FOR PAYMENT.</u>

	M.G.O.F. £	M.of S. £	Total £
Year ended 30th June, 1942	388,113	7,897	396,010
" " 30th June, 1943	635,034	90,967	726,001
" " 30th June, 1944	691,317	594,533	1,285,850
" " 30th June, 1945	136,668	884,792	1,021,460
	£1,851,132	£1,578,189	£3,429,321

The above invoices are for all S.O.E. stores other than Radio, Drugs and local purchases by E Section, plus raw materials for use at Station XII.

(d) <u>STRENGTH OF STATION (EXCLUDING ATTACHED PERSONNEL).</u>

	MILITARY Officers	O.Rs	A.T.S. Officers	O.Rs	Civilians	Total
30th June, 1942	19	29	1	25	45	119
31st December, 1942	25	118	1	91	59	294
30th June, 1943	23	211	2	116	74	426
31st December, 1943	26	263	2	108	86	485
30th June, 1944	27	318	2	110	87	544
31st December, 1944	24	322	2	109	70	527
30th June, 1945	20	334	2	109	59	524

HISTORY OF THE RESEARCH AND DEVELOPMENT SECTION OF S.O.E.

DEVICES AVAILABLE BY MIDDLE OF 1940

TIME FUZES

1. <u>Pencil Time Fuze</u>: A silently operating time fuze the size of a pencil, giving delays of from 10 minutes up to five days.

2. <u>Cigarette Time Fuze</u>: A time fuze the size of a cigarette giving delays of a few hours; for use with potassium chlorate/ sugar mixtures.

3. <u>Water Time Fuze</u>: A time fuze for underwater demolitions, giving delays of from one hour to forty-eight hours. (This fuze was used in the "Limpet").

4. <u>Clock-work Fuze</u>: Various time delay actions based on clocks. These were for use only in special circumstances where very exact timing was required. Clock-work mechanisms need careful handling and usually require to be connected to electric detonators.

EXPLOSIVES

5. <u>Plastic Explosives</u>: This is a high explosive having the appearance and consistency of putty. It is not detonated by a rifle bullet, but does not require a primer. It is about twice as effective as guncotton or TNT for demolition purposes. Plastic explosive lends itself to camouflage; for example, it was su plied as kegs of putty; it was dyed black to simulate Chatterton compound, and in one rather ambitious scheme it was made up in German cartons exactly like those containing plasticine. For this purpose it was necessary to dye the plastic explosive so that it had exactly the same colours as the plasticine manufactured in Germany. This was a somewhat tricky research, mainly carried out under the direction of Dr. Drane. It will be appreciated that the stability of a high explosive has to be carefully checked when it is adulterated, e.g., by the mixture of dyestuffs.

6. <u>Cheddite</u>: This is a high explosive that can be made at

home from potassium chlorate and candles.

7. <u>Potassium Chlorate/Sugar</u>:   This is an explosive that
can be made at home from innocent ingredients (it was possible
at that time to purchase in most countries potassium chlorate
as throat lozenges, weed killer, etc.).

8. <u>Blasting Gelatine</u>:   This is one of the strongest
commercial explosives.   By arrangement with I.C.I. Section D
were supplied with B.G. made up in continental type cartridges.

9. <u>Detonators</u>:   All the explosives issued were of a type
capable of being detonated by the normal commercial detonator
that is used almost universally in all mines and quarries.
A large supply of detonators made in Germany was obtained from
South Africa before war was declared.

INCENDIARY MATERIALS

10.   <u>Small Incendiary Bombs:</u>   These weighed about two
ounces and gave excellent effects when placed among inflammable
material.

11. <u>Large Incendiary Bombs</u>:   These weighed about two pounds
and were capable of doing nearly as much damage as the service
thermite bomb, although made from raw materials that were
readily available.

12. <u>Incendiary arrows</u>:   These resembled large safety matches
about 18" long with a percussion fuze at the head.   They
weighed about $2\frac{1}{2}$ ozs. and could be fired at a range of about
50 yards from a bow or catapult, or dropped from aircraft.

13. <u>Incendiary Liquids</u>:   Sundry incendiary liquids were
supplied, the most effective probably being a liquid phosphorus
compound.

DEVICES

14. <u>Fog Signals</u>:   This was an adaptation of the common railway fog signal arranged to fire an explosive charge which
shattered the rail when run over by a train.   This device was
intended for use at night when it would not be seen on the rail.

15. <u>Pressure Switch</u>:   This device was buried in the permanent way and was actuated by the pressure caused when a train passed over it.   It was invisible and so could be used by day for derailing trains.

16. <u>Limpets</u>:   These were about the size of a steel helmet. They were filled with explosive and fitted with magnets so that they would adhere to iron or steel surfaces.   When used for underwater work against ships or canal barges, they were fitted with the water time fuze mentioned in (5) above;   when for above water purposes they could be fitted with the Pencil Time Fuze.

17. <u>Coal Borer</u>:   This was a small specially designed hand borer for making holes in lumps of coal or in briquettes. The hole was filled with black plastic explosive together with a suitably arranged detonator so that a lump of coal, after treatment, had an absolutely normal appearance.   These treated lumps of coal could be dropped, for example, into railway loco- motive tenders and, when finally thrown into the furnace, would explode generally with sufficient violence to damage the boiler, or, at least, to render the profession of locomotive driving highly unpopular.

18. <u>Tree Spigot</u>:   A spigot weighing about 2 lbs. that could be screwed into a tree trunk and which would fire an h.E. demoli- tion charge into a target (such as a munition dump) about a hundred yards away.   If used with a Pencil Time Fuze, the discharge would take place days or hours after the spigot had been concealed in the tree.

19. <u>Secret Signalling</u>:   Means of signalling over distances of a mile or two using polarised light were supplied.   It con- sisted merely of a sheet of celluloid-like material a few inches square and could be used wherever black-out regulations were not in operation, i.e., over most of Europe except Germany at that time.

CHEMICAL WARFARE

20. <u>Abrasives:</u>   Various types of abrasives were produced for
introducing into lubrication oils, railway axle boxes and other
analogous points so that the bearings of machinery, railway
engines, etc., would be ruined.   They were mostly supplied
in "toothpaste tubes".

21. <u>Noxious Liquids:</u>   Various noxious liquids were produced which, when inserted in small quantities in grain stores
and bulk food supplies or the like, rendered them unfit (not
poisonous) for human consumption.   Considerable assistance
in this work was afforded by Dr. Roche Lynch of the Home
Office.

ITEM	WORK TO BE DONE
Home-made Bombs:	
A. Acetylene Bomb	Trials and recipe for home manufacture required
B. Use of chlorate mixtures as bomb fillings	Trials of mixtures that can be home-made
C. Bombs filled with B.E., Gelignite, P.E., Shot gun powders	Trials of fragmentation and with various "shot" fillings and with various casings, e.g., cast iron, steel, cement
S Mortar	Design and trials of production unit
J Flare	Full-scale trials of adhesion etc., required

Appendix B:
Site Plan of Aston House, 1945

Traced by the author from an item in a private collection.

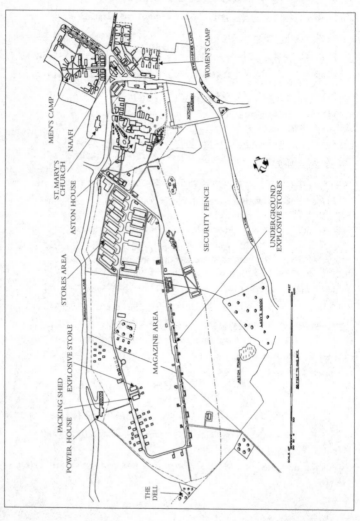

Bibliography

Documents

National Archives (formerly the Public Record Office), Kew:

PRO HS 2/224 Claymore. First Lofoten raid.

PRO HS 7/7 Development of FANY unit in SOE.

PRO HS 7/16 V-weapons.

PRO HS 7/27 Bliss, J.L. Lt Col, History E.S.6. (WD) Station XII, 1945.

PRO HS 7/28 & 30 Special equipment used by SOE agents.

PRO HS 7/49 History of the camouflage section; special weapons;
plastic surgery for agents.

PRO HS 7/108 Assassination of Heydrich.

PRO HS 7/117 Special Forces Development Centre, Poona.

PRO HS 7/179 Norway. Attacks on heavy water plant and ferry.

PRO HS 7/181 Norway. Attacks on heavy water plant and ferry.

PRO HS 7/287 SOE War Diaries, miscellaneous.

PRO HS 8/897 Churchill memo on heavy water attack.

PRO HS 8/955 Intelligence Norway, Rjukan, bombing raid.

PRO ADM 226/48 Baby mobile mine.

Department of Documents, Imperial War Museum, London:

IWM 76/151/1 Langley, Arthur John G., Lt-Cdr, Memoir typewritten
in 2 vols., Ottawa, 1974.

Books

Amess, John, *Mission 179*, Stevenage Society for Local History, 2000

Boyce, Fredric and Everett, Douglas, *SOE: The Scientific Secrets*,
Stroud, Sutton Publishing, 2003

Cruickshank, Charles, *SOE in Scandinavia*, Oxford University Press,
1986

Dear, Ian, *Sabotage and Subversion: Stories from the Files of the SOE and OSS*, London, Arms and Armour Press, 1996

Dugan, Sally, *Commando: The Elite Forces of the Second World War*, London, Channel 4 Books, 2001

Eyewitness Visual Dictionaries, *Dictionary of Special Military Forces*, London, Dorling Kindersley, 1995

Farrington, Karen, *Secret War: Spies, Traitors, and Weapons of Doom*, Leicester, Blitz Editions, 1995

Foot, M.R.D., *Special Operations Executive, 1940–1946*, London, Pimlico, 1999

Gunston, Bill, *The Encyclopedia of the World's Combat Aircraft*, London, 1978

Haukelid, Knut, *Skis Against the Atom*, London, William Kimber, 1954; also revised edition: North Dakota, USA, North American Heritage Press, 1989

Healey, Tim, *Secret Armies: Resistance Groups in World War Two*, London, Macdonald, 1981

Huggett, Frank, E. *Goodnight Sweetheart*, London, W.H. Allen, 1979

Lampe, David, *The Last Ditch*, London, Cassell, 1968

Lumley, Joanna, *Forces Sweethearts*, London, Bloomsbury, 1993

MacDonald, Callum, *The Killing of Obergruppenführer Reinhard Heydrich*, London, Macmillan, 1989

—— and Kaplan, Jan, *Prague in the Shadow of the Swastika*, Prague, Melantrich Publishers, 1996

Mackenzie, William J.M., *The Secret History of SOE, 1940–1945*, London, St Ermin's Press, 2000

Macrae, R. Stuart, *Winston Churchill's Toyshop*, Warwick, Kineton, The Roundwood Press, 1971

Melton, Keith H., *Ultimate Spy*, London, Dorling Kindersley, 2002

Messenger, Charles, *The Commandos, 1940–1946*, London, William Kimber, 1985

Miller, Russell, *The Resistance*, Virginia, USA, Time-Life Books, 1979

Ogley, Bob, *Kent at War*, Westerham, Froglets Publications, 1994

Parker, John *Commandos*, London, Headline, 2000

—— *SBS: The Inside Story of the Special Boat Service*, London, Headline, 1997

Pattinson, Juliette, *Secret War: A Pictorial Record of SOE*, London, Caxton Editions, 2001

Pawley, Margaret, *In Obedience to Instructions: FANY with the SOE in the Mediterranean*, Barnsley, Leo Cooper, 1999

Philby, Kim, *My Silent War*, London, Grafton Books, 1989

Phillips, C.E. Lucas, *The Greatest Raid of All*, London, Pan Books, 2000

Russell, Francis, *The Secret War*, Virginia, USA, Time-Life Books, 1981

Ryan, Chris, *The One That Got Away*, London, Century, 1995

Seaman, Mark, *Secret Agent's Handbook of Special Devices*, London, Public Record Office, 2000

Sparks, William and Munn, Michael, *The Last of the Cockleshell Heroes*, London, Leo Cooper, 1992

Stafford, David, *Secret Agent: The True Story of the Special Operations Executive*, London, BBC Worldwide Limited, 2000

World War II Magazine, Orbis Publishing

Verity, Hugh, *We Landed by Moonlight*, Manchester, Crécy Publishing

Warwicker, John, *With Britain in Mortal Danger*, Bristol, Cerberus Publishing, 2002

Wilkinson, Peter, *Foreign Fields*, London, I.B. Tauris.

Wilkinson, Peter and Astley, Joan Bright, *Gubbins & SOE*, London, Leo Cooper, 1997

Wilkinson-Latham, *Wilkinsons and the F.S. Fighting Knife*, Pooley Sword Limited, 2008

Index